More Experts Praise
Succeeding As An Expert Witness
by Harold Feder

"For those already anointed, this book will affirm what they have been doing; for those just beginning, or thinking about it, it will be a valuable primer on what to look forward to and how to proceed... The author underscores the need for 'professionally correct and ethical methods' to be employed by (expert) witnesses."

> William A. Morgan, *Research & Exploration,*
> *National Geographic Society*

"This 'how-to' book succeeds in capturing and holding the interest of what should be a wide audience... not just a book for the expert witness, but everyone involved in the dispute resolution process."

> John F. Spisak, President and CEO, Industrial Compliance

"Particularly useful to the new expert, an individual knowledgeable in his or her field, but having no experience as a witness."

> Mark R. Thompson, Attorney
> Foret & Thompson
> *Law Practice Management*

"More a serious text than a simple how-to, this book is valuable for all types of expert witnesses, and for attorneys as well."

> Willa Westbrook Smith, *Communique,* Newsletter of the
> National Association of Document Examiners

"A most valuable addition to the toxicologist's library."
> *Journal of Veterinary and Human Toxicology*

"I wish I had this book when I was an expert witness... (this book) should provide a needed service, and I hope many, many people read and assimilate its contents."

> Dr. Elmer Koneman, Professor of Pathology
> University of Colorado Health Sciences Center

"A one-of-a-kind book written by a one-of-a-kind trial lawyer... I have given this book to each expert I have worked with since I found out about it."

> Steven Zapiler, Attorney
> Zapiler & Ferris

SUCCEEDING
AS AN
EXPERT WITNESS

ROLLAND OSBORNE
"The Consummate Expert"

Succeeding
as an
Expert Witness

Increasing Your Impact
and Income

Harold A. Feder

Second Printing with Revisions

Tageh Press
Glenwood Springs, Colorado

Copyright © 1991, 1993 by Harold A. Feder

Library of Congress Card Number pending.
ISBN 0-9638385-0-4 (previously ISBN 0-442-23728-6)

First printing 1991.
Second printing1993 with revisions.

Manufactured in the United States of America

Published by Tageh Press
P.O. Box 401
Glenwood Springs, CO 81602

Graphic Design: Ackerman/Ohnmacht, Inc., Carbondale, CO
Cover Illustration: Lev Ropes, LCT Graphics, Inc., Denver, CO
 *A firm specializing in presentation graphics for science,
 technology and litigation.*
Printing: Publishers Press, Salt Lake City, UT
Back Cover Photo: Portrait Gallery, Northglenn, CO

Library of Congress Cataloging-in-Publication Data

Feder Harold A.
 Succeeding as an expert witness: increasing your impact an
income / Harold A. Feder. Second Printing with revisions.
  p.   cm.
 Includes bibliographical references, appendices and index.
 ISBN 0-9638385-0-4
 1. Evidence – United States. 2. Expert Witness – United States. 3.
Witnesses – United States. 4. Expert Testimony – United States. 5.
Forensic Evidence – United States. 6. Investigative Research – United
States. 7. Scientific Evidence – United States.

CIP number pending.

DEDICATION

This text is dedicated to Rolland Osborne, an expert who epitomizes the highest professional and ethical standards of the forensic field. Mr. Osborne served for 26 years with the United States Secret Service. He has examined more than 100,000 questioned documents and has been engaged as an expert examiner in more than 1,000 cases. He has been deposed more than 200 times and has testified at trials on more than 250 occasions. He has been qualified in state and Federal courts and other dispute resolution forums of more than 14 states of the United States.

He is meticulous in his preparation and articulate in testimony. His conviction for or against a particular fact situation is unshakable, with no bearing whatsoever on which of the parties in an adversarial proceeding might have engaged his services. I am sure he would rather die than lie.

Every forensic witness could well aspire to his reputation for excellence, integrity, ethical conduct, credibility, and humility, which have been evidenced during the more than 40 years of "Rollie" Osborne's professional career.

It is to those standards and that degree of excellence that this book is dedicated.

CONTENTS

FOREWORD

*by Thomas T. Noguchi, M.D.**

Those of us who are forensic witnesses often sail in frigid and hostile waters. This book is a real icebreaker. For the first time, there is a text that grapples with every significant aspect of the process and practice of forensic testimony.

The place of the expert in the adversary system is explored. We are then given an overview of the tasks of the expert witness. Every phase of the procedure is explored, from engagement through investigation, discovery, and testimony, even including practice building for the expert witness who seeks to expand testimonial opportunities.

Subjects are presented in an organized and readable way. The book will provoke keen interest from expert witnesses, attorneys, judges, hearing officers, arbitrators, professors, and those interested in how expert witnesses work in a proper and ethical fashion.

Several interesting and unique topics are contained in this material, some of which have never been previously addressed.

First, we are introduced, for the first time, to a survey of forensic witnesses who responded with candor and detail to a unique forensic expert questionnaire. Appendix D contains the questionnaire, significant explanations of how the survey was conducted and some major conclusions. Other results are placed throughout the book to introduce, explain, or expand on the author's points.

Second, the text and appendices contain a series of valuable and usable checklists, forms, and formats which should prove of value to any professional, technical, scientific, or skilled person who must accomplish tasks in an orderly and organized way. Noteworthy among the tools presented are the Case Plan in Chapter 5 and the Action Plan in Chapter 9.

Third, because of the insights provided by responses to the forensic experts questionnaire, the author's observations of the process, and contributions to the textual materials by experts, the material takes on a realistic flavor not heretofore seen in other attempts to address the subject.

---

*Dr. Noguchi is the former Chief Medical Examiner-Coroner for Los Angeles County, California. He is a Fellow of the American Academy of Forensic Sciences and author of the New York Times best seller *Coroner* (Simon & Schuster, 1983) and numerous other publications including *Coroner At Large* (Simon & Schuster, 1985) and *Unnatural Causes* (Putnam, 1987). He is an internationally recognized forensic expert, having testified hundreds of times in various courts of the United States.

Fourth, the book is generic. It is applicable to all fields of forensic testimony. While examples are presented in many scientific, technical, professional and skilled fields, the lessons are clear and all apply with like force to every area of forensic endeavor.

Fifth, the material is well-organized and readable. The author's original ideas are blended and interwoven with the best thinking and writing of other lawyers and expert witnesses. The glossary, bibliography, footnotes, and appendices serve to make the text more useful.

Sixth, the case examples, most of which are from the author's trial practice experience, enliven the book's themes and serve to drive home its objectives. These illustrations make for informative reading even for the nonexpert and nonlawyer.

Seventh, the entire text provides a continual focus on ethical aspects of expert witness service, from engagement to marketing for additional assignments. Of special value are the guides for several difficult ethical configurations, areas where even the most seasoned forensic witness may stumble without proper guidance. A proposed code of professional conduct and an interprofessional code provide additional leads for proper conduct in various settings.

Ability to teach, candor, simplicity, and the need to illustrate and exemplify are continual themes of this work. This book is a total resource for expert witnesses, experienced or novice. Lawyers will use the work for self-education and as a tool to educate and train expert witnesses with whom they work. Professors and libraries at professional, technical, scientific and skill schools, colleges and universities will use it to prepare students in all fields for what will surely be their expanding role in the dispute-resolution process. Finally, the text is an easy read for those who want to learn more about the inside workings of our court, arbitration and hearing processes, as those systems rely to an ever-increasing degree on the testimony of forensic witnesses.

Thomas T. Noguchi, M.D.
Beverly Hills, California

PREFACE

This book is intended to improve the role and function of the expert witness within the dispute resolution process. My objective is to emphasize professionally correct and ethical methods to be followed by expert witnesses through the mileposts of a forensic undertaking, including engagement, investigation, discovery, trial testimony and file closure. This presentation is generic in that the information applies to all fields of expertise. The material applies to the court and administrative hearing systems and various alternative dispute-resolution vehicles, all of which call for increasing reliance on expert testimony.

Expert witnesses and attorneys who approach this text should consider this admonition: "The human mind is like a parachute. Neither works unless it is open." If impediments to learning can be set aside, I genuinely believe the material contained in this text will enhance the effectiveness, in an ethical manner, of the expert witness as a key participant in the dispute-resolution processes.

I refer throughout this book to the Federal Rules of Civil and Criminal Procedure and the Federal Rules of Evidence. That is a studied determination, on the assumption that the Federal Rules constitute the mainstream of current thinking for both Federal and state court systems. Many exceptions to those rules can be found in various states. Reference to particular local rules of civil or criminal procedure or rules of evidence and practice as annunciated by codes, case decision, statute, and other dispute resolution vehicle rules should be made on a case-by-case basis.

In 1993, the United States Supreme court decided the landmark case of *Daubert v. Merrell Dow Pharmaceuticals, Inc.*, _____ U.S. _____, 113 S. Ct. 2786, 125 L. Ed. 2d 469 (1993).

While the Court's discussion will likely prompt controversy for some time, the holding is significant in providing further guidance regarding what standards should be applied to test admissibility of forensic testimony.

In *Daubert*, the U.S. Supreme Court rejected the prior rule of "general acceptance," which had been the court standard for years. The Court found:

> '[G]eneral acceptance' [by peer review or technical writings] is not a necessary precondition to the admissibility of scientific evidence under the Federal Rules of Evidence, but the Rules of Evidence - especially Rule 702 (Appendix E, Page 209) - do assign to the trial judge the task of ensuring that an expert's testimony both rests on a reliable foundation and is relevant to the task at hand. Pertinent evidence based on scientifically valid principles will satisfy those demands.

The expert witnesses, texts, organizations, and directories mentioned in the material do not constitute any particular endorsement of the person, firm, or corporation, but rather serve as examples of who and what is available to assist the serious student of the subject. Appendix D describes my forensic expert questionnaire, the first known attempt by survey to better understand the forensic testimony process.

Throughout the text, I refer to many specific cases for purpose of exemplifying substantive material. To protect the privacy of clients, attorneys, experts, and opposing parties, I have not identified the parties in these cases. I have also slightly modified facts to protect individual privacy.

I hope the material contained in this book will enhance ethical and professional competence for expert witnesses and attorneys working within all phases of the dispute-resolution processes. It should stand as a constant reminder that advocacy is for the attorney and objectivity is for the forensic expert.

Harold A. Feder
Denver and Eagle, Colorado

ACKNOWLEDGMENTS

Special thanks is extended to my agent and friend Robert Ubell of Ubell & Associates, Inc., New York, who initially conceived this book and encouraged the project. Helen Hyatt accomplished the major word processing and production effort which allowed this text to be completed. Donna Jacobsen did the proofreading. Florie and Harlan Feder provided manuscript review, proofreader service, and advice on chapter content and text organization. The Association of Trial Lawyers of America and the Defense Research Institute generously provided reprint permission and publication of valuable materials in *Trial Magazine* and *For the Defense*, respectively. Sociologist Martin M. Kretzmann assisted in compiling and evaluating the survey results contained in Appendix D. The American Academy of Forensic Sciences, with its continued dedication to improvement of the forensic testimony process, has been and is a continuing source of inspiration.

A final word of thanks is extended to the law firm of Feder, Morris, Tamblyn & Goldstein, P.C., Denver, Colorado, and all of its attorneys and staff members for continued encouragement, assistance, and support.

SUCCEEDING
AS AN
EXPERT WITNESS

1 EXPERT WITNESSES: AN OVERVIEW

INTRODUCTION

Succeeding as an expert witness requires a basic understanding of who and what experts are. Our dispute-resolution process permits certain witnesses to render opinions based on data rather than merely reciting information. These opinions are sought to explain past, present, and future events. You are such a witness. In this book, you will learn why you are unique and how you are selected to be a forensic witness (see the Glossary for definitions of this and other legal terms). I will suggest ways in which you may better accomplish your tasks as an expert. Yours is a special, often controversial, position in our court and hearing procedures. An overview of the relationships, practices, procedures, and ethical considerations of the process will provide a backdrop for the remainder of this book.

A recent article defines an expert as:

> a person who, by virtue of training and experience, is able to do things the rest of us cannot. Experts are not only proficient in what they do, but are also smooth and efficient in the actions they take. Experts know a great many things and have tricks for applying these things to problems or tasks. Experts are good at plowing through irrelevant information in order to get at basic issues or actual problems. Experts are also good at recognizing problems as instances of ones with which they are familiar, generalizing alternative solutions and making good choices among the alternatives.[1]

Those authors indicate that experts can be found from a number of sources:

- Recommendations from others
- Published works

---

1. Johnson, Johnson, and Little, "Expertise in Trial Advocacy: Some Considerations for Inquiry into its Nature and Development," *Campbell Law Review*, Vol. 7, No. 2, Fall 1984, p. 125.

- Technical products
- Academic degrees
- Formal credentials such as licenses, awards, or honors
- Teaching experience
- Supervisory work with others
- Membership in specific organizations[2]

Federal court jury instructions advise juries as follows concerning expert witnesses:

> The rules of evidence ordinarily do not permit witnesses to testify as to opinions or conclusions. An exception to this rule exists as to those whom we call "expert witnesses." Witnesses who, by education and experience, have become expert in some art, science, profession, or calling, may state an opinion as to relevant and material matter, in which they profess to be expert, and may also state their reasons for the opinion.

> You should consider each expert opinion received in evidence in this case, and give it such weight as you may think it deserves. If you should decide that the opinion of an expert witness is not based upon sufficient education and experience, or if you should conclude that the reasons given in support of the opinion are not sound, or that the opinion is outweighed by other evidence, you may disregard the opinion entirely.[3]

HOW THE PROCESS WORKS

Preliminary Stages

Before you are selected as an expert, the conscientious attorney interviews you, sometimes at the scene of the technical challenge or at your working environment. You may also be selected without interview based on criteria previously listed.

You should have adequate time and sufficient basic information to prepare for that first interview. Approach it with appropriate questions and sufficient technical preparation to assess the degree of professional excellence required by the assignment. If your qualifications meet the needs of the case, you should confirm the relationship in writing. Critical terms are discussed and established in express detail.

The client, a person, company, or government agency, should be involved in selecting and confirming you in your role as expert witness. The client ultimately bears financial responsibility for your services and

---

2. Johnson, Johnson, and Little, p. 125.

3. Devitt and Blackmar, *Federal Jury Practice and Instructions*, 3rd ed., Vol. 1, (West Publishing Company, 1977), §15.22, p. 482.

should sign or guarantee the engagement letter. If you can choose whether to take the assignment (and many times you cannot, because of your employment), you should feel comfortable with both client and attorney.

A popular misconception should be dispelled at the outset. Dramatic courtroom testimony is not the only use made of experts. Often you will be engaged for other purposes, such as arbitration, consultation, administrative hearing, office negotiation, long-range planning, or internal investigation. The process is the same regardless.

You should be made aware of all available facts, the client's understanding of the case, technical reports, research papers, official investigative records, and witnesses' statements. If the case involves places or objects, you should inspect both as soon as possible.

In cases that involve a specific protocol, locate the best, most current version. That guide will be the format for future investigation. Compare events of the case with the standard for flaws, negligence, omission, oversight, and compliance. But do not assume that only one protocol exists. Many an expert has been blindsided by that misconception.

Throughout all stages of the case, you should keep a running list of additional information required for follow-up investigation. A sample things-to-do list and follow-up sheet is found in Appendix A. Use it as a guide for preparing your tracking devices, either manually or as part of a computer program.

You and the client's attorney should discuss the legal principles involved in the case before you render an initial opinion about factors such as liability, culpability, fault, defect, negligent practice, or propriety. At this point, you may have developed a series of alternative hypotheses to be tested against known data, reserving final conclusions until all data are available. Your initial evaluation should be flexible and questioning. At this point, it is inappropriate for you to reach anything but tentative conclusions, and those should be kept verbal and probably private.

A cautionary word is in order. Attorneys in our system are advocates, relics of the champions of jousting fields of the past. As such, their duty is to put forward a set of facts and proofs that support the client's position. Occasionally, zeal for the cause may shade professional and intellectual independence. It is not improper for the advocate to give you a wish list stating the most desirable conclusions from the attorney's and client's viewpoint. This does not mean, however, that you must support that view. Your integrity, reputation, and personal and professional self-esteem require that the conclusions you reach and opinions you espouse be supportable based on the available body of facts and operative knowledge. Follow the scientific method regardless of the path it forces you to take.

In a case involving more than one expert, all expert witnesses on your side should be called together for a meeting. Each should bring results of preliminary studies and fact-gathering efforts for an exchange of data, ideas, and theories. The attorney should open the meeting by explaining that subjects about to be discussed will be part of the attorney's work product and thought process. As such, the materials should not be discoverable by opposing counsel if discovery ensues. This precaution is mandatory, particularly at early stages when various hypotheses are proposed, some of which will be discarded for lack of evidence. If the attorney does not call such a meeting, you might initiate it, just as you would do in an ordinary investigation. A collateral benefit of the first meeting is that all experts begin to appreciate reciprocal strengths, weaknesses, and information. This is particularly necessary in multidisciplinary cases that demand a blend of sciences, skills, and expertise.

The client should be intimately involved in preparing the case and should attend the conference. At these meetings, the client will understand the amount of effort each expert must expend, and the client may then find your financial and other requests more reasonable.

Minutes of the meeting should be kept in a separate file marked "confidential" and retained by the attorney. In addition, headings on the minutes should indicate that the meeting is part of the attorney's work product and thought process. Confidentiality may be enhanced by having the client present, making the communication subject in part to attorney–client privilege and possibly not discoverable. Some existing law protects conferences such as this from discovery.

Discovery and Deposition

If the assignment is court-oriented, you may play an important role in pleadings and discovery preparation. You may be called on to word technical parts of a pleading. You can also review discovery requests and responses for completeness and technical consistency. In some cases, you can help uncover a body of technical data, forms, procedures, protocol, notes, and research materials. It is often essential that you participate at this stage to ensure that requisite technical materials are available before deposition, and to assist in reducing the costs of discovery.

Preparing for deposition, as well as interrelating previously obtained materials, should be a joint effort between you and the attorneys. But if no attorney is available, proceed as indicated nevertheless. Essential items to consider in planning for your depositions include a basic understanding of what a deposition is and what its purposes are. A deposition is sworn testimony before trial, usually made in an office or at your place of work. It is designed to accomplish certain specific objectives:

- Gather information
- Uncover weaknesses in testimony
- Lock you into a position
- Assess your ability as a witness

The examination is usually done by opposing counsel, with few if any questions by your sponsoring attorney. The setting is generally informal, scheduled in advance, and conducted in the presence of a certified court reporter. Recording by video, as well as stenographic notes, is common. You may also assist the examining attorney at deposition of opposing experts by assessing their qualifications, capabilities, and demeanor and framing questions for them.

The guidelines for courtroom testimony sketched in this chapter and treated in depth later in the text and as Appendix L will help guide your performance as a witness. Before your deposition, you should review the following:

- Technical and fact data from the client
- Your investigative and technical materials
- Pleadings on file in the case
- Products of discovery, such as interrogatories, document production, and depositions
- Standard scientific works relevant to the subject
- Appropriate legal authorities

Agreement of counsel or court approval is usually necessary before you may be deposed. The pleadings must show that the information sought by deposition cannot be obtained by other traditional and less expensive means of discovery. This is particularly true under the Federal Rules of Civil Procedure and in states that have adopted similar rules.[4] Depositions may be taken either for discovery or in lieu of testimony in court because you are beyond the jurisdictional limits of the court's subpoena power.

Obtaining prior court approval for your presence at deposition is an effective precaution. In some jurisdictions, such matters would be referred to local counsel, who would then determine whether you should attend the deposition. Hearing such matters in foreign territory is risky. The attorney should, at your suggestion, obtain either stipulation or a trial court order in advance of the deposition which you are expected to attend.

---

4. See, for example, Rule 26(b)(4), Federal Rules of Civil Procedure.

Preparation for Trial

Before trial, you will assist in preparing exhibits and demonstrative charts, tests, and documents. Any demonstration must be tested before the trial or hearing. Trial exhibits should be shown to opposing counsel in advance of trial, and either stipulation or court order approval should be obtained. These are easy ways to guarantee the admissibility of a key chart, exhibit, document, or demonstration. It is proper for you to ask the attorney calling you if these details have been satisfied. Nothing can be as disappointing as preparing costly demonstrations or exhibits that are rejected at trial because of inaccuracy or lack of foundation. Exhibits and demonstrations must be accurate and technically correct. Demonstrations must be substantially similar to the subject under litigation to be admissible.

You, the attorney, and the client should be present at the final pretrial conference of experts. The client's presence allows testimony to be sharpened and blended. Often clients forget essential facts. You can ask probing questions to remind the client of events of technical significance or inquire as to facts which will be presented at trial and may be necessary foundations for your opinions.

At this conference, all weaknesses in the case should be exposed and all strengths of the opposition examined. You and the other experts coordinate testimony among yourselves. A recalcitrant expert can be identified at this time. Inconsistencies in expert testimony should be disclosed. This conference is a dress rehearsal. All staging and timing should be practiced. Experts, attorney, and client should be brought to a peak of performance, using video or audio monitoring if necessary to identify flaws, weaknesses, and idiosyncratic behavior.

Unnecessary exhibits and testimony should be eliminated before trial. Your calculations should be rechecked. Data should be summarized whenever possible: have the raw data available in the courtroom but refer to summaries of voluminous documents or material. New rules of evidence allow this use of summary data.[5]

The large amount of raw material you have evaluated before trial can enhance the weight of testimony. The data from which summaries are made must in all cases be available for examination by opposing counsel. Good practice dictates that such information be made available well before trial and be in court for opposition examination.

Preparation for trial is somewhat different from preparation for deposition. The attorney should explain to you the objectives of testimony and describe the physical setting of the hearing room in detail, including positioning of the parties, the attorneys, and the dispute resolution

---

5. See, for example, Rule 1006, Federal Rules of Evidence.

forum. The attorney should outline the functions of the witnesses, attorneys, jury, or other factfinder. But if you do not receive that preparation, the information in this text should suffice.

At Trial

During the trial, you should be aware of the importance of careful testimony, particularly the hazard of inconsistent testimony between deposition and trial. You are admonished to tell the truth and to prepare for deposition or trial testimony by reviewing the facts of the case and your work effort. You should not lose your temper. Speak slowly, clearly, and naturally. If you are familiar with the process, you will not fear the examining attorney or the setting. You must answer only the questions asked, never volunteering information beyond the scope of the question presented. You need not have an answer for every question.

Remember that most questions asked by the opposition can be answered "Yes," "No," "I don't know," "I don't remember," "I don't understand the question," or by a simple factual answer. You should not memorize your story or testimony. Avoid such phrases as "I think," "I guess," "I believe," or "I assume." These are weak and insufficient to meet scientific and technical burdens of proof of reasonable probability.

Taking a breath before answering a question is always a good idea. This allows you to appear deliberate and gives you time to digest the question and frame an answer. Be careful of trap words such as "absolutely" or "positively"; be cautious about estimating time, space, and distance. If technical information is involved, give specifics—not estimates—in the answer. Refer to files or notes to refresh your recollection.

Avoid fencing, arguing with, or second-guessing examining counsel. You should not deny having had prior discussions about testimony in the case if such is the fact. If you make a mistake, correct it as soon as possible. If a negative or apparently damaging fact or omission has been elicited, admit it and move on quickly. To fence, hedge, argue, equivocate, or become angry only exposes you to further cross-examination and a resultant loss of credibility. It also draws attention to the weakness. One way to handle the situation is to answer the question and then add: "But please let me explain." The examining attorney will probably not let you do that. But the attorney for whom you are working will certainly ask you to explain on redirect examination.

You should never answer too quickly or look to counsel for assistance. Testimony in court, deposition, or hearing should never be turned into a joke. Exaggeration, underestimation, or overestimation are all indications of unwary and ill-prepared witnesses. You must translate

technical terms into common, understandable language at every opportunity. Your demeanor and behavior before, during, and after testimony
should be the subject of care. You should review your clothing, stance,
and posture with the attorney before trial. You should know the hazards
of discussing testimony in hallways, restrooms, or public areas around
the hearing room. Conversations with opposing parties, attorneys, and
jurors must be avoided.

A court order may be necessary to allow you to remain in a court or
hearing room during trial, if either side has sought to exclude witnesses.
Your assistance during trial may mean the difference between success
and failure. If you continually pass notes and confer with the attorney,
the client's case will appear weak to the factfinder. It is better for you to
take notes and confer with the attorney during recess. At all costs, you
must be viewed as a professional interested in a factual presentation, not
as an advocate for either side. This is not to say your testimony is to be
given without conviction. The contrary is true. Courtroom tools and
gadgets which make your testimony more effective should be used.
Lapel microphones, overhead projectors, and telescoping pointers allow
comfort of movement and clarity of presentation.

At trial your testimony will be divided into five main parts:

- Your qualifications as an expert to render opinion testimony
- Your assignment and how it was performed
- Findings of fact based on your research
- Your expert opinions
- The reasons that support your conclusions

Your opinions may be based on facts found, research conducted, or a
series of hypothetical questions developed with you by the sponsoring
attorney based on facts, evidence, and proof developed at trial.

CONCLUSION

You as an expert, because of your knowledge training and experience,
are allowed to render opinions about controversial matters during the
resolution processes. You may be called on to assist in all phases of
investigation, preparation, discovery, and trial of contested matters.
Your role is to transmit specialized information and knowledge to the
factfinder. In many cases. your effectiveness will determine the outcome
of the controversy. As in any stimulating setting, the expert is likely to
be questioned. Anticipation of cross-examination will facilitate your
persuasive response. Of particular concern are those areas which you

isolate as weak. You should prepare for cross-examination and frame a strategy for answering vulnerable areas.

As in all aspects of dispute-resolution, three standard rules apply to your forensic testimony:

- Prepare!
- Prepare!
- Prepare!

2 THE EXPERT'S PLACE IN THE DISPUTE RESOLUTION PROCESS

INTRODUCTION

The tribal councils of ancient societies frequently sought guidance from designated magicians, sorcerers, and tribal wisemen. These persons did not possess divine gifts or supernatural powers. Rather, they had the ability for keen observation of nature, physical facts, animal behavior, contents of roots, plants, and herbs, and the uniformity of times, tides and seasons. By focusing attention on this body of data, they were able to correctly predict a number of future events. This gave them a position of superiority in primitive society. On analysis, we have not really come that far. Today you are, for similar reasons, considered to hold a special place in the dispute resolution process.

THE EXPERT IN TODAY'S SOCIETY

Contemporary application of the expert can be found in the highest halls of government and industry. Presidential and legislative panels regularly provide the executive and legislative branches of government with technical guidance. National disasters such as the Space Shuttle catastrophe of 1986 led to the convening of a blue-ribbon panel of space scientists searching for causes of the tragic flight of *Challenger*. Congressional panels seek scientific, technical, and fiscal experts to testify before investigating committees which attempt to unravel mysteries or develop legislation.

Administrative boards and tribunals call on forensic experts for technical guidance. Examples are the Interstate Commerce Commission, Public Utilities Commission, Federal Trade Commission, Federal Aviation Administration, Federal Reserve Board, Department of the Interior, Department of Defense, and Department of Energy. Administrative boards and agencies are composed of technical experts who call on other experts for study, opinion, and reasoned predictions as to present, past, and future events.

Local governing bodies make frequent use of experts. Among the many areas are land use, air and water pollution, zoning, building code, industrial and mining operations, wet lands, aviation, forestry, budget, economic growth, tourist and visitors' bureaus, school boards, departments of public safety, public health, safety, and welfare, liquor control, drug and alcohol abuse units; the list could go on.

Last but not least are judicial and dispute-resolution bodies. In traffic courts, the arresting or investigating officer is the lead forensic expert, and engineers, toxicologists, and accident reconstructionists are all frequent witnesses.

Municipal courts likewise use forensic experts such as zoning code interpreters, construction experts, electric code enforcement officers, plumbing and sanitary experts, and welfare officials. Specialists of every department of the municipality are frequently called upon for expert opinion, testimony, and guidance.

Our juvenile and children's courts frequently see the child psychologist, social worker, probation officer, and guidance counselor, whose expert opinions often determine the course of a young person's life. In our probate, family, and domestic relations courts, we seek advice of economic experts, accountants, marriage counselors, therapists, physicians, and clergymen.

As an expert witness you are sought either to explain what happened in the past or predict what is likely to happen in the future. How do you do that? Because you are experienced and trained in a specialized field and a keen observer, you can reach conclusions and opinions from skillful observation of events and phenomena. These events may seem routine and commonplace to you but mysterious to the rest of the world.

In state and federal courts of general jurisdiction, not counting the areas previously enumerated, it is anticipated that at least one-third of all matters going to trial entail the use of some forensic expertise. As an example of the breadth and scope of expert testimony areas, see the list produced by the Technical Advisory Service for Attorneys$_{SM}$ (TASA®), in Appendix B.

TASA® was formed in 1961 by trial attorneys who recognized the need for a central source of expert witnesses. In 1988, TASA® received 16,000 requests for expert assistance. The TASA® international pool of experts lists over 8,000 persons who are expert in more than 3,000 substantive areas. TASA® represents neither plaintiff nor defendant parties, but rather provides a service to the legal profession, industry, business, and government.

The influence of the forensic expert in our lives today, helping shape not only future decisions but resolving present controversies over past events, assumes unusually vital proportions. But there are some philosophic impediments the forensic witness must overcome before becoming truly effective.

- If forensic investigation suggests a result scientifically, technically, or factually irrefutable, why all the hassle? Why can't we experts gather around the table and resolve the dispute in a spirit of collegiality and fraternity?
- Why must I as an expert be subjected to grueling and rigorous cross-examination when the facts are so clear? After all, I am an expert, I have studied the facts, I am educated and trained in this area. I know the answer to the problem.
- I am appalled that there is an expert witness who studies the same facts and reaches a conclusion contrary to mine. How can that be? The other expert must have been imposed upon by opposing counsel.
- How can the attorney know in advance the result of my study without the benefit of the weeks or months necessary for me to arrive at those conclusions? I refuse to have my profession insulted or my integrity challenged by an attorney who makes such a quantum leap.

These four misconceptions lie at the root of most fundamental misunderstanding between forensic witnesses and attorneys. As this text will explore every aspect of the expert witness and testimony process, these misconceptions should evaporate, eliminating the major basis for combat between the professions.

It has been observed that jurors generally take to ordinary people but they do not always like and trust experts. In other words, experts tend to depersonalize themselves through their methodology, vocabulary, or general demeanor. The end result is trial presentation by a robotlike creature who has become devoid of human attributes. That situation can be reversed.

QUALITIES OF THE EFFECTIVE EXPERT

Eight qualities identify the effective, credible expert witness:

- The expert must perform a thorough investigation.
- The expert must be personable, genuine, and natural.
- The expert must have an ability to teach.
- The expert must be generally competent.
- The expert must be believable.
- The expert must persuade without advocacy.

• The expert must be prepared.
• The expert must demonstrate enthusiasm.

Thorough Investigation

The expert must go the extra mile. Study all reports. Survey the general body of relevant data. View all relevant objects and places; interview all relevant witnesses. Maintain field notes and investigative tracks, and make sure your time records reflect this. Conduct tests for both inclusion and exclusion of your hypothesis. Draw and follow an investigation plan. Use the most current professional thinking, writing, and practice to develop appropriate investigative checklists.

As an expert, you should be aware of the well-recognized *Daubert* rule which comes from a case dealing with evidence from new scientific theories.[1] *Daubert* requires that expert opinion testimony be based on a reliable foundation and be relevant to the case at issue. You must be prepared to show that the professional, scientific, or technical premise on which you rely has a scientifically valid principle base.[2] The Federal Rules of Evidence presented in Appendix E probably represent the mainstream of current legal thinking about admissibility of expert testimony, according to the United States Supreme Court.

Personable

What qualities make you want to socialize with other people? How do you decide whom you will bowl with or take on a fishing trip? What determines whom you invite to your home?

Human beings tend to associate with those we like, those who exude feelings of warmth, friendliness, and concern. We gravitate toward people who let us talk, think, and grow for ourselves. We tend away from lecturers, know-it-alls, and people who lack humility.

What causes you to say, "I like that person"? Think about the factors that make you want to spend time with some people and not others. Be natural; be yourself. Your job as an effective forensic witness is to leave the witness stand and have the commission, court, or jurors think, "That seems like a nice person."

---

1. *Daubert v. Merrell Dow Pharmaceuticals, Inc.*, _____ U.S. _____, 113 S. Ct. 2786, 125 L. Ed. 2d 469 (1993).

2. But see Gass, "Using the *Frye* Rule to Control Expert Testimony Abuse," *For The Defense* (Defense Research Institute, Feb. 1989), p. 23, referencing the prior rule requiring "general acceptance" from *Frye v. U.S.* 293 Fed. 1013 (D.C. Cir. 1023).

Ability to Teach

Think back to high school or college days. Recall a favorite instructor or coach. Recollect the qualities that made you want to learn more from that person. Visualize those attributes, and try to act like that person. This partial listing of a few of those qualities might assist your recollection:

- Well-informed
- Uses demonstrative aids
- Nonintimidating
- User of example and analogy
- Questioning
- Humble
- Nondirective
- Provides opportunities to test knowledge
- Honestly admits information gaps
- Friendly
- Sense of humor

Competence

Demonstrated ability and competence in the subject field is a mandatory element of effective expert testimony. Competence is demonstrated by thorough knowledge in the field, appropriate experience or credentials, currency of information, ability to perform as well as teach, proven results, and an ability to recognize problems, elect alternatives, and make good choices among them. Competence is the demonstrated ability to do something very well.

Believability

You have to believe to be believable. You are not merely a mirror of the position established for you by an attorney or client. You are presented with a problem, afforded opportunity to investigate and evaluate the facts, and asked to reach a supportable conclusion. As a witness dedicated to a particular conclusion, reached independently and based upon available data, you will be believable because you believe in what you are saying. On the other hand, if the conclusion you espouse is that of counsel or client, or is not supportable or supported by available data, you will not demonstrate belief. You will not be believable.

Ability to Persuade

Do you remember the last time you changed your mind on any subject? What caused you to do that? Did you read a book, attend a lecture, watch a television program, or exchange ideas with persons who had more information than you? As human beings we change our minds for various reasons. One of your objectives as an expert witness may be to cause the factfinder to change an opinion about a scientific, technical, or factual proposition. Your task frequently is to analyze what beliefs are likely to be held by the trier of fact, decide why those beliefs are held, ask yourself what it would take to convince someone that the previously held beliefs were incorrect, and then set out to convince. Your task is to persuade without becoming an advocate, to convince without argument, and to encourage a conclusion based upon irrefutable data presented in an interesting way. Effective persuasion is subtle. A person is most strongly convinced if he or she can mentally develop the ultimate conclusion rather than it being spoon-fed by the persuader.

Preparation

Thorough preparation is a relative task. It may involve detailed and extensive notes, findings, and calculations or a general knowledge of relevant literature. It is like this story of snow peas and shrimp. Once a witness was asked her opinion about whether a man and a woman who had frequented her restaurant were married. The witness was emphatic in her recollection. She knew the people. They had appeared at her restaurant every Tuesday night for years. She had regularly served them. Her foundation testimony to that point was totally convincing. Not satisfied with the overwhelming presence of preparation and knowledge evidenced by the witness, the examining attorney pressed forward.

QUESTION: And are you absolutely certain you served these people every Tuesday night?

ANSWER: Yes.

QUESTION: Then I suppose you even remember what they ordered?

ANSWER: Yes.

QUESTION: What did they order?

ANSWER: Snow peas and shrimp.

QUESTION: Every Tuesday night?

ANSWER: Every Tuesday night.

The witness concluded her testimony with her opinion that the couple was married. Her thorough preparation and familiarity with the facts, even on a collateral subject, carried her testimony on the primary issue, marital status, to a point of complete believability.

Enthusiasm

Enthusiasm for the task at hand, the subject matter, and the conclusion, can be demonstrated in many subtle ways. Facial expression and body language tell a great deal about the witness's enthusiasm for the subject. Tone of voice and inflection can suggest boredom or conviction. Imagine the difference in perception between a witness who answers simply "Yes" and the witness who at the right moment says, "You better believe it."

The Illinois State Police Bureau of Forensic Sciences has developed an excellent trial rating evaluation form (see Appendix C). In essence, it encompasses the eight factors just described and expanded. Test yourself against the categories of the rating form from your last testimonial opportunity. How would you rate yourself in each of those twenty-three categories?

The Forensic Expert Questionnaire

There is an opportunity to learn from experiences of other experts. A Forensic Expert Questionnaire was prepared and sent to over 160 experts throughout the United States. The questionnaire and an explanation of the survey process and results is found in Appendix D. Responses to various questions contained in that survey have been tabulated and are used throughout the text to explain relevant chapter materials.

Experts questioned about how the quality of forensic testimony could be improved rendered some thoughtful suggestions:

- Upgrading of qualifications, standards, and training
- Better review of qualifications of experts
- More accountability for performance
- Developing a list of incompetent or unethical experts
- Institute educational programs for judges
- Institute educational programs for attorneys
- Use more demonstrative visual aids
- Let experts question experts
- Work more closely with attorneys
- Change question-and-answer process to allow more explanation

A Brief Introduction to Cross Examination

We have seen the qualities of good expert witnesses. Another part of the process involves cross-examination. What is it all about? How does it work?

Cross-examination is the most misunderstood aspect of the adversary system. It need not be a fearful experience for you. It is designed to guarantee a fair trial. Cross-examination has six general purposes. These are to establish your:

- lack of perceptive capacity or application (Stated another way, failure to do your homework)
- inadequate recollection of the applicable facts
- bias, prejudice, or interest in the outcome or motivation for particular testimony
- questionable character, reputation, or qualifications
- prior inconsistent statements or conduct (stated another way, if you testified to different conclusions in another case in which the facts and evidence were approximately the same, that can be used to impeach your testimony)
- inconsistency with recognized published authorities, so-called "learned treatises"[3]

Do not be afraid of cross-examination. It will allow you to solidify the impression you left through prior testimony. Be a good witness. Be honest. Follow the skilled, technical, professional, or scientific method. Meet the eight criteria of credible and effective expert testimony. You should be able to use cross examination in a positive way. (See Chapter 21 for further information.)

RULES ARE RULES

Almost every forum in which you testify, will have rules to guide you as an expert witness. Most reflective of current thinking on the subject are typically the Federal Rules of Evidence, Rules 701 through 706. The Federal Rules of Evidence characterize the rules in the federal courts, and they are similar to rules enacted by many state courts. The Federal Rules also generally reflect case and common law decisions in many jurisdictions which have grappled with aspects of expert testimony. Federal Rules of Evidence 701 through 706 inclusive are found in Appendix E.

In synoptic form, the Rules provide:

Rule 701. General reference for the use of scientific, technical, or specialized knowledge.

Rule 702. A liberal approach to the admission of expert testimony if that testimony will "assist the trier of fact" to understand the evidence or determine an issue. This rule also sets forth a liberal standard to the

---

3. *The Expert Witness in Litigation*, Defense Research Institute, 1983, No. 3, p. 6.

question of who is an expert, leaving the determination to the discretion of the trial court.

Rule 703. Experts may base their opinion or inference on facts or data which are not necessarily admissible or admitted into evidence at the trial.

Rule 704. You may give testimony on any ultimate issue to be decided by the trier of fact.

Rule 705. You may state your opinions and conclusions without disclosing the underlying facts or data of your opinion unless the court requires you to do so.[4]

Rule 706. A court may appoint its own expert witnesses to assist the dispute-resolution process.

CONCLUSION

A general understanding may help alleviate some of your fear of the adversary system and our dispute-resolution process. If the evidence in a particular case is subject to only one conclusion and is cast in terms of absolute proof, the matter will probably not proceed to trial or hearing. It is the case involving questionable evidence, doubtful outcome, or conflicting exhibits and testimony that requires adversarial presentation. That presentation and its ultimate objective, the dispute-resolution process, will be aided immeasurably by your service as a forensic witness. It should be comforting to know that 88% of the experts responding to the survey in Appendix D generally believe the forensic area is worthwhile.

As a reminder, justice is for the philosopher, truth is for the sage. However, it is a wise and practical society that endeavors to use the adversarial system and your expert testimony to assist in the dispute-resolution process.

---

4. Inker, "A Practical Guide to Using Expert Testimony under the Federal Rules of Evidence," *The Practical Lawyer*, Vol. 31, No. 5, July 1985, p. 21.

3 CASES THAT MAY REQUIRE EXPERT TESTIMONY

INTRODUCTION

Expert witnesses are called on whenever specialized information will assist the trier of fact to understand the evidence or decide facts in dispute. Some engagements involve testimony relating to investigation and conclusions derived from independent research. Others require you to reach expert conclusions, including the ultimate conclusions in issue, based on an overall analysis of general precepts and concepts.

Your opinions will be sought, based upon a reasonable degree of professional scientific or technical certainty, as to what has previously happened and why it happened. You may also be asked what is likely to happen in the future and why that prediction is accurate.

POSSIBLE AREAS FOR EXPERT TESTIMONY

The survey responses, combined with trial experience with hundreds of cases using experts, suggest the kinds of cases that may require expert testimony. This list is illustrative and by no means inclusive. As you review the outline, place yourself in settings where you could be a forensic expert.

Administrative Law
- Compliance with environmental laws
- Franchise and specialty permits
- Health or zoning code violations
- Land use
- Personnel retention, promotion, or termination
- Revocation of professional licenses

Business Organizations
- Banking or business activity
- Dissolution of corporations or partnerships

- Liquidation or market value of a going concern
- Lost profits
- Securities regulation and violation

Constitutional Law
- Application of federal regulations
- Appropriateness of warrant and warrantless searches
- Customs matters
- Discrimination
- Immigration issues
- Pornography issues
- Search and seizure

Consumer or Commercial Transactions
- Banking practices and legal requirements
- Commercial usage and custom
- Express or implied warranty

Contract Law
- Assessing damages for breach of performance
- Contract meaning and interpretation
- Determining whether a breach has occurred

Criminal Matters
- Ballistics
- Biology
- Chemistry
- Criminology
- Odontology
- Pathology
- Psychiatry
- Questioned documents
- Toxicology

Domestic Relations
- Accounting examination of financial statements
- Appraisal of real and personal property
- Child custody and visitation matters
- Psychiatric and psychological evaluations

Employment Compensation
- Calculation of statutory or contract benefits
- Causation for termination of employment
- Construction of employment agreements
- Questions of wrongful termination

Environmental Matters
- Air, soil, and water quality and contamination

- Clean-up procedures and costs
- Gas and chemical migration

Insurance Law
- Actuarial evaluations
- Causes of fire, flood, or other casualty
- Coverage questions
- Propriety of claim procedures and damages

Juvenile Matters
- Potential for treatment and rehabilitation
- Psychological or psychiatric opinion

Labor Laws
- Compliance with collective bargaining agreements
- Grievance procedures
- Wages, hours, and conditions of employment

Mining and Public Land Use
- Environmental and ecologic damage and restoration
- Methane gas infiltration
- Mine safety
- Mining operating hazards
- Proper procedure for strip mining
- Source of mineral specimens
- Technical logs and drilling data

Municipal Law Disputes
- Accounting and budgetary matters
- Method of expenditure of public funds
- Public services and franchises

Oil and Gas
- Construction of oil, gas, and mineral leases
- Failure of drilling rigs or pipe
- Fire causation
- Oil field production allocation
- Property ownership

Patent, Copyright, and Trademark
- Damages for violation
- Infringement
- Issuance

Professional Negligence and Ethics Violation
- Accounting
- Dental
- Education

- Engineering
- Legal
- Medical
- Scientific

Real Property Litigation
- Boundary disputes and title defects
- Condemnation
- Flood causation
- Land use regulations
- Property valuation

Taxation
- Value of property for tax purposes
- Calculation of tax formulas
- Meaning and construction of tax laws
- Taxability of particular transactions

Tort Law
- Anatomical functions
- Assessment of causation
- Child or spousal abuse
- Chemical analysis
- Chemical substances
- Construction defects
- Dangerous premises
- Dynamics of machinery
- Explosion or fire causation
- Lost economic opportunity
- Material testing
- Migration of gases and materials
- Motorized vehicle collision and dysfunction
- Personal injury of all types
- Product liability
- Safety guarding
- Surgical procedure
- Valuation of businesses or property

Trusts and Probate Law
- Accounting
- Appraisal
- Construction of trust and testamentary documents
- Handwriting analysis

Water Law Disputes
- Aquifer and watershed sources
- Contamination of water

- Quantity and quality of water for irrigation
- Well and drilling permits

Workers Compensation
- Cause of work-related injury
- Probability of rehabilitation effort
- Safe working conditions
- Value of statutory benefits

SOME SUCCESS STORIES

Examples of successes made possible by expert witness testimony provide fascinating vignettes. These situations were derived from actual cases. Some come from the recollection of experts who responded to the survey (Appendix D, question 15). Visualize how your expert testimony might have provided a key to the results described.

Case No. 1. A taxi driver picked up a female fare at a tough bar. The woman entered the cab; a semiintoxicated male patron of the tavern tried to remove her. The driver came to her rescue. A fight commenced with six male patrons of the tavern. The driver was kicked, beaten, and finally murdered in the tavern parking lot.

Two defendants were convicted of first-degree murder. Another pled guilty to conspiracy. Other assailants were either minors or escaped. The driver's widow brought an action against the tavern for negligent maintenance of a dangerous premise and dram shop law violations. Expert testimony was provided by the investigating police detective, who served as a security expert. In his expert opinion, had the tavern provided parking lot lighting and a security guard in the area, the victim would not have been murdered. Substantial recovery was ultimately made by the widow and her children against the tavern and its insurance carrier.

Major changes in the way property owners protect persons on their premises have been brought about by cases such as this. In particular, protection of women and children from sexual assault in poorly lighted or unpatrolled buildings has been greatly enhanced.

Case No. 2. A fourteen-year-old semidelinquent youth who had evidenced behavior problems was sent by public social service caseworkers to a remote mountain camp. The stated purpose of the wilderness experience was to build character and correct personality and behavior deficits. Instead, the camp operator and one male and three female companions subjected this youth and nine others to many days of physical and sexual abuse, beatings, restraint, psychological abuse, threats, fear, intimidation, and mental domination. The children were forced to engage in sex acts with each other and to witness open sex acts between the adults.

Psychology evaluation testing and testimony by a treating psychologist established the extent of damage done to the youth by this treatment. The doctor projected the resulting psychological impact on the young man. A substantial settlement was recovered, which assisted the claimant in regaining his self-esteem.

Discovery often reveals major gaps in the way some systems work. This case focused on the lack of checking or verification by social service placement agencies. Often, major changes follow publicity surrounding these kinds of cases.

Case No. 3. A gynecologist prescribed a drug for a posthysterectomy patient who evidenced depressed behavior. The patient developed extrapyramidal symptoms, an ailment called "hunting jaw." This ailment is characterized by joint pain, lack of control of the jaw and tongue muscles, slurred speech, drooling, and difficulty chewing. The ailment was permanent. The drug manufacturer claimed no duty to warn of the risk of adverse reaction to the drug, asserting it had no actual or constructive knowledge of the possibility.

Expert testimony and reports of the U.S. Food and Drug Administration established that adverse drug reaction reports had existed for seventeen years before the claimant sustained the reaction. According to plaintiff's counsel, it was the testimony of the expert witness, "without a doubt," that was the key factor in establishing the case against the drug manufacturer.[1] A substantial recovery was obtained.

Society is complex. As situations present themselves in which an individual has suffered severe injury, only expert testimony can unravel the proof, which may or may not affix culpability.

Case No. 4. Part of the marital estate in a dissolution proceeding was commercial industrial and development real property and related companies owned by one of the parties. The value of the properties exceeded $800 million. Valuation was necessary to assist the court in entering permanent orders for property division. The valuations submitted to the court by one real estate appraiser were accepted, with general disregard for the value opinions of opposing experts.

What causes the opinion of one expert to be accepted over the opinion of another given the identical set of facts? Your testimony can become the accepted version if the suggestions in this text are followed.

Case No. 5. Over fifty private homes began to settle, sink, crack, and deteriorate in a suburban housing development. The issue presented to soils and structural engineering experts centered on the water source which infiltrated into expansive soils surrounding the homes. By pin-

---

1. *Hermes* v. *Pfizer, Inc.*, 848 F. 2d 66 (5th Cir. 1988).

pointing the actual parties at fault, the homebuilder was able to recover most of the damages it had paid to the homeowners. Recovery was ultimately made from the responsible subdivision developers, based on expert engineering and soil analysis and investigation.

In this case, not only was the dispute resolved, but the experts developed a solution. Experts who actually accomplish corrective work seem to acquire more credibility than those who merely opine from afar.

Case No. 6. An infant, as a result of a traumatic birth event, was rendered essentially brain dead. However, the child's family was required to care for the child twenty-four hours per day. It was the task of an economic evaluator to determine the financial loss to the family as a result of its care efforts for the child. The testimony resulted in a substantial dollar award for the family.

That was a case of substantial financial need. That need would have not been met had it not been for the team of experts working for the family.

Case No. 7. The defendant in a criminal case had been charged with murder. The victim had died as a result of a drug overdose. Two sources of drugs were determined to be present in the victim's body: drugs administered by a medical facility as well as street drugs provided to the victim by the accused. A toxicologist working closely with the pathology team concluded that the hospital-administered drug, not the street drug, caused the death.

It is not uncommon for claims or defenses to be dropped or withdrawn following rendition of well-supported expert opinions. Often all experts involved agree on the conclusion. In such cases the process works, based only on the expert opinions and reports, without the need for trial.

Case No. 8. Two companies were involved in litigation concerning damages from a business closure involving an overseas mining venture. Due to a casualty, accounting records of many years' duration had been destroyed. The accounting expert had to reconstruct the financial records based upon examination of five foreign currencies and numerous bank transactions by the use of specially developed accounting software. The program recreated the accounting records from the banking activities of the business claiming damage. The expert's report resulted in a highly favorable resolution of the case.

This is an example of the expert bringing state-of-the-art technology to the forensic arena. It demonstrates the need for you, as an expert, to stay current in your field and applicable technology.

Case No. 9. A concrete building exploded, demolishing the structure and destroying evidence of causation and structural soundness of the building. The pivotal issue turned on relevant strengths of certain corrugated asbestos cement.

A building materials expert established that the defendant's product had the lowest impact strength as compared with six other manufactured products. Crucial to that conclusion was the expert's collection of photographs of the concrete product following the explosion and analysis of those photographs. Testimony at deposition concluded the matter without the need for trial.

The following two cases, in vastly different areas of expertise, validate the process of dispute resolution. Whether at trial or by the investigative process, the forensic witness carried the day.

Case No. 10. A plane took off with no indication of any aircraft defect. At the moment the plane was airborne, it became suddenly uncontrollable. The plane lacked a backup system to correct the deficit, and the crash resulted in the pilot's death. According to expert testimony, the manufacturer had been aware of the defect and had proposed a corrective measure, which was itself defective. The corrective measure did not provide adequate protection for the problem, thereby impressing liability on the manufacturer not only for the defect, but also for the secondary defect.

Case No. 11. An adult male was enjoying a Sunday afternoon outing on an off-the-road motorcycle. He dressed carefully for the activity, including putting on a pair of gloves. He experienced a sudden unexpected and rapid acceleration of the motorcycle. The operator attempted to use the kill switch, a push-button device.

Expert tests established that excessive force was necessary to activate the kill switch button at any angle greater than 10 degrees from dead center, if the operator was wearing gloves. The expert established that the defective switch, coupled with the psychological stress of accelerating unexpectedly and rapidly toward an obstruction, caused the injured plaintiff to believe he was depressing the kill switch button when in fact he was not. A substantial settlement for the quadrapalegic victim resulted from the expert's tests and evaluation of the human-factors engineering problems.

In some of the instances described, experts established major defects. The social utility of elimination of those defects has dramatic effect on consumer, manufacturer, and the general public.

CONCLUSION

The listing of potential areas requiring expert testimony is intended to be representative. New fields and cases in which expert forensic testimony is necessary occur almost daily. Having reviewed these case examples and itemized potential testimony areas, it becomes easy to see yourself in a forensic witness setting.

An important underlying concept emerges from a review of the case sketches. Expert testimony is of critical import in the continued function and improvement of our social, judicial, administrative, and other dispute-resolution processes.

4 KEEPING CURRENT AND COMPETENT

INTRODUCTION

Humankind's collective knowledge in the last fifty years equals perhaps one-half of our knowledge accumulated during recorded history. It is therefore awe-inspiring to consider the amount of new knowledge we will witness in the next twenty-five years.

As you undertake the challenge of expert testimony, you have an obligation to stay current in your profession. You cannot rely on outdated and outmoded theories, methods, concepts, or equipment.

Whether you intend to pursue a forensic witness career aggressively or are called upon incidentally for that service, you must maintain and improve your current credentials. At the very least, you owe that obligation and duty simply to those who rely upon you for expert advice.

The process of preparing a case for trial or hearing is itself a learning exercise. Because you must examine all aspects of the case, you must become and stay competent and current within the parameters of the forensic investigation's subject matter. But our reference here is to general overall competence.

The survey generated a wide variety of answers to the question about keeping current. The eight categories of response include:

- reading professional literature
- being active in the field
- continuing education/certification
- research and publishing
- teaching, lecturing, and consulting
- attending seminars
- attending professional conferences
- peer review

Memberships in professional associations were also considered useful by 83 percent of the survey respondents. Benefits include:

- making contacts
- stimulating interaction
- keeping current
- educational opportunities
- new ideas
- publishing opportunities
- enhanced credibility

However, there were some negative points made. Society membership is seen by some as too social and political, with little relevance to the experts' area of work.

CONTINUING EDUCATION AND TRAINING

With our current information explosion, it is difficult to stay competent in any professional or technical field. As a result, you may tend to become more competent in a gradually narrowing field. The specialization of fields of endeavor and the hoped-for increase in knowledge and competency in those narrow fields are trends which will probably continue.

Most professional, technical, and scientific societies provide continuing education and training. Some make ongoing learning mandatory. Others sponsor seminars and workshops as part of an effort to maintain professional responsibility. Some organizations, however, provide training and education solely to generate income.

Whatever the motivation behind the programs, they are certainly a fact of life. The benefits to the forensic witness of participating in such programs are significant.

JOURNALS AND PUBLICATIONS

The flow of technical, scientific, and professional journals is also multiplying. Here too it is necessary to be selective. Determine which journals you will read on a regular basis. Unfortunately, there is a tendency to put all the journals in a stack and leave them there, year after year.

A better process is to survey the available field, consider your area of current interest and endeavor, and then select the publications that are most relevant to your specialty area. Make a personal commitment to finding time to review your chosen publications.

PROFESSIONAL SOCIETIES AND ASSOCIATIONS

All of us have known people who boast of membership in a string of professional societies and associations. However, on careful examination, their involvement consists in the payment of annual dues.

Because of the proliferation of professional and technical organizations, you should select your organizations carefully, again depending on your particular specialty area. Then participate actively and energetically in the organizations you have chosen.

Assume leadership roles. Undertake chairperson roles on committees or research projects. A forensic expert who is a structural engineer has for years been a major drafter of scientific and technical papers for the American Concrete Institute. Another expert, a certified public accountant, has provided input for twenty-five years into research publications of the American Institute of Certified Public Accountants. These achievements go far to enhance witness-stand qualification. Also, it is often professional society research or publication that brings the forensic expert to the attorney's attention in the first place. What better witness could there be in a case involving posttraumatic stress disorder than one of the authors of §309.89 of *D.S.M.-III-R*?[1]

Organizations that selectively invite membership are of great value to the forensic witness. Membership in associations that require an examination for membership, such as the American College of Surgeons, is even more valuable.

The professional societies and associations available to you may not be organized on an invitation basis or require examinations for entry. Still, your aggressive participation will dramatically serve to keep you current and competent within your area of specialty.

TEACHING AND WRITING

Professors are both popular and effective in the courtroom as expert witnesses, because the academic world relies on commitment to knowledge rather than commitment to a particular client or cause.[2] Professors are accustomed to addressing audiences. They are natural and confident. They do every day what the testimonial process seeks to achieve: to teach.

---

1. D.S.M.-III-R., §309.89 (American Psychiatric Association, 1987). D.S.M.-III-R is the diagnostic manual of the American Psychiatric Association.

2. Kingson, "The Professors Who Make a Case," *New York Times, Sunday Supplement, Education Life*, Nov. 6, 1988, pp. 41–77.

Preparation of articles for publication has the same benefit as classroom teaching for the forensic witness. The article, monograph, book, chapter, or text cannot be properly and correctly produced without substantial research effort.

Classroom teaching is itself a learning opportunity. So is professional, technical, or scientific writing. The motivation for both undertakings is to advance knowledge in a particular field. Often an investigation which is part of a forensic testimony assignment becomes the subject of a paper, article, or textbook chapter.

ACTIVELY PRACTICE IN THE FIELD

The forensic witness who does nothing but forensic testimony is a less desirable and effective testimonial witness than one who actively practices in the specific field and only incidentally testifies in the dispute-resolution process.

Opposition attorneys relish the opportunity to cross-examine a forensic witness whose full-time occupation is forensic testimony. Such a witness can be an easy target. Therefore, some attorneys will not engage the services of a professional forensic witness. The problem is credibility.

As an example, expert testimony from someone working in the field was offered in a courtroom on the issue of the age of an automobile. The opinion as to car's age was tendered not by a metallurgist or automotive engineer but by a tow-truck driver who based his opinion on the condition of the undercarriage. During his professional career, he had personally towed and recorded the odometer mileage of more than 10,000 vehicles.

This witness was able to render an opinion as to whether the vehicle had been driven 30,000 or 130,000 miles. He was also able to support that opinion with specific investigative facts gained over his many years of work in the field. The witness's testimony carried the day on the issue, though he had never before testified as an expert witness.

GROW WITH THE FLOW

A leveling process exists with all human endeavor. Civilizations, nations, groups, and individuals tend to remain on a plateau after reaching a certain level of competence. It is the individual who refuses to accept a cap on capability who achieves excellence. Always search for the better way. Seek the more certain laboratory test or engineering solution. Probe and explore. Do not be afraid to challenge established thinking in your field. The opportunity for improvement, innovation, and creativity exists in every area.

MAINTAIN PHYSICAL, MENTAL, AND EMOTIONAL BALANCE

While it is crucial to move forward in your selected field, it is also important to maintain contact with the world in general. Do not neglect the arts, literature, and music. It is impossible to function as an effective and alert forensic witness in a vacuum. You must be cognizant of the world and use everyday examples to support your testimony.

Of even greater significance is the need to maintain physical, mental, and emotional health. None of us can function in any field unless we have the strength and balance to perform effectively. Stress avoidance in both personal and professional life will go a long way toward enhancing your testimonial performance.

CURRICULUM VITAE

Your curriculum vitae, or resume, tends to address the past. For the reader's benefit, it suggests your ability to analyze prior events for causation and effect and to predict a course of activity or conduct in the future. Many things make up that ability, the most important of which is your investigative experience in the field, gathering facts and digging out in meticulous fashion relevant information on the subject under inquiry.

Your resume speaks of your ability to do that kind of extensive study and labor. The theory is that after the concentrated fact and information-gathering effort, problem-solving solutions will become apparent. Each part of your resume should be designed to lead to that conclusion. The sections should suggest an ability to wade through the morass of factual and technical detail to reach conclusions.

Your areas of professional emphasis speak to your experience. Special admissions, memberships, and technical or professional ratings suggest excellence and other experts' opinions of your abilities. Special recognitions, honors, and awards likewise evidence professional or societal recognition.

Your educational history is evidence of your academic inquiry and tenacity. So is your teaching, writing, and lecturing. Your publications witness your ability not only to gather and process information but also to pass it on to others in an effective way.

A potential outline for your resume might include these major sections:

- current position or title
- professional education and training

- government and public service
- employment history
- details of continuing education and training
- areas of professional or technical concentration and professional highlights
- honors, ratings, recognitions, and licenses
- professional memberships and affiliations
- teaching, lecturing, and seminar or workshop presentations
- publications, including books, articles, and seminar or workshop papers
- expert witness experience, either specific or generic
- volunteer and special activities, projects, and programs
- personal and family data, including avocational activities

Your curriculum vitae must be factually accurate in all respects. Resist any tendency to expand your credentials beyond the absolute fact. And if your resume is not correct and up-to-date, update it now. Imagine the courtroom chagrin which would attend the exposure of errors in your resume to cross-examination. That attack might involve nonexistent degrees, improperly stated ratings and licenses, undisclosed disciplinary proceedings or suspensions, or plagiarized articles. Do not let it happen to you.

CONCLUSION

You have ample opportunity to stay current and competent in your professional, technical, or scientific field. You owe that duty to your profession, your client, and the dispute-resolution process. Maintain your skills and knowledge. Growth, maturity, and success in the field of forensic testimony does not come easily. It does not come overnight.

5 ARE YOU RIGHT FOR THE CASE?

INTRODUCTION

Forensic testimony is challenging, difficult, and important. It requires honest introspection. Before deciding to take on a case, you must examine your conscience and your professional and technical experience for conflicts of interest or professional inabilities.

Your qualifications must be examined from the perspective of the critical eye of the opposing counsel and the ultimate factfinder, be it judge, jury, arbitrator, or hearing panel. Also determine whether you have time to undertake the task and the energy and ability to fully prepare for it. Being available for the assigned hearing date is itself critically important.

Examine the philosophical prohibitions that might impede your effective testimony or any moral or ethical objection you might have to the position you are being asked to support. Finally, ask yourself whether your testimony will ultimately help resolve the dispute.

You must consider a number of factors before you decide to accept a case for forensic investigation and testimony. Careful examination of those factors will avoid professional disappointment for you and disaster for your client.

This chapter deals with the best of all possible worlds. It assumes that you can decide whether to accept particular assignments. Many professional occupations are so structured that the forensic witness has no such choice. Acting as a witness is just part of the job. However, even within public service, where choice and selectivity are limited, some of the ideas explored in this chapter have application.

Survey results indicate that 91 percent of the respondents turn down cases from time to time. Of greater interest than the percentage are the reasons listed for rejection of forensic assignments:

Unethical case, client, or attorney	13
Fell outside area of expertise	12

Time constraints	12
Case lacked substantive merit	11
Conflict of interest	8
Disagreed about facts of case	8
Fee problems or disagreement	6
Personality clash	6
Do not take certain types of cases	3
Case was not interesting	2

Responses to question, "What makes a case worth your effort?" are likewise revealing:

Interest or challenge of case	13
Merit of case and issues involved	13
Appropriateness of case to area of expertise	13
Size of fee	11
Time it will require	8
Quality and reputation of attorney	4
Size or magnitude of case	3

The following sections explore these and other considerations.

SPACE AND EQUIPMENT

Consider whether you have adequate laboratory, test, or work space to perform the assignment. If space is not available as part of your regular organization, can you gain access to appropriate space elsewhere? Should the assignment entail particular laboratory equipment, facilities, or computer capability, can it be readily obtained?

SUPPORT STAFF

Consider the personnel necessary to assist you in field work, fact gathering, testing and data correlation. Do you have the staff necessary to accomplish the assignment? If not, can you engage them temporarily? The personnel working on the case must be equal to the challenge.

TIME

The time constraints involved in the case, together with possible deposition and trial schedules, must be considered before you undertake a forensic assignment. If you do not have the time available to do the job, you and the case will be better served by letting the assignment go to someone who does.

CONFLICTS

Strictly speaking, a conflict of interest prohibits your testimony in a specific case. A conflict arises if prior relationships, testimony, or assignments exist that suggest you could not give your undivided loyalty to the cause and the client in the present assignment.

Thoughtfully examine the parties and products involved in the assignment. Conflicts of interest can be embarrassing, to say the least, and disastrous in some cases, if they are not uncovered early. Consider whether you or your organization has been contacted previously on the case or represented either party in prior matters. Conflicts of interest can be subtle, but the effect of an undisclosed or undiscovered conflict can come crashing into the courtroom at a most inopportune time.

CREDENTIALS AND EXPERIENCE

Examine your own background and qualifications to carry out the assignment. If your training and experience do not qualify you for the assignment, pass it on to a more qualified expert. Develop a network of professionals to whom you can refer cases and who can refer cases to you. Such networking allows the right case to be placed with the right witness, raising the probability of a salutary result. The mark of a true professional is to acknowledge one's limitations.

FUNDING

You should examine the funds available for the assignment. Can they realistically be expected to accomplish the client's goals? Evaluate the magnitude of the case in relation to the funds available. It would be unfortunate if thousands of dollars were spent for expert investigation and testimony when only a few hundred dollars were at stake.

SIGNIFICANCE OF THE CASE

Consider whether the case has sufficient professional or societal significance to justify your becoming involved. Many cases are too small or insignificant to justify the cannonades that will be generated if you step into the fray.

PRIOR CONTRA WRITINGS OR TESTIMONY

Before taking on a forensic assignment, consider prior testimony you have tendered in trial or deposition. Review your writings as well. Compare your contemplated investigation, conclusion, and testimony with the cross-examination effect which might occur if you have written or testified in a similar case contrary to the position you will be tendering.

One of the major areas of deposition examination is to determine the extent of prior inconsistent writings or testimony by the expert (see Chapter 17). Opposing counsel will spend countless hours and great effort in uncovering inconsistent prior testimony or writings which can be used to impeach you as the testifying expert. It is difficult to remember everything one has said or written in the past. To help you remember devise some method of categorizing prior testimony and writings and always consult your records at the outset of a potential assignment. This system can avoid professional embarrassment to you, destructive effect on the case, and the potential of legal liability for nondisclosure.

Possibilities include listing materials by name of client; location of property or event; description of the product, object, or event; date of event; and area of expertise involved. The system should include reports rendered, articles or books written, and transcripts of deposition or trial testimony. Extensive cross-indexing while the matter is fresh in your mind will prove valuable later.

CASE PLAN

An organized approach to case analysis before undertaking an assignment will alert you to some of the skeletons that could be lurking in the closest. Consider use of a case plan format before or after undertaking a forensic assignment. Working through the case plan will help you decide whether you are right for the assignment. It will also help you get started with the requisite analytic steps if you accept it.

Take a moment to examine the twenty-seven points in the case plan. See how contemplating these points would have assisted you in determining whether to undertake your last forensic assignment. Consider how the case plan might help you organize the work necessary to accomplish your present forensic assignments. The points in the case plan are:

1. Name, address, and phone number of client
2. Name, address, and phone number of attorney

3. Type of case
4. Opposing parties and attorneys (conflicts check)
5. Client's objectives
6. Rationale of the case—why this case makes sense
7. What information is needed
8. Types of documents, exhibits, and witnesses to be developed
9. How will you get information needed
10. What are the forensic issues—what research is needed?
11. What is your overall strategy?
12. Time frame for investigation, preparation, and testimony
13. What resources will you need—people, support centers, materials, equipment?
14. Estimated number of hours you will devote to this case
15. Available staff people
16. Outside resources, consultants, experts, technicians, space, and equipment needed
17. Importance of this case in terms of forensic issues involved
18. Importance to the client or society
19. Prior testimony or writings to the contrary position
20. Analysis of claims of plaintiff
21. Analysis of defenses and possible counterclaims of defendant
22. Possible liability of persons or entities not joined in the present matter
23. Budget for funds and time
24. Goals and action plan, including specific task assignments and time schedules
25. Action plan monitoring and follow-up
26. Periodic evaluation with client and counsel
27. Conclusion (trial, settlement, or alternative dispute-resolution activity)

CONCLUSION

You have a high ethical duty to examine each tendered case against your background and ability. The concepts and tools described will help you through that process. Of major value in making that determination is the case plan, a pragmatic approach to the undertaking. Examine your time, availability, skill level, and support mechanisms. Be certain you can make the total commitment necessary to properly investigate, prepare, and testify for the client.

6 INVESTIGATING CREDENTIALS OF EXPERT, ATTORNEY, AND CLIENT

INTRODUCTION

Various methods are available to you as a potential expert witness to investigate the credentials of the attorney and client by whom you are about to be hired. Some of the same devices are available to the attorney and client who are attempting to verify your credentials. Both from the standpoint of avoiding disappointing relationships and establishing yourself in the forensic community, it is important to know how this verification process works.

Fifty-four percent of the survey respondents stated they check out the attorney or client by whom they are about to be engaged. Most verification is accomplished by personal networking. The experts believe the attorney should have the duty to check out a client. All responding experts considered the attorney's reputation of prime concern. This chapter covers, first the attorney's investigation of the expert and, second, the expert's investigation of the attorney.

INVESTIGATION OF THE EXPERT

The first thing an attorney will do is examine your curriculum vitae, which should state your credentials accurately. The result of overstatement in the resume can have disastrous effects in the courtroom.

Case No. 1. The resume of the expert, an electrical engineer, was slick, clear, and seemingly complete. Trial was underway. It was time for cross-examination. The expert, when faced with two basic types of wire samples, incorrectly identified both. He thereby established for the trier of fact a lack of the most basic knowledge. But he had a great-looking resume.

A mechanical engineer, purporting to be an expert in all things mechanical, including safety guarding of grinder equipment and printing presses, failed to qualify as a witness in both categories in separate cases.

The expert had never dealt with the particular types of equipment involved. He was not allowed to render expert opinions as to either item.

Fortunately, the lack of qualification became apparent before trial in one case. In the other, the witness was examined by a process called *voir dire*, which can be used to test the qualification of an expert even before testimony on direct examination. The cross-examination *voir dire* out of the jury's presence went like this:

QUESTION: You are a mechanical engineer?

ANSWER: Correct.

QUESTION: As such, you deal with matters of machine guarding?

ANSWER: On occasion.

QUESTION: Does that include information about the design and function of machine-guarding devices?

ANSWER: Yes.

QUESTION: Are all machine-guarding devices the same?

ANSWER: Obviously not.

QUESTION: Even with machine guarding, workers must be careful with equipment which could injure them?

ANSWER: Yes, but guarding is for the forgetful or careless worker.

QUESTION: The equipment in this case, a meat grinder, did not have a guard, isn't that correct?

ANSWER: That's correct.

QUESTION: Have you ever dealt with a meat grinder before?

ANSWER: No.

QUESTION: Did you ever design or modify a guard on a meat grinder?

ANSWER: No.

QUESTION: Have you ever designed a machine guard for a hamburger grinder?

ANSWER: No.

QUESTION: Do all meat grinders have guards?

ANSWER: I don't know.

On the strength of those answers, the witness was not allowed to render expert opinions in the case. This case was tried long before enactment of the Federal Rules of Evidence, which contain more generous guidelines for who may render expert opinions. A contrary result could be expected today, with the *voir dire* going to the weight of the expert's opinion, not its admissibility.

A second excellent evaluation technique involves examination of your writings, books, and articles. It is incumbent on you to maintain an up-to-date bibliography of your publications, seminar papers, and workshop presentations.

Affording an opportunity to a potential client to observe you in an actual testimonial setting can be an excellent audition. In one case, an expert testifying in deposition in an explosion disaster was hired by other claimant's counsel following settlement of the primary claim. Deposition performance, thorough preparation, and articulate presentation provided an excellent basis for engagement, not only in that case but also in numerous subsequent cases involving explosions.

Courtroom testimony by an expert, whose testimony was found by the court to be incredible would dissuade any attorney from engaging the services of that expert in the future. In one such case, the unbelievable testimony was tendered based on inadequate information provided by counsel, with disastrous result. The expert had a duty to verify the data, however, and failed in that responsibility.

A personal meeting is usually mandatory before confirming an engagement. There is a lot to learn from observing and speaking with you as an expert, as well as observing the condition of your office or laboratory. Premises in disarray suggest a similar mental condition. The in-person visit also affords an opportunity to uncover personal or behavioral idiosyncracies which might diminish your ability to communicate effectively with a factfinder.

Your demeanor and attitude during personal visits may signal a successful or unsuccessful future relationship. First, you must convey whether you are an affirmative person. Second, can you transmit that attitude effectively to others.[1] You must be familiar with existing standards and rules. The attorney will look for evidence of that familiarity early in the hiring process.[2] The hiring attorney or client will consider your time in the field. They will want to know the number of forensic cases you have handled[3] and will compare them to their case.

---

1. Leonard Ring, "Choosing and Presenting Your Expert," *The Brief*, Summer 1985, p. 37.

2. *Ring*, p. 38.

3. Bridgers, "The Selection, Preparation and Direct Examination of Expert Witnesses," *The Docket*, Vol. 2, No. 4, p. 7.

The in-person visit should uncover any mannerisms or behavior characteristics which the client or attorney find objectionable. Humility is a useful trait for a persuasive forensic witness. Sharpness of mind should be combined with mildness of tongue, projecting a demeanor that is enthusiastic and informed, yet not combative or argumentative.[4]

A history of cases you have successfully handled may be one of the best investigative devices available to the attorney or potential client. There is a lawyers' network of expert witnesses in various fields. You become a member of that group by doing good work every time; thus your name will be circulated among attorneys.

Case No. 2. An attorney who had successfully used a team of experts in a mass disaster case recommended the same team for a subsequent multiple toxic tort damage-injury case. The team had by this time been the subject of several complimentary books, which allowed the attorneys and clients to evaluate the success potential of the expert group.

Previous case histories are necessary for adequate credential investigation. You should keep a record of all cases and their outcomes. Be able to explain your test procedures. Have they been used before? Are your processes scientifically recognized? Your ability to answer such questions reflects well on your qualifications.

On occasion, an expert has particular knowledge of the underlying facts of a case. For example, you might have been an active participant in the operative events. That knowledge must be weighted for potential bias, particularly if you are an in-house expert. If observation of the facts as they unfold provides an adequate basis for you to render subsequent opinions, that source of potentially powerful testimony should not be overlooked.

Case No. 3. In a premarriage contract contest case, the expert hired by plaintiff was the attorney who prepared the agreement in the first instance. He was candid, forthright, and articulate. He was able to testify as to the advice given to the testator and the contestant at the time the contract was made, to the effect that the document was probably invalid. The result of that testimony carried the day.

Attorneys often verify experts' references with other experts, prior clients, and other lawyers. Because references are checked, it is important for you to do a first-rate job in each case. Lawyers look for testimonial experience.

---

4. Bridgers, p. 7.

In many cases, outside experts determine the outcome of a case. Staff experts do not always stand up as well under cross-examination. They are by definition not independent. Also, experts who had served as independent witnesses for a lengthy period are more highly valued.

One of the things an attorney looks at is your proximity and availability to do the job. If long distances are involved, it is difficult and sometimes uneconomical to engage you, even though you may be the best person for the case. However, sometimes experts need to be retained from foreign countries. The subject matter of the case may be overseas, or the particular expertise may be found only at great distances. Locating you as a foreign expert, going through the examination and investigation process, and finally preserving your testimony for trial (or arranging for your presence in the courtroom) represent major logistic undertakings. You can prove of major value if your professional network extends overseas. Today, video equipment is often used to preserve testimony of such an overseas expert.

Case No. 4. In a mining case, it was necessary to establish the original location of certain mineral crystals within a foreign mine. Spark source mass spectrography (SSMS), utilized for the general purposes of identifying content of substances, accomplished this forensic task. With known samples for comparison and unmarked samples for suspected product, it was possible for the expert to pinpoint, with reasonable scientific certainty, the general location within the specific mine which was the situs of the specimens.

Available time to do the job is an essential part of the investigation. Sometimes you are called on with little or no notice. Regard such an assignment with skepticism. Unless adequate time is available, your results are likely to be disappointing to everyone involved.

It is the attorney's task at the outset of a case to establish the existence of sufficient time. As with funds insufficient time usually leads to disappointing results.

If, by virtue of employment or otherwise, you have an interest in the outcome of a contested matter, you will be approached with care. Make your disclosure early. That interest not only shades the investigative and testimony process, but also affords substantial opportunity for damaging cross-examination. Government and staff forensic witnesses face this problem almost by definition. The question of indirect interest can be eliminated by the following series of questions on direct examination:

QUESTION: Doctor, you are employed by the state crime lab, is that correct?

ANSWER: Yes, for eighteen years now.

QUESTION: And of course, the state does pay your salary?

ANSWER: Certainly.

QUESTION: Could that payment cause you to slant or shade your testimony in favor of the prosecution?

ANSWER: Absolutely not!

QUESTION: Why is that, Doctor?

ANSWER: There is a vast and significant difference between paying for my time and paying for my integrity, honesty, and reputation. Those factors cannot be the subject of payment — ever!

Case No. 5. Because of costs and time, the only expert available was the claimant himself, a civil engineer. He testified as to standard procedures utilized by a municipality in annexing property and adjusting survey lines in that growth process. The municipality failed to produce contravening testimony, notwithstanding the claimant's interest in the outcome. The testimony carried the day. That case stands as a marker to the exception, not the rule.

As an expert, you must be able to work with other experts in a multidisciplinary case. For example, petroleum engineers, chemists, toxicologists, explosion experts, medical and psychiatric witnesses, and sometimes sociologists or real property appraisers may be called on to assist in presentation of mass disaster cases. The experts must be able to give and take, support and enhance each other's testimony. They must work as a team in fact gathering, preparation, and presentation.

Sometimes experts are engaged not because they have the experience in a field themselves but rather because they have been trained by a known and recognized professional. That training, at the feet of an established master, is valuable reference information for the hiring attorney or client.

A nationally known accountant and forensic witness had spent years training several associates, using the associates to assist in preparation of major cases. Because of the constraints of time and money, the experienced witness was not able to testify in a particular case, but referred the client to a well-trained, but courtroom-inexperienced associate. The associate was able to follow established procedures, emulating and even surpassing the demeanor and persuasiveness of the experienced expert.

Local color is necessary to properly present your testimony. Do you speak the language of the community? Is the forum likely to accept your background and credentials? As a forensic witness from afar, you may need a local expert as a support witness to vouch for your credibility.

INVESTIGATING THE CREDENTIALS OF THE CLIENT AND ATTORNEY

It is to your advantage to determine whether the attorney and client about to engage your services are honest. Some rare cases involve false claims or perjury. Various insurance-industry computer databases can identify professional claimants or attorneys who have presented fraudulent claims.

Newspaper articles and morgues are excellent sources of data concerning the events for which your testimony is sought and the client and attorney who are seeking the engagement. Lawyers' professional associations can be consulted. You should meet the attorney and client in person. Give due consideration to your instinctive likes and dislikes.

Personality conflicts disclosed in an early meeting might indicate that you should pass up a particular case. When people dislike each other at the outset, it may be difficult, if not impossible, for them to work together.

Pay particular attention to the client's version of the facts. If incredible circumstances are suggested, you may wish to reconsider the engagement. Body language, eye contact, and behavioral mannerisms are all worthy for consideration. The general reputation of both attorney and client are areas of fruitful inquiry.

The best-known legal directory, *Martindale-Hubbell*, is a source of information about attorneys. This legal directory provides a wealth of information about attorneys, including peer ratings. In addition, the directory includes a telephone number you can call for further information.

Professional references are also available to you through bar associations and other attorneys in the community. The best references come from other experts who have successfully worked with the hiring lawyer.

To summarize, among the things you want to know about the engaging attorney and client are:

- general reputation for integrity
- organizational ability to get the job done on time and in an orderly fashion
- creative use of demonstrative aids
- professional courtesy and recognition of interprofessional codes
- preparation effort for investigation, discovery, and trial
- reputation and result in the substantive area
- prompt bill paying

CONCLUSION

The forensic witness, the client, and the attorney all benefit from mutual investigation and credential verification. Some assignments are just not meant to be. The relationship between expert witnesses, attorneys and clients is intense; there is little margin for error. Many avenues for inquiry are available. Your confidence in the case and ability to work with the parties involved will benefit from liberal use of the investigative opportunities.

YOUR ENGAGEMENT AND COMPENSATION

INTRODUCTION

You can take a number of steps to make your life easier during the course of an assignment. Most importantly, clarifying possible areas of misunderstanding through an engagement letter or directive will eliminate later confusion and possible areas of disagreement. Forty-six percent of the responding experts regularly use engagement letters.

Fifty-three percent of the experts surveyed reported occasional problems getting paid. Sources of problems included:

- difficulty with attorney
- simple delay
- case lost and hence no funds
- absence of written engagement letter
- erroneous work by the expert
- possibility the fee was too high
- additional work called for beyond the agreement
- lack of clarity as to who was responsible for paying the fee

The following methods of resolution of fee disputes were reported:

- negotiated settlement
- suit (mostly won by experts)
- grievance procedures
- severed relationship with the attorney
- accept the loss and move on

The remainder of the chapter addresses these issues in depth.

INITIAL CONTACT

The first contact you have concerning a case may come by telephone, letter, or an in-person visit from the potential client or attorney. At this time, write an intake memo. That memo should include certain minimal information:

- date
- name, address, and phone number of client
- name, address, and phone number of attorney
- name, address, and phone number of opposing party
- name, address, and phone number of opposing attorney
- date of the subject event
- location of the event or things involved
- location of relevant documents and information
- brief description of the problem or situation
- statement of terms of initial assignment

Many initial contacts do not result in cases. It is well to maintain a file of contact memos entitled "Pending Matters Not Yet Cases." The memo could be important in checking for possible conflicts should you later be contacted by an adverse party.

Who Is the Client and Who Is the Opposition?

One critical determination to be made is who is the entity or person for whom you are to render your services. Are you working for the attorney or directly for the client? Is the client an individual, a partnership, or a corporation?

It is equally important to determine who the opposing parties are, to eliminate any potential conflict of interest. The problem of conflict of interest becomes particularly acute as your engagements and associations become extensive.

Case No. 1. A recent attempt to engage certified public accountant representation in a testimonial setting required the accounting firm to inquire of all its national and international offices as to whether the opposing party was or had ever been represented by the firm. The accounting firm's careful scrutiny revealed a prior representation of the corporate opponent in another city, which disqualified the firm from the potential forensic undertaking.

A conflict of interest question extends to second tier inquiry. If the opposing party is a corporation, determine who the officers and directors of that corporation are, again to clear conflicts. You should accept no information about the potential assignment until the conflict of interest question has been fully investigated. The reason is obvious: if you obtain information about the opposite side of a current case, that information could disqualify you from continuing with a present assignment.

The particularly skilled or widely known expert will be frequently contacted, though not all those contacts will result in engagements. Previous contact by the opposing party might be forgotten but for your retention of the case intake memo. That brief inquiry, which did not mature to an engagement, may be sufficient to disqualify you from later representing the opposing party.

Nature of the Assignment

Expert engagements are generally undertaken in two distinct ways. First, you may be hired as a consultant to guide the investigation of the client and attorney in a technical field, possibly even before an adversary case has matured. In that role, you may assist in averting a full-blown dispute.

Second, you may be engaged as a witness to testify during trial or other dispute-resolution proceedings. Often the consultation witness matures into a testimonial witness.

Different rules apply to consultation and testimonial witnesses. In general, consultation experts cannot be deposed by opposing counsel. Their work with the attorney is covered by privilege, and only in the most unusual circumstances can the results of the consultation be made available to the opposing party.[1]

In addition to the distinction between consultation and testimonial experts, give attention to the specific assignment to which your services are directed. Assignments are described in various ways. Following are some typical examples:

- In your expert opinion, did a real estate developer pursue requisite annexation zoning and development in a careful, proper, and prudent way?
- What was the instrument which caused puncture wounds in the chest of the deceased victim of a barroom brawl?
- Did the attorney render erroneous advice concerning application of a statute of limitations so as to deprive a party of a right to appeal an adverse trial court judgment?
- Was the negligence of the structural engineer by inadequately designing support columns the proximate cause of a building collapse?
- What was the cause of a sudden unexpected jamming of a bicycle wheel, causing the rider to be thrown to the ground and sustain severe personal injuries?

---

1. Rule 26(b)(4)(B), Federal Rules of Civil Procedure; *DelCastor, Inc.* v. *Vail Associates, Inc.*, 108 F.R.D. 405, 407 (D. Colo. 1985); *Ager* v. *Stormont Hospital*, 622 F. 2d 496 (10th Cir. 1980); *Phillips* v. *District Court*, 194 Colo. 455, 573 P. 2d 553, 556 (1978).

Your assignment should be clearly and carefully stated. The attorney and client must tell you what they need. You must have the specific statement to guide your work and keep it focused.

Specific Responsibilities

In addition to a statement of general assignment, an itemization of specific duties is sometimes appropriate. For example, if your assignment involves investigation of an explosion scene, the listing of specific duties could include any of these:

- inspection of the scene, including photography
- examination of official reports
- sampling of debris
- removal of possible explosive fragments
- interviewing key witnesses and victims
- cooperating with local officials
- formulating preliminary causation thesis
- preparing final cause-and-effect report

The benefit of an itemized list of specific responsibilities is that both you and the client or attorney will go through the thought process necessary to bring your service into proper focus within the framework of the overall case. In addition, opportunity for misunderstanding is reduced.

Dates and Deadlines

A clear understanding of the timeframe within which you must do your work should be established. If trial dates or statutes of limitation are involved, they should be noted at the outset to avoid later misunderstanding. Some cases require preliminary expert reports at an early date. The overall strategy of the case often revolves around the timing of your investigation.

Administrative and judicial dispute-resolution processes frequently involve a carefully timed sequence of steps. Your clear understanding of the time requirements will avoid the last-minute crunch which often attends discovery and production matters.

Engagement Letter or Directive

Whether you work for a public agency or are a private consultant, you should use a directive or engagement letter to commence your assignment. This is true even for routine assignments. A typical engagement letter is found in Appendix F. The sample may be more detailed than your purposes require; consider it as a guide only, but make the use of such an agreement part of the commencement of each case.

The engagement letter or directive may be a discoverable item by opposing counsel. It may contain instructions to you. Under current case decisions, any information relied on by you as an expert to help you formulate opinions is a discoverable item, certainly in court proceedings.[2] Therefore, phrase the document carefully, avoiding any hint of direction to you to reach a specific conclusion. The document should clearly state that you are to reach your conclusions based only on your professional opinion after full inquiry and investigation.

COMPENSATION

As an employee of a governmental laboratory or forensic facility, your compensation is routine and part of your employment agreement. If you become engaged in private practice, compensation must be included in your engagement letter. The rate and method of compensation should be carefully spelled out. The engagement letter frequently fails to spell out who is responsible for paying your fees, the client or the attorney. Often the attorney is known to the expert and the client is not. As a result, it is to your advantage to have the attorney guarantee the payment.

Expert fees may range from $25 per hour to $2,500 or more per day. Find out what experts like you are actually charging in your community. Your fee may be determined by your experience, the complexity of the assignment, or time constraints placed on you. Consider whether your fee is net or gross: in other words, who pays the expenses you incur in performing your assigned duties?

AN IMPORTANT ETHICAL CONSIDERATION

Part of the engagement process between forensic expert and attorney or client may involve a preliminary discussion based upon hypothetical facts, in order to determine the expert's general opinion in a given professional area. Specifically, the attorney or client may wish to determine whether an expert is predisposed to a certain conclusion.

A typical initial contact dialogue may involve discussions like this:

ATTORNEY: Doctor, as a thoracic surgeon, I know you have performed a number of operations involving first rib resection.

---

2. Rule 26(b)(4)(B) Federal Rules of Civil Procedure; *DelCastor, supra* at 407–408; *Phillips, supra* at 556; *U.S.* v. *McKay,* 372 F. 2d 174 (5th Cir. 1967).

DOCTOR: Yes, that's correct. That surgery has often been used to alleviate what's called the thoracic outlet syndrome.

ATTORNEY: Doctor, my previously healthy client sustained an injury requiring a first rib resection following an automobile collision. After surgery, all symptoms of the thoracic outlet syndrome, including diminished radial pulse, were alleviated. Doctor, if I can establish for you the facts which I have just recited, and if after you have made an investigation of the medical records and a clinical examination of the patient you conclude that those facts are accurate, what sort of conclusions would you make as an expert testifying witness about the car crash being the proximate cause of the thoracic outlet syndrome necessitating a first rib resection?

DOCTOR: If you can establish the facts you just indicated and if the medical records, the history, and a clinical examination of the patient support that conclusion, it would generally be my belief that, absent other intervening or contraindicative causes, the car crash probably caused the thoracic outlet syndrome and resulting first rib resection surgery.

This sort of inquiry is proper. The inquiry and dialogue allow the expert to determine the general area of testimony which will be required, require the attorney to state the client's situation accurately, and ensures that the expert opinion will meet the attorney's and client's expectation, assuming the facts stated are established.

The following dialogue, as distinguished from the previous scenario, would constitute an improper imposition by an attorney on an expert's independence. Having been forewarned, you are now forearmed about such unscrupulous tactics.

ATTORNEY: I know you have testified in a number of cases about property valuations in condemnation. The state in this case has offered our clients $100,000 for their property. The client believes the property is worth $300,000. It's important for me to know at the outset whether your expert opinion can support a $300,000 valuation. If you can't support such an opinion, I'm going to have to find another expert for our client.

WITNESS: Well, I'd have to look at comparable sales in the neighborhood, consider the income stream generated by the property, and examine the cost of construction of the property less appropriate depreciation in order to reach a value opinion.

ATTORNEY: No. I'm not concerned at this point about the standard approaches to the value. What I want to know is, can you tell me now that you can support a valuation of $300,000 for this property? If you can't, I'm just going to have to hire someone else.

That type of examination is unethical and improper. You are being asked to venture a position for a client which is either not supported by the pragmatic data or has been entirely suggested by an attorney. However, you can definitively reach a conclusion only upon careful, professional, factual, and technical investigation. Tendering unsupported opinions suggested by a client or attorney is unethical and contrary to the goals of the dispute-resolution process.

CONCLUSION

Starting the engagement in an orderly and businesslike way indicates your competence. Intake memos and engagement letters reflect your attention to duty. They also serve to eliminate possible conflicts of interest and fee disputes. Your general and specific assignments are important parts of the initial engagement. Certain permissible areas of inquiry and dialogue between you and the client or attorney are proper, so long as you maintain your right to reach an independent judgment and opinion.

8 THE INVESTIGATIVE PROCESS: PEOPLE, PLACES AND THINGS

INTRODUCTION

Traditionally newsgathering involves some well-established principles of who, what, where, when, and why. The investigative process you will follow in your forensic assignments involves precisely those same five elements. Who are the actors, the victims, or the investigators? What are the relevant facts? Where did these events occur? When did the events occur and in what time sequence? Why did all this happen the way it did?

A case begins with an event involving people, places, events, and objects. In most cases, you will become acquainted with those four fundamental elements. It is said that the combination of people, places, and things in a chance moment of time creates an accident, injury, damage or event which may precipitate need for forensic services. The unique bonding of people, places, and things within a defined timeframe constitutes the unusual element of almost every forensic engagement. Jung called this meaningful coincidence synchronicity.

This chapter will present some case examples showing unusual investigative techniques and results. They suggest the importance of using a standard investigative technique in all your forensic assignments. If you do not have such a standardized approach, this material will help you formulate one. All the material in this chapter can be used in conjunction with the case plan described in Chapter 5.

Meeting the people involved in the case refers not only to the actors or victims but also to official investigators, law-enforcement personnel, and the clients and attorneys involved. What is meant by site inspection and investigation of tangible objects is self-explanatory. Expert witnesses should always visit the scene and inspect the physical property involved in a forensic assignment. Many is the disappointed advocate whose expert has been either disqualified or given little credibility because he or she failed to view the site or physically inspect the materials involved in the case.

The survey suggests that almost 50 percent of the responding experts turn first to the technical literature when presented with a new forensic assignment. The next source of information is the public or institutional records (24 percent). Then comes specialized data: that is, information about the specific subject, followed by consultation with the attorney who engaged the expert.

In general, there are fifteen steps to the investigative process:

- Obtain from the client or attorney a preliminary statement of what happened
- Read and view the client's materials
- Survey the technical literature
- Develop an early working hypothesis
- Investigate the physical evidence involved in the case
- Group the data obtained into logical categories
- Process the data obtained and determine what it shows
- Record all tests and evaluation steps
- Plan graphic displays of the information you have gathered
- Relate your findings to a nonprofessional person and listen to his or her questions and comments
- Package the results of your effort. This includes developing verbal or written reports, together with supporting drawings, models, charts, or tables
- Highlight and follow up on what is yet to be accomplished in the investigative process
- Preserve your data for discovery and trial
- Present your conclusions to the appropriate dispute-resolution forum
- Close your file, retaining what might have value for later use as part of your library; return to attorney and client those items which are no longer necessary for you to keep

The remainder of this chapter elaborates on and explains these steps.

GETTING STARTED WITH YOUR INVESTIGATION

As in other phases of your work, a checklist of things to do will establish your credibility and ensure your thoroughness. If you do not have one, design it now. If you do, compare your protocol with the following ideas.

This checklist is intended as an example. Your format should be based on your needs and fields of expertise. It should be everchanging and expansive as your experience suggests modifications. At a minimum, it should include the following steps:

- Meet the client, or the client's representative if the client is an entity
- Visit the client's attorney
- Visit the client's place of residence or occupation, if relevant
- Visit and inspect the event scene, if physically possible
- Examine all available public and private records and investigative reports
- View and photograph, or otherwise record, tangible items for quantity, quality, and condition
- Survey the professional literature

What is the purposes of each of these steps?

Meeting your client will ensure interpersonal compatibility and enhance communication. In most cases, you will obtain the initial version of the facts on this visit. Meeting the attorney will afford initial guidance through the issues of fact, law, and relevant rules of evidence. Meeting the client at the place of residence or business, or both, can prove instructive. Some small clue, observation, or impression can often be a key to a solution, proof, or disproof.

Site investigation is a mandatory step. It allows you to investigate accident debris and to obtain relevant samples for analysis. While you are on the scene, attempt to visualize how the events occurred. Place yourself in the position of the actors. Determine whether doors were opened or closed, windows locked or unlocked. Anticipate, if you can, why victims were found in particular postures. Relive the events in question to help you determine what really happened.

Because our society and judicial process are complex, a number of reports about the event may already be in existence before you are engaged, or you may be the author of those investigative reports. In any case, be aware of the standard operating procedures of organizations and entities that produce reports of extraordinary events. Reports you should seek initially are those from the attorney and client and the internal investigative reports of the client's organization, police, fire department, or other governmental bodies.

Insurance investigations generate useful information. Reports of safety officers, investigators of industrial commissions, and government investigations will prove useful. It is important to identify all persons and organizations that have probed the event. Usually public reports are available for the asking, on payment of a minimal fee. Reticent officials sometimes respond to subpoena for deposition. Various freedom of information acts are often useful in obtaining these reports. Obtain all tangible results suggested by those investigative efforts.

The survey of literature should include technical bulletins on the product or process involved in the case. Internal operating and procedure manuals should be reviewed. Standard textbooks for the industry and articles in professional journals provide excellent sources. Finally, media coverage of the event may provide additional clues to causation.

Excellent investigative information can be provided by the client or attorney. They are uniquely able to summarize important data. They can often cut directly through the maze of available information, pointing you toward the source of the problem.[1] There is, however, one danger. Unfortunately, clients and attorneys sometimes write history as they wish it occurred, rather than as it actually happened. Remember, there are at least two sides to most stories. The matter would not be in controversy if there were no one on the other side with well-supported contrary views.

As you undertake field and laboratory investigation, try to visualize how the data could best be presented to a factfinder. Keep in mind that one fundamental of forensic testimony includes the ability to convey complicated information clearly, understandably, and persuasively. The pedantic approach to teaching just will not do before a jury of laypersons or an administrative panel composed of nontechnical members.

DEMONSTRATIVE PREPARATION

Experts tell us we learn 15 percent from what we hear and 85 percent from what we see. Therefore, you must translate complex principles into visual presentations. You must clearly demonstrate how those principles can be applied to the facts of your case. A list of possible vehicles for visual presentation of technical data is included at this point because these materials must be planned early in your investigation:

- Drawings, for use during testimony
- Photographs, including black and white and color enlargements and slides
- Films or videos
- Charts and graphs summarizing voluminous data[2]
- Time-lapse still photography
- Photographic enlargements or overhead projection of critical documents

---

1. Bridgers, "The Selection, Preparation and Direct Examination of Expert Witnesses," *The Docket*, Vol. 2, No. 4, Fall 1987, p. 18.
2. See, for example, Rule 1006, Federal Rules of Evidence, specifically allowing, if not encouraging, use of such summary charts and graphs.

- Parts, samples, or specimens of tests which were performed
- Microscopic examination of slides enhanced by video presentation; this technique is particularly effective for cellular or fiber analysis
- Models and mockups of the site
- Holographic presentations
- Computer-generated or enhanced animation to demonstrate movement, time, and sequences of events
- Computer-enhanced displays to portray otherwise difficult-to-observe features
- Digital retouching of photographs (be sure to state that retouching has been done)
- Three-dimensional computer graphics

This list has relevance to Chapter 20, on techniques for the witness stand. It is the truly great witness who uses demonstrative and graphic aids for maximum effect, working with counsel to obtain appropriate rulings to allow use or admissibility.

It is always effective to produce the actual item at issue: the knife, valve, coupling, electric switch, burnt fabric, or deteriorated timber. In a case involving an allegedly defective item of heavy equipment, jurors were taken to a warehouse and afforded an opportunity to see, sit in, and view the vehicle from the position of both operator and injured fellow employee.

Models can be equally effective. In one case, a full-scale model was prepared of a building that exploded in part because of a defectively installed liquified petroleum gas regulator valve. In another case, a scale model was prepared of a giant crane which had collapsed, causing a workman's death. In a third case, a topographic model was prepared of an acreage subject to a partial condemnation, where resulting road elevations caused substantial damage to the remainder of the owner's land. The models described were the focal points of each of these cases.

A number of national companies can provide three-dimensional digital animation and interactive video production services. Possible uses for this type of graphic display include cases involving radio tower and takeoff procedures; runway scenarios, including aircraft incursions; vehicle-operating errors; and complex assembly procedures.

SOME EXAMPLES OF AN ORGANIZED APPROACH

An engineering firm that does construction claim analysis shares its scope of services outline, which appears as Appendix G. This organized approach to claim analysis is instructive. Included as part of Appendix G is a critical path method (CPM) developed to graphically display hypothetical responsibility for project delay. It is included in Appendix G both for its own value as an expert's opinion and for your use as an investigative tool to track your own critical path analytic approach to the case assignment. The CPM is particularly useful when your investigative process involves many steps undertaken sequentially.

Another example of an organized approach to a forensic assignment is found as Appendix H. An engineer has analyzed the steps necessary to investigate vehicular malfunction, accident reconstruction, and vehicle arson. Adapt appendices G and H to help you develop your own format for the investigative phase of your forensic assignments.

CHAIN OF CUSTODY

As with all graphic presentations and demonstrative materials, the expert must give meticulous care to the source of the data and methods of combination. Unbiased techniques of enlargement and enhancement are combined with fundamental fact gathering details such as date, time, and place of initial data gathering. These techniques of backing up and supporting the accuracy of graphic presentations are tied closely to the entire chain-of-custody procedure followed in all criminal and some civil cases. Chain of custody literally requires each person who touches an item of evidence to sign for its possession. Generically it refers to the ability to track tangible evidence items.

A typical chain-of-custody checklist would include the following items:

1. *Field location of the item:* the geographical location where the item was found or observed, including a careful log entry and, if necessary, a photograph of the location.
2. *Preserving the item:* bagging, packaging, or otherwise handling the item in such a fashion that the evidentiary value is not destroyed. Appropriate containers, again with tags and labels, should be used.
3. *Chain of physical custody:* Each person who handles the item should make a log entry and receipt of the handling. As the item passes from person to person, ultimately to laboratory or storage area, a chain of receipts should be executed. No question should ever exist at trial or hearing as to missing items, mishandling of items, mislabeling of items, or destruction of items other than in special circumstances where destructive tests are required.

A typical chain-of-custody guideline is included as Appendix I, provided courtesy of the U.S. Department of Justice, Federal Bureau of Investigation.

INVESTIGATING TANGIBLE OBJECTS

Some examples of effective view and inspection of tangible objects may stimulate your thinking for a present or future forensic assignment.

Case No. 1. In a notable murder prosecution, officials in and around Lake City, Florida, spent months combing a vast area seeking the remains of a victim. Ultimately, analysis by a skilled forensic expert of some discarded cigarette butts proved the key to narrowing the site search, ultimately revealing the child's remains. Analysis of fibers from the victim's clothing and the suspect's vehicle was sufficient to tie the victim to the accused, resulting in the conviction, sentencing, and ultimate execution of serial killer Ted Bundy.

Case No. 2. This case involved massive structural defects to a 104-unit apartment complex. The defects were causing buildings to shift, doors and windows to jam, fireplaces and chimneys to pull away from building walls, and surface water to collect in low areas, stairwells, and basements. The swimming pool shell cracked. Boilers and mechanical equipment, instead of resting on concrete floors, were literally hanging from pipe connections.

A team of forensic structural engineers meticulously excavated and then photographed foundations, caissons, grade beams, and voids. At trial, the photographs dramatically portrayed missing caissons, caissons that were "belled" at the top, absence of void materials, grade beams in direct contact with soil, and heavy boilers suspended as much as five inches from the concrete floors on which they were to have rested. The investigation also led to a plan of corrective action, which was carried out under direct supervision of the forensic expert team.

Case No. 3. A motorcyclist proceeding on an open highway at about 60 mph was observed to suddenly lose control of his vehicle. It fishtailed violently and threw him to the ground, causing him to die instantly of a broken neck. No road condition was observed which caused the accident. Investigators combed the roadway and recovered debris from the accident site, including three-quarters of the motorcycle's front wheel hub. The wheel spokes had been attached to the hub.

The debris was delivered to the forensic expert, a metallurgist. Electron microscopy revealed that the front wheel hub had cracked due to metal fatigue rather than impact. It was later established that the hub was made from a defective metal alloy which led to the fatigue. That evidence would never have been obtained had it not been for the careful gathering of debris, coupled with forensic investigation and opinion as to the cause of the metal fracture.

In 1983, Paul D. Rhinegold and Robert Vilensky complied an all-inclusive procedure to guide the expert and attorney in conducting discovery in a products liability action.[3] That analysis constitutes the basis for the following checklist of steps in investigating tangible objects:

- *Identification of the item:* serial number, ingredients formula, quantities and qualities, specifications, markings, trademarks or logos.
- *How the item works:* how does the product do what it is supposed to do? What are the functions of each part and the relationships of the parts to the total item?
- *Use:* intended use and possible misuse or abuse of the product or item. Does its present condition suggest abuse or misuse?
- *Conduct of parties:* the actions of various individuals with regard to the tangible items you are seeking and locating. Consider handling, mishandling, design, in-house testing, quality control, manufacture, sale, promotion, packaging, misuse or modification.
- *Patent:* patents constitute a guide to the inner workings of an item. Often the patent drawings will explain a function which is not otherwise observable.
- *Composition:* wood, metal, plastic, gas; solid or liquid?
- *Markings and labels:* carefully record and photograph all markings and labels. Hazardous warnings, color coding, and visibility become critical. Do not overlook the obvious.
- *Instruction and warranty:* is warranty, guarantee, or instruction information available? Is the information clear? Is it readable? Has it been obliterated?
- *Promotional and sales effort:* how is the object advertised, photographed, sold, and promoted? Who is doing the advertising and sales effort? What photographs exist concerning the product item or evidentiary material?
- *Location:* how did the item get to the place it is found? Does it belong where it is found? If the item is not packaged, should it have been?
- *Parts and components:* study the interrelationship of the components and subparts. What specifications attend the subassemblies?
- *Configuration and design:* the design or misdesign of an object may be highly relevant.
- *Overall safety consideration:* was the item used in a safe or unsafe way? Are necessary guards, interlocks, and coverings in place?

---

3. Rhinegold and Vilensky, "Discovery in the Products Case: A Checklist," *Trial Magazine*, November 1983, pp. 124–128.

- *Related and collateral items:* What items were to be used with the item at the time of the operative events? What debris is found with the observed item?
- *Tests and inspections:* preuse tests should be considered. Your tests may be operational, physical, or chemical. If destructive testing is undertaken, different evidentiary problems are presented.
- *History:* consider prior events that may bear on the subject of inquiry. For example, has a particular location been a frequent scene of auto accidents? Evidence at the site may provide clues to these important questions.

The following three cases illustrate particularly unusual field investigations. Each demonstrates some of the steps just described.

Case No. 4. Careful investigation of a crash between a large truck and a Volkswagen produced the following items of conclusive evidence:

- Police officers' investigative report indicated failure of the truck to stop for a stop light.
- Truck driver's statement to witnesses disclosed alleged brake failure.
- Police officers' tests of the truck's brakes following the collision found them defective.
- Shop repair tickets revealed brake restoration after the collision.
- Vehicle history records showed seven separate operator's complaints about defective or inadequate brakes.
- Recovery of the actual brake shoes showed they had been worn through to the rivets.

Case No. 5. Fifteen homes were flooded after a road construction project. A natural drainageway overflowed its banks during a period of heavy rains. The water engineer studied topography drawings and elevations and engineering plans, interviewed neighbors and victims, and inspected photographs.

The pictures revealed the problem. At the time of highway construction, a sixteen-inch water conduit had been destroyed by heavy equipment. Photographs of construction excavations revealed the damaged conduit. Upon completion of the project, the construction company had failed to reestablish the conduit. The new construction literally created a dam across the natural drainageway, with the inevitable result of flooding.

Case No. 6. After a successful coronary bypass operation, a patient sustained sudden, unexplained convulsions. He was comatose for twenty-eight days and ultimately died. Investigation by a forensic team including a cardiac surgeon, an anesthesiologist, a recovery room nurse, a mechanical engineer, and a pathologist disclosed these events.

After surgery, the patient was moved to the recovery room. Standard procedure called for commencement of 100 percent oxygen for a period of twenty-four hours. The hospital house oxygen supply was utilized. As the operating room recovery nurse affixed the oxygen mask to the patient, a tank truck outside the hospital was in the process of filling the house oxygen system.

Investigation revealed that the hospital had called for an oxygen supply truck. The gas company had dispatched an oxygen supply truck. The driver selected and drove a nitrogen-filled tank truck to the hospital. He proceeded to physically force the tank fitting, which was supposed to prohibit nitrogen from being pumped incorrectly, into the oxygen tank. As a result, nitrogen was introduced into the house oxygen system, creating a mixture of 60 percent nitrogen and 40 percent oxygen. That mixture was inadequate for the patient, and the inadequate oxygen supply triggered the convulsive event, ultimate coma, and death. The chain of events and causation was uncovered only through meticulous investigative inquiry.

This case exemplifies the social utility of your services as a forensic witness. As a result of the investigation, corrective steps were instituted nationally. The forensic team probably saved hundreds of lives.

TESTING

Testing refers to the ways you might examine a tangible object or process in preparation for courtroom presentation.

The following case examples illustrate the utility of laboratory and test procedures. In many situations, the clinical, laboratory, and testing procedures establish the data you need to premise your conclusion and opinion.

Case No. 7. A criminal defendant was charged with first-degree murder. Metal-detection tests performed by the prosecution on the defendant's operative hand were inconclusive as to whether the defendant had held the suspected murder weapon. The defendant's criminalist established that the prosecution's tests were suggestive of holding a beer can rather than a knife. The defendant was acquitted, although the case did not turn on that single item alone.

Unfortunately, not all testing is honestly done. Some crime labs, because of the crunch of demands for drug testing, have reported the presence of controlled substances, based only on a presumptive screening. That test would not justify a scientific conclusion. While some defendants might plead guilty based on such inadequate evidence, such shallow work does not well serve the process.[4]

Case No. 8. Various defendants in a methane contamination case attempted to allege that existing residue in the soil created the pollution. The plaintiff insisted that the contamination was caused by the defendant's abandoned landfill. Gas chromatograph analysis of the methane product from the landfill against that found in the contaminated areas established without doubt that the defendant's product caused the contamination.

Case No. 9. A man operating an automobile lost control of his car for no apparent reason and collided with an obstruction. Subsequent thoracic surgery revealed a ruptured aortic aneurysm. The forensic issue was whether the aneurysm ruptured through trauma or spontaneously. Pathologic examination of the blood, heart tissue, and sac surrounding the heart on autopsy established traumatic rather than spontaneous rupture.

FORMULATING A WORKING HYPOTHESIS

After investigation and testing have established the facts of a case, the next step is to formulate a working hypothesis. The following cases show how this is done.

Case No. 10. Two men, licensed pilots, were killed when their small plane crashed in a snowstorm. Only one was IFR (instrument flight rated) qualified. It was necessary to establish why the aircraft was in the snowstorm and which of the two was piloting the craft at the time of the crash.

The working hypotheses were:
- The aircraft had been misdirected by the FAA controllers to a weathered-in airstrip
- The IFR-rated pilot was at the controls

The first hypothesis was established by expert analysis of radio transmissions between the aircraft, the FAA controller, and the tower at the weathered-in airstrip to which the aircraft had been directed. Further, examination of the actual weather records, the plane's location when it radioed for FAA assistance, weather reports at the crash site, and

---

4. *Scientific Sleuthing Review #1*, Vol. 13, Winter 1989, p. 2.

weather reports at another open airstrip established that the air controller had not given sufficient care to the weather reports available.

The second hypothesis was established by three items of expert analysis:

- The weather conditions were such that experienced pilots would have turned the aircraft over to the flyer with the instrument rating
- The right rudder pedal was severely bent on impact, consistent with the position of the aircraft when it hit the ground
- Autopsy analysis of both victims, who had been ejected from the aircraft upon impact, revealed that the right leg of the IFR-rated pilot was shattered

The facts of this case emphasize the need for a working hypothesis in a forensic case and application of that hypothesis to the discovered facts. Sometimes the hypothesis is not readily apparent and considerable investigation is required before a specific theory can be developed.

Case No. 11. The prosecution hypothesis was that the defendant, charged with burglary, was (1) the perpetrator of the burglary and (2) the seller of the stolen goods to the state's prime prosecution witness, who had purchased the recently stolen materials from the defendant. The prosecution forensic fiber expert was able to analyze and conclusively establish fiber remnants from stolen materials in both the defendant's van and in his home closet.

There is a sense of satisfaction when a working hypothesis is established. It represents an essence of the scientific method.

USE OF A STANDARD PROTOCOL

Another available investigating device is the standard protocol, if one exists. Comparison of that standard to your facts may reveal significant oversights or discrepancies.

In a thoughtful article, attorney Richard Bostwick carefully analyzes a protocol for management of a medical malpractice case involving malignant hypothermia.[5] The standard protocol included fifteen steps that a physician must follow in a usual case to properly treat and care for the patient. Therefore, in preparing defense of an anesthesia malpractice case involving malignant hypothermia, the defense team can compare the standard protocol described with the steps that were or were not

---

5. Bostwick, "Anesthesia Malpractice Today: Defense Preparation Management." *International Society of Barristers Quarterly*, Vol. 18, No. 4, October 1983, p. 428.

taken in the particular case. Their investigation tells the defense team what areas of the defense require concentrated attention.

Many scientific, technical, and professional tasks are the subject of standard protocols. Your task as an investigating forensic witness is to locate that standard protocol and examine the case against it. Your conclusion may be that standard procedures were followed. Or you may determine that important steps were omitted. The question then becomes, did the omitted items create civil or criminal culpability?

CONCLUSION

Investigation is the process by which you gather the data on which your opinions and reports will be based. Many ideas and lists can be used to make the process more efficient. Plan your work and work your plan. Develop your own standard fact gathering and investigative checklist. See how others do their work, and follow those examples. As you gather the facts, give consideration to graphic displays which will help you later present the material in an understandable and effective way. As your findings are developed, communicate them to non-technical and non-professional people. Listen to their comments and questions. Constantly strive to translate your findings into nontechnical layman language. The most complete investigation will be of little importance if the result cannot be relayed in a clear, effective, and understandable way.

9 AVOIDING SELECTIVE FACT GATHERING: THE ACTION PLAN

INTRODUCTION

In presenting facts to an expert, attorneys and clients sometimes tell their story the way they wish it had been rather than the way it actually was. Since trial of a disputed matter in any forum is often the retelling of past events, accuracy of recitation is essential. If you do not get it right, your adversary might, often with disastrous result to your client.

An ethical obligation attends the fact gathering process for all concerned. Our dispute-resolution processes cannot survive if experts, attorneys, and clients attempt to create biased results through selective fact gathering. Attorneys have a responsibility to provide you with complete and accurate information about the case.[1] Your responsibility is to refuse to be satisfied with incomplete information. Press to obtain all available factual information.

CAUSES OF SELECTIVE FACT GATHERING

A recent news story focused on certain physicians who are regular defense witnesses: so-called "medical prostitutes."[2] It highlighted the fact that there are physicians who sometimes forget the Hippocratic oath, sell out to the pressures of the legal system, are hired to render the "right" opinions in certain cases, subrogate money for medicine, and can become torn between service to the patient and the patient's employer. These are all examples of selective fact gathering by an expert witness.

In the final analysis, there are four causes of selective fact gathering or selective fact presentation:

---

1. Postol, "A Legal Primer for Expert Witnesses," *For the Defense*, February 1987, p. 24.
2. Locke, "Medical Prostitutes," *Up the Creek*, Vol. 14, No. 21, April 7, 1989, p. 1.

- Willful mispresentation in an attempt to shade your conclusions
- Willful selection of only those facts that support the conclusion reflective of one side of the controversy
- Selective presentation of facts and evidence through the expert, by the attorney or client, because in retelling the story, they have shaped the events as they hoped they had occurred ("Selective recollection")
- Genuinely erroneous field, clinical, or investigative preparation which did not disclose salient evidence

Selective fact gathering is contrary to the scientific method. It should go against your judgment. Such a process will impede your ability to reach valid, supportable, professional, and ethical conclusions.

WAYS TO AVOID THE PITFALLS

There are some key steps you can follow to avoid the pitfalls of selective fact gathering or fact presentation.

- Keep an open mind
- Do not approach a case with predetermined conclusions as to causation, culpability, fault, or damage
- Remember that attorneys and clients come to you with facts which may be slanted, either accidentally or purposefully
- Carefully follow your own well-established investigative steps; develop forms, procedures, and processes which will ensure that you do not overlook evidence
- Observe the ethical guidelines of your profession
- Recognize that you have a vital role in the dispute-resolution process

THE EFFECT OF SELECTIVE FACT GATHERING

The examples which follow are derived from actual cases. In each, critical evidence was either not made available to the expert or was overlooked or disregarded. Each situation will reflect the nature of the case, the missing or overlooked evidence, the cause for its not being considered, the effect on the outcome of the case if the evidence had been known, and finally, how the unhappy circumstance could have been avoided.

Case No. 1

Case: Plaintiff's claim was for professional negligence arising from undisclosed conflict of interest by an attorney.

Evidence: Defendant charged with the alleged conflict had publicized its existence in the presence of several persons, including plaintiff.

Cause: The client, unintentionally, had forgotten the public statement of possible conflict of interest.

Effect: The effect in court was to undercut plaintiff's expert, probably resulting in a defense verdict.

Avoidance: The missing evidence could conceivably have been made known to the expert through more aggressive questioning of plaintiff by the expert or counsel prior to trial.

Case No. 2

Case: A condemnation case involved valuation of a fleet of vehicles.

Evidence: The condemning authority's expert had applied an erroneous depreciation rule and slanted discount rate.

Cause: The cause was an erroneous and intentional instruction to the expert by the client.

Effect: The result was that calculations were in error by approximately $500,000. Cross-examination of the expert and revelation of the correct standards at trial resulted in a substantially increased recovery for the property owner.

Avoidance: The effect could have been avoided had the expert done independent research concerning the depreciation standard and discount rate to be applied, rather than allowing the client to mandate those critical factors.

Case No. 3

Case: Defendant in a criminal case pled not guilty by reason of insanity.

Evidence: The state psychiatrist missed or overlooked significant evidence of insanity. In attempting to establish mental competency, he had spent less than forty-five minutes of interview time with the defendant. The psychiatrist failed to obtain a history from the accused of prior incarceration for mental illness or to interrogate any collateral witnesses, including family, friends, and jailers. The state psychiatrist did not observe defendant in the courtroom evidencing hallucination episodes.

Cause: The state's expert had apparently seen so many cases of feigned insanity, he simply did not do the job.

Effect: Revelation during cross-examination of numerous events of bizarre behavior by the accused, including the fact that he consumed his own excreta while a prisoner in a county jail, ultimately resulted in a finding that the accused was insane. Credibility of the state's examining expert was demolished.

Avoidance: The adverse effect could have been avoided had the expert approached the task with an open mind and followed the basic procedures dictated by the scientific method. At the least, the adverse effect of failure of proper investigation could have been blunted had the expert not steadfastly held to an incredible position when confronted with a series of adverse facts at trial.

Case No. 4

Case: The case involved a corporate buy/sell agreement which could have had bearing on stock valuation in a divorce.

Evidence: Discovery uncovered alteration of corporate minutes and the buy/sell contract. Certain dollar values had been covered with typing correction fluid and new dollar values inserted. Photocopies of the altered minutes and contracts were then produced as part of the discovery package. Defendant's expert relied on the altered documents to reach valuation conclusions. Plaintiff's expert, suspicious because of the unlikely values found in the altered documents, demanded to examine the original corporate minutes and contract. The alteration was discovered. On examination of the original documents, the original numbers were still visible through the correction fluid.

Cause: Cause of the problem was the intentional alteration of relevant documents by unknown persons.

Effect: Effect of the disclosure was to discard the conclusions of defendant's expert. Ultimately, the altered minutes and contracts were given no consideration in the ultimate valuation.

Avoidance: Careful examination of original documents could have eliminated the adverse fallout.

Case No. 5

Case: In a criminal prosecution, conduct of the victim before his death became relevant. The prosecution was led to believe that the deceased had spent many hours at home assisting in the care of the family and doing household repairs and chores before he died.

Evidence: During trial, defense counsel found evidence in the victim's jacket pocket that established that the victim not only had not been at home during the hours preceding his death, but had in fact been at a tavern.

Cause: Inadequate police investigation (failure to go through the victim's pockets) proved the unraveling of the erroneous scenario.

Effect: Defendant's pleas of self-defense and intoxication by the victim were established, resulting in a verdict of acquittal.

Avoidance: Thorough investigation of defendant's clothing would have revealed the information prior to trial. The district attorney could have eliminated the aspect of the deceased's conduct from the case.

Case No. 6

Case: In a case involving alleged damages for wrongful attachment, plaintiff claimed defendant's conduct in attaching rents before judgment caused plaintiff's commercial project to be thrown into foreclosure. Plaintiff acted as his own expert in so testifying.

Evidence: While on the witness stand, plaintiff was confronted with his own correspondence to the foreclosing lender. There he had requested, before the alleged wrongful attachment, additional funds due to "cost overruns caused by architectural and contractor errors."

Cause: Cause of the surprise at trial was pure oversight and plaintiff's selective recollection.

Effect: Confrontation of the plaintiff with this damaging written statement against interest resulted in an adverse judgment for plaintiff.

Avoidance: The dramatic effect of the courtroom revelation could have been avoided had plaintiff, acting as his own expert, carefully reviewed each page of each document that was to be tendered as an exhibit at trial.

As these cases indicate, the cause for adverse trial results from selective or inadequate fact investigation is either:

- Attorney oversight in failing to ask the client the right questions
- Misstatement of fact by the client either due to faulty recollection, lack of appreciation of the significance of fact, or intentional nondisclosure of fact
- Inadequate investigation by the expert due to failure to explore evidence fully, lack of proper direction, inadequate time or money, or inadequate direction pursued by attorney or client

Regular use of a case plan, standard investigative procedures, and an action plan, will go far in eliminating this hazard of the investigative process.

GETTING THE JOB DONE: THE ACTION PLAN

The most difficult part of any task is getting started. You should do four basic things as you approach a new forensic assignment:

- Develop alternative hypotheses
- Survey applicable literature
- Review your own private files
- Develop one or more action plans

"Action plan" is just a catch phrase for an organized way to break a large project into steps and sub-steps. It is an easy way to track progress and spot what needs to be done.

The expert survey found that 68 percent of the respondents follow some type of procedure for tracking effort through a forensic assignment. Responses indicated that attorneys sometimes develop the tracking system. Other experts use schedules, notes of items that require follow-up, and checklists. Some experts regularly use a standard procedure, while others do so informally or when circumstances require.

DEVELOPING POSSIBLE HYPOTHESES

Once you have been retained on a case, obtained initial information from the client or counsel, and done a preliminary investigation, your next step will be to formulate a series of test hypotheses. A given case may involve one or more preliminary propositions. Regardless of the number, the process is the same. Some examples of preliminary statements are as follows:

- The cause of the fall was metal fatigue of the tenth rung of the ladder under inspection.
- The loader operator's failure to use a seat belt was the cause of his death.
- The presence of contaminants in cattle feed was caused by storage of pesticides and feed in the same area.
- Improper medical procedure was the cause of erroneous diagnosis and unnecessary surgery.
- Proper collateral control methods were followed in estimating the number of cattle present at a feed lot.

The following case demonstrates the effective use of a working hypothesis, followed by proof of the supporting facts.

Case No. 7. Nine hundred head of cattle were delivered to a feed lot for custom feeding, to be redelivered to the bailor-owner "when ready." The owner delayed taking redelivery of the cattle, choosing to leave them on feed for an inordinate period of time, while cattle prices were rising. The feed-lot owner sold the cattle to another buyer and was forced to defend breach of contract claims. The forensic expert's working hypothesis was that by pragmatic study of initial weight, weather, feed composition, and time, it is possible to determine when 900 heifers and steers were "ready."

The working hypothesis was developed by the forensic expert, the client, and counsel. The investigative process involved amassing data necessary for the expert to make calculations. He concluded that the cattle were "ready" on the date asserted by the feed lot owner, who was found by the court to have been entitled to sell the cattle to the third-party buyer.

LITERATURE SURVEY

In the just-described case, the forensic expert did an initial literature survey before applying the raw data to the hypothesis. The areas studied included the following generic categories:

- Professional and technical journals
- Dissertations
- Commercial literature
- Manufacturers' product bulletins
- Relevant test procedures and laboratory studies
- Other experimental studies
- The expert's own files, including lecture notes, laboratory tests, reports prepared in prior forensic assignments, and prior depositions in similar cases

By carrying out the review, the expert followed standard procedures in the animal-husbandry community. The literature survey varies in each case, however depending on your field and the specific assignment. Your own library of reports, surveys, articles, lecture notes, and testimony transcripts should be studied for guidance and cross-examination preparation.

THE ACTION PLAN

A large project must be broken into manageable tasks. Those small tasks must then be assigned priorities. Each task must be well-defined, including how it is to be accomplished, by whom, and when.

In Chapter 5, we looked at an overall case plan. That vehicle contemplates a broad case analysis and a listing of the major elements of a forensic assignment. The action plan is designed to concentrate on particular parts of a case plan, blow up the ones that need attention, and break those steps into manageable modules.

Appendices G and H are examples of other organized approaches to various forensic assignments. A preset format will see you through any complex assignment. If your file is examined in discovery or at trial, the presence of an action plan should enhance your credibility. But if you have action plan forms available and do not use them, you may be open to criticism and cross-examination for not observing your own procedures.

Development of an Action Plan

The following case example illustrates the development of an action plan.

Case No 8. Three young men, all friends, took a plane ride on a Saturday afternoon. One was a pilot who had logged 160 hours of flying. The others had also flown. The licensed pilot had filed a flight plan. The plane took off routinely and maintained a position near the airport. Ground observers noted the plane flying figure-eight patterns and making sharp turns and steep banks. Because of its erratic flight pattern, the aircraft attracted considerable attention from casual ground observers.

At one point, the engine was heard to stop and then restart while the plane was in a glide pattern. The plane banked sharply to the right and headed steeply downward. Due to rolling terrain, ground observers could not see the impact. No fire or explosion followed the crash. One victim was found in a passenger seat. The other two had been ejected from the pilot and co-pilot positions upon impact. There were no survivors. The aircraft wreckage was impounded by Federal authorities. The local coroner performed autopsies on all of the deceased victims. A partially smoked marijuana cigarette was found in the clothing of the only licensed pilot. The hypothesis was that the licensed pilot was at the controls at the time of the crash. The action plan is shown on p. 75:

Preparation and Use of the Action Plan

An action plan is prepared by the expert before undertaking detailed work in the field. The plan should be sufficiently flexible to allow for additions and deletions as the project progresses. For maximum flexibility, the action plan should be prepared on computer or word-processing equipment.

It is a good idea to provide copies of the action plan to the client,

Action Plan

Steps	Who to Do	By When	Where	Conclusions	Completed
1. Eyewitness statements	Burns	10/10	Field		
2. Inspect aircraft	Matthews	10/12	Field & photo		
3. Inspect cockpit controls	Matthews	10/12	Field & photo		
4. Record control position	Matthews	10/12	Field & photo		
5. Photograph cockpit instruments	Matthews	10/12	Field & photo		
6. Examine clothing	Matthews	10/14	Field		
7. Review autopsy reports	Burns	10/12	Office		
8. Interview pathologist	Burns	10/12	Field		
9. Confirm flight plan filing	Burns	10/15	Office		
10. Review NTSB preliminary report	Matthews	1/15	Washington, D.C.		
11. Report to client (verbal)	Matthews	1/17	Phone		
12. Review NTSB guide	Burns	12/1	Office		
13. Prepare written report	Matthews	1/20	Office		

attorney, and possibly other experts. This gives the client and counsel a sense of the tasks you are performing and helps avoid duplication of efforts among other experts. Also, others who review your action plan may be able to suggest new areas of inquiry.

If the action plan is prepared by the attorney, it may be an item of work product—the lawyer's thought processes—and should receive very limited distribution. As such, it may be privileged and not discoverable. Without the attorney work-product blanket of protection, confidentiality may not attend the action plan.

CONCLUSION

The effect of overlooked or previously undisclosed evidence can be dramatic. Evidence and facts may be intentionally withheld or carelessly forgotten. Use of a standard fact-gathering checklist and protocol will help eliminate missed or overlooked evidence. The dire effects of withheld or forgotten facts should not occur if you follow a standard protocol, keep an open mind, dig for all the facts all the time, and never assume anything. In situations where action plans have been used, cases are usually ready for trial on time. The chance of a successful result is significantly increased by a well-organized, pragmatic approach to the project by all concerned. Because some forensic assignments are so massive, it is necessary to break the task into manageable parts. If you do develop an action plan, failure to use it may result in a claim of improper procedures.

10 YOUR PRELIMINARY REPORT

INTRODUCTION

There comes a time when your opinions and conclusions are properly converted to your initial or preliminary report. At this point, you have not yet finished your investigation. Discovery steps, such as interrogatories, production of documents, and depositions, may still be underway. Tests may not have been concluded. Your literature survey may still be unfinished, and you are still obtaining witnesses' statements. Your preliminary report must reflect these open areas of inquiry.

LIMITATIONS OF THE PRELIMINARY REPORT

At this stage of your assignment, caution and wisdom would dictate five limitations of your preliminary report:

- Only a preliminary opinion is required.
- The report should not be reduced to writing.
- Your findings may be tentative at best.
- Your statements should be substantially qualified and limited.
- The report is subject to a list of remaining investigative tasks.

At the same time you make your preliminary report, you will be restating, reevaluating, and possibly recasting your preliminary hypotheses. The investigative process may have taken a surprise turn. Stay in touch with attorney and client. Facts uncovered may require further discovery or investigation and you need to know the unfolding events. The client or attorney may wish to put you on hold for a period of time, pending receipt of further factual information.

EARLY TERMINATION

On occasion, the preliminary report will expose your inadequacy in the particular case. You may not be qualified or you lack a particular area of expertise.

Sometimes the preliminary report creates a conflict between you and your client or counsel. Some clients and attorneys may terminate your services upon receipt of an adverse preliminary verbal report. They may believe that your conclusions are heading in the wrong direction or your methods are inordinately impartial. Have faith! Hang in there! Continue to follow the method and standards you know to be correct. If your preliminary report seems to suggest dissatisfaction with your methods or conclusions, it may be best for all concerned to terminate the assignment.

A few examples of case direction change as a result of the preliminary report serve to emphasize the importance of this checkpoint in the process.

Case No. 1. A bicycle accident resulting in the rider's quadrapalegic condition was subjected to extensive forensic investigation. Examination of the front bicycle wheel revealed wood fragments at several locations on the spokes and the internal aspect of the front wheel fork. The expert was able to conclude in a preliminary verbal report that a stick had slipped into the front wheel spokes and had been carried to the fender strut, causing the front wheel to jam and throw the rider violently over the handlebars. That preliminary finding justified terminating the injury claim process.

The preliminary report may not totally resolve the conflict. Even if a portion of the case is resolved by early findings, substantial benefit for the system results.

Case No. 2. In a criminal prosecution for assault with a deadly weapon and robbery, three defendants were charged with firing weapons at pursuing police officers during a running gun battle. Each defendant was tried separately from the others.

The criminalist analyzed the police officers' statements, statements from the three defendants, bullet holes in a police vehicle, position of all three defendants in the fleeing car, and gunpowder residue tests on the hands of all three defendants. He also interviewed the defendants. It was determined whether each defendant was right- or left-handed. The preliminary verbal report was that one defendant did not and could not have fired any of the weapons during the chase. Resulting dismissal of the assault charges against that defendant paved the way for a plea bargain disposition of the robbery charges.

Another purpose of the preliminary report is to obtain guidance from the attorney or client about other facets of the case which you may be uninformed about. You should also list further areas of inquiry you believe are necessary to complete your task. At that same time, you ought to project a timetable for completion of research and your final report.

Case No. 3. Defective and inadequate lighting was the alleged cause of an elderly woman's fall on a stairway, resulting in a permanently disabling fracture. The lighting expert's preliminary verbal report revealed that available light was 70 percent less than code requirements. On receipt of this information, counsel instructed the expert to conclude his study with complete examination of all available light from various angles, documentation of code requirements, filming of the accident site to replicate the extent of available light, and finally calculation of the cost of installing adequate lighting. The final report was sufficiently thorough to support an early and favorable settlement.

FORMAT OF THE PRELIMINARY VERBAL REPORT

This section provides two examples of preliminary, verbal reports. The reader should note that both examples emphasize the preliminary nature of the results and highlight the factors which might induce you either to change or confirm your views. The second example lists the elements necessary for you to reach a final and more conclusive view.

EXAMPLE 1:   I have completed a preliminary inspection of the drain cleaner which you sent to me for analysis. The product is approximately 70 percent hydrochloric acid and certainly sufficient to cause severe burns to human tissue. I think what we ought to do at this point is run an analysis on the clothing of the injured child to see if we can match chemical compound of the drain cleaner with residue that might be available on the clothing. If I can make that match, I think you have a case.

EXAMPLE 2:   I've done a preliminary review of the hospital records. At this point, it is clear that the nursing staff, by its own notes, was aware of the deceased's depressed condition the night before he committed suicide. I think the next step is to interview the nurse who made the hospital record entry and the deceased's wife, who saw him the night before he died, and then review hospital records for prior admissions of the deceased over the last five years.
  If the continuity of depression is evident, I think we have good basis to conclude the hospital was on notice of the man's depressed condition. At that point, I'd want to take a look at the regulations and standard practices published by the hospital outlining procedures to be followed when a patient has evidenced depression and suicidal tendencies. If the hospital didn't follow its own procedures, with the notice it had, I think we'll be able to conclude the hospital is at fault for this death.

  Your preliminary opinion should track the fundamentals of your investigation: Who is involved? What happened? Where did it happen?

Why and how did it happen? When did the events occur? Answering as many of these questions as possible at a preliminary stage will be exceedingly helpful to your client and the attorneys.

Remember the distinction between your initial role as consultant, from that of a testifying forensic expert. In usual practice, the consultant's research file is not discoverable by the opposition. The purposes of obtaining a consultant's report may be to guide the client through a particular process or to make changes in a product and not for courtroom trial purposes.

There are good public policy reasons for not exposing consultation reports as part of the discovery product. If parties could not use confidential consultants, public health, safety or welfare could be jeopardized. However, if you as a consultant become a testifying expert, your entire start-to-finish file may be open to the discovery process. The opposition is generally entitled to use everything that constitutes a basis for your opinion. Good cause exists to solidify your role prior to preliminary report preparation.

Appendix J is a checklist of what can be included in a preliminary report. As with all the appendices, this item is offered as a guide. The format you develop should be an expandable, ever-improving vehicle that gets better as you do.

Discuss with your client and counsel whether they prefer a written or verbal preliminary report. If they do not seem to have preference, make it verbal. Certain tactical considerations may dictate the form. An early settlement may follow a written preliminary report. Change of investigative direction may be suggested by a verbal report and that modification may not be helpful if later uncovered.

THE WRITTEN REPORT: LANGUAGE TO AVOID

Certain phrases, if included in the preliminary report, are sure to open areas for cross-examination during deposition or trial. If possible, avoid the following phrases in the preliminary report:

- "Draft Copy Only"
- "Preliminary Copy"
- "For Discussion Purposes Only"
- "Working Draft"
- "May I Have Your Comments Please?"

The problem with the noted language is that opposing counsel will make it appear that the attorney or client who hired you had input into your independent professional judgment. Do not provide counsel with an opportunity to imply that this was the case.

STAYING FLEXIBLE

Two publications, by professionals in vastly different fields, underscore the importance of keeping the preliminary report verbal. In a monograph entitled *The Expert Witness Handbook: A Guide for Engineers* this synoptic view of the preliminary report is given:

> You will eventually write up the results of your investigation in a report. However, you should not commit anything to writing until asked to do so by the attorney. Instead, you should discuss your findings with the attorney. . . .
>
> If, on the basis of your investigation, you will not be able to give testimony favorable to your client's case, the attorney will probably decide not to designate you as an expert, and will not ask you for a written report. Your findings may or may not persuade the attorney to seek settlement out of court. On the other hand, if your findings appear to be useful, the attorney may ask you for a report of your findings and opinions, and at some point in the preparation for trial, will designate you as an expert.[1]

A similar view of the same problem is referred to in an AICPA manual dealing with litigation services. In referring to oral reports, the authors state that:

> Some lawyers do not want a written report, even when the CPA is retained as a consultant to the attorney and the CPA's work is protected by the attorney work-product privilege. There are two reasons for this. First, the attorney work-product privilege is not absolute. . . . Therefore, there is a slight [sic] chance that a written report, which may include possible negative implications for a client's case, may be turned over to the opposing party. . . .
>
> Second, the attorney may change his mind and designate the CPA who was previously retained as a consultant, as an expert. The attorney may then be forced to turn over the CPA's report to the other side because it may no longer have the protection of the attorney work-product privilege . . . The CPA . . . may have included statements that are adverse to the client's interest.[2]

Facts change along the way to render moot your prior opinion. The client benefited by the continual contact between the attorney and expert and the absence of a written report in the following case.

Case No. 4. In a methane gas migration case, an expert structural engineer rendered a preliminary verbal opinion concerning blocking of the methane gas flow from underground sources. He concluded that the

---

1. Sunar, *The Expert Witness Handbook: A Guide for Engineers* (Professional Publications, 1985), p.13.
2. Wagner & Frank, *Technical Consulting Practice Aid No. 7* (AICPA, 1986), p. 28.

only way the gas could be efficiently blocked was to excavate a trench down to bedrock and then build an underground concrete wall which would force the migrating gas around the affected property. The cost of such a construction was very high.

The opposing party developed a scheme to vent the gas to the atmosphere, thereby alleviating the need for the underground barrier. The cost to ventilate the gas was less than one-half the expense entailed with the underground excavation and barrier construction. As a result, the barrier correction device was abandoned. The proper measure of damages, in this case the least expensive method of correction, was used for trial purposes. The structural engineer did not testify at trial.

Checking with counsel during your preliminary work will afford guidance to you concerning the rules of law applicable to your part of the case. Knowing what evidentiary or substantive law applies can steer you clear of major hazards.

CONCLUSION

Verbal preliminary reports are desirable for many reasons. Your preliminary report should suggest areas of further inquiry. It should also make clear that neither the attorney nor your client had any meaningful input into your conclusions. The report should state what still remains to be done. At this point, it is important to stay flexible. The facts change, and the law is not always apparent at the outset of your engagement.

TESTS, EXPERIMENTS, DEMONSTRATIONS, AND MODELS

11

INTRODUCTION

The task of doing tests, conducting experiments, or building models may involve substantial expenditure. As a general matter, you will not carry out these further steps until after you have made your preliminary report. However, some forensic assignments start and end with laboratory tests.

Numerous types of expert witness assignments primarily involve testing. These include the following areas:

Air and water pollution
Alcohol or drug ingestion
Bacteria content
Ballistics
Botany testing
Chemical compositions
Concrete strength
Document examination
Fingerprint analysis
Gemstone identification
Glass fracture
Handwriting analysis
Light measure

Metallurgy
Noxious fumes
Nuclear contamination
Odontology
Pharmacology
Soil tests
Sound and noise pollution
Thermography
Tire blowout
Toxicology
Vaccine contamination
Virology
X-Ray analysis

CONDUCTING TESTS

The conduct of tests and experiments or model construction should be carried out, or at least supervised, by the testifying expert. Inability to verify test and experiment procedures and results impinges on the credibility of the opinion expert.[1] It has been a fatal defect on some occasions.

The difference between permitted and excluded testimony occasionally centers on the conduct of tests. For example, if the issue is the speed of vehicles involved in a collision, the expert who personally tested the road surface to determine its coefficient of friction, examined the vehicles, and measured the skidmarks would certainly be permitted to testify. By contrast, the expert who merely formulated opinions by examining photographs of the road and the vehicles three years after the accident and inspecting the road surface at that time might be precluded from testifying altogether.[2]

DESTRUCTIVE TESTING

Testing requires scrupulous attention to detail. You must maintain impeccable records of your procedures at every point. Memory fails. Write, draw, photograph, videotape or otherwise record the various steps of your investigation.[3]

Testing is often a prerequisite to expert testimony. Occasionally, destructive testing must be undertaken. The expert must weigh benefits and drawbacks before beginning any such tests and must confer with the attorney and the client to be sure the results will be admissible. Strict compliance with rules of practice will protect not only your processes but also the dispute resolution system. Disastrous results can result from destructive testing which has not been concluded in accordance with these guidelines. You may become a defendant if a party claims your conduct was negligent, under a civil action called "spoiliation of evidence."[4]

Here are some simple steps to follow when destructive testing appears to be necessary:

- Consult with attorney and client first.
- If an opposing party is known, notice should be given to the party. This simple step will avoid many problems and objections.
- If the matter is subject to court or administrative procedures, rules of the forum must be reviewed and observed.

1. Bridgers, "The Selection, Preparation, and Direct Examination of Expert Witnesses," *The Docket*, Vol. 2, No. 4, Fall 1987, p. 18.

2. Pemberton and Hirsch. *The Defense Lawyer and The Expert: Finding, Preparing, Discovering, and Counteracting Expert Witnesses*, (Defense Research Institute: The Expert Witness in Litigation, 1983), No. 3, p. 10.

3. Sunar, *The Expert Witness Handbook: A Guide For Engineers* (Professional Publications, 1985), p. 11.

4. See the *ATLA Law Reporter*, August 1989.

- Good practice dictates obtaining an actual court or administrative order before destructive tests are undertaken.
- Maintain meticulous documentation. Show precisely what you did, how you did it, and what your findings were. Record the process with photographs or videotape.
- If appropriate, make sound recordings as well, particularly if you observe results or the process is one that can be heard.
- Follow the scientific method of preservation, marking, labeling, and evaluating to preserve the residue of the test.
- If the process is a lengthy one, time lapse photography is an alternative method of recording.

The following case shows what can happen when these steps are not followed.

Case No. 1. In a defective motorcycle case, the manufacturer was able to obtain possession of the vehicle. From all available information, the motorcycle had not only been taken from the city where the event occurred, but it had been removed from the United States and shipped overseas for destructive tests of certain metal parts. The vehicle was never again found. The defense was induced to settle the case because of the missing vehicle and absence of opportunity for plaintiff and his expert to conduct tests and inspections of the machine.

Inability of a party to produce documents or objects which in the ordinary course of events should be produced raises a legal presumption that production would be contrary to the interests of the party failing to produce. Simply stated, if you cannot produce what you should be able to produce, the law is going to imply the worst anyhow, so you might as well produce.

Destructive testing presented some problems for the experts responding to the survey. Among the helpful admonitions culled from the survey results were the following:

- Use documentation
- Obtain written authorization
- Use photos or video to record the events
- Arrange for witnesses to be present

TRIAL DEMONSTRATIONS

If you use a demonstration at trial, make certain the display works correctly. Your credibility will sink if a demonstration fails during hearing or trial.

Case No. 2. In a toxic burn case involving a caustic product, the forensic expert determined that he could graphically demonstrate the potency of the product by applying the product to a pigskin sample. The idea was that severe burns to the pigskin would dramatically demonstrate to the jury how injuries had been sustained by the claimant. Tests attempted before trial revealed that, for reasons unknown, the pigskin did not react in a positive fashion. The demonstration effort was abandoned.

Some tests work well and prove their point with shocking effect. But the process must be tested and retested before deciding that the test will be beneficial.

Case No. 3. Detection devices used for determining the presence of ambient gas had been rigged in the courtroom. The demonstration was to show the sensing equipment and warning devices in place at claimant's property. Several practice applications of gas to the sensing device revealed that the equipment worked well. The warning buzzer was shockingly loud and startled the jury. The demonstration was graded a success.

TEST RESULTS

Not all testing results and demonstrations are as dramatic as the preceding case. The usual test involves painstaking laboratory work, minute examination of materials, substances, and compounds, and the reporting of those results. Testing has resulted in noteworthy trial determinations, both for and against claimants.

Case No. 4. Tests of an elevator established the presence of interlocks that made it impossible for the elevator doors to open unless the elevator was at floor level. Expert testimony to that effect was positioned against the testimony of an eyewitness who asserted that the elevator was two feet above floor level at the time of claimant's fall. That direct conflict caused the case to be settled. Both expert and eyewitness were fully credible.

Case No. 5. Industrial contamination was claimed to be the cause of a worker's chronic obstructive pulmonary disease. The worker had prevailed at a worker's compensation hearing. Later respiratory testing was inconclusive as to whether the industrial contaminant or the claimant's twenty-year history of cigarette smoking was the cause of the disease. The hearing result was overturned.

Case No. 6. An expert created a model of an injury-producing ramp which collapsed under the claimant's weight. The model was the determining factor in a dangerous-premises litigation. The expert, using photographs and measurements taken by an investigator the day after the injury, created an exact scale model of the injury-producing structure. The dynamics of the collapse and the fall were readily demonstrable from observation of the desktop scale model.

INADEQUATE FOUNDATION

Not all tests and demonstrations have happy endings. For example, unless meticulous care is taken to ensure that the events portrayed in a demonstration are substantially similar to the facts of the case, the results of costly re-creations may be disallowed as evidence at trial.

Case No. 7. In a product-liability action involving the alleged defective function of an item of heavy equipment, the defense spent $30,000 to create a film which purportedly depicted the defense view of the procedures that should have been followed by the injured plaintiff but were not. The vehicle used in the film was the same one involved with the injury. However, the procedures, practices, warnings, and other portrayed steps had not occurred at the time of the injury. Because of the dissimilarity between the film and the events that occurred at the time of the injury, the court rejected the tendered evidence.

ADEQUATE FOUNDATION

Because courts will reject tests based on inadequate foundation, be sure to re-create exactly all essential elements as they existed at the time of the events. Only in that way will such information be admissible. Court procedures are available for *in limine* (preliminary evidence limitation) rulings concerning the proposed testing, experiments, demonstrations, or models. The effort to obtain tribunal approval in advance will not be wasted. Coordinated work with counsel will enhance the probability of admissibility. While this disclosure does take away the element of surprise, it also provides a compensating element of certainty. The modern dispute-resolution process seeks to avoid trial by ambush. Preliminary clearance of tests and experimental procedures is certainly the prudent course. In most cases, evidence must pass opposition scrutiny before it is used at trial anyway. This is true of both real evidence and demonstrative material.

EVIDENTIARY VALIDATION

In order to prepare useful demonstrative or evidentiary materials, the forensic expert and attorney must carefully analyze every possible objection that could be made to the tendered evidence. The evidence tendered must be relevant.[5] Relevant evidence is that which has a tendency to make the existence of any fact that is important in the case more or less probable than it would have been without the evidence.[6] However, some evidence, and this includes tests, experiments, models, and demonstrations, may be relevant and still not admissible. Such evidence may be inadmissible because it is prejudicial, confusing, or misleading. It may take too long to present or repeat other evidence.[7]

The current rule requires forensic evidence to have a reliable foundation, be relevant to the case at hand, be based on scientifically valid principles, and satisfy the trial judge as to these three elements.[8]

In addition, the tendered evidence must not be objectionable because of the existence of a confidential privilege.[9] Usual rules of evidence do not permit witnesses to testify about anything that is not the subject of the witnesses' sensory perceptions. The law makes an exception for experts, who are allowed to render opinions. That probably would not excuse a forensic witness from the requirement that tests and experimental data be based upon the witness's own personal knowledge of the matter.[10] Careful adherence to evidentiary rules involving experts is required. See Appendix E.

ELEVEN STEPS TOWARD ADMISSIBILITY

To increase the probability that your tests, experiments, demonstrations, and models will be admissible, follow the following steps:

- Be thoroughly familiar with the facts of the case
- Have available accurate measurements
- Be familiar with the progression of events which occurred

---

5. Federal Rules of Evidence, Rule 104(a) and (b).
6. Federal Rules of Evidence, Rule 401.
7. Federal Rules of Evidence, Rule 403.
8. *Daubert v. Merrell Dow Pharmaceuticals, Inc., supra.* But compare the prior rule of "general acceptance" in *Frye v. United States*, 293 Fed. 1013 at 1014 (D.C. Cir. 1923); see also Ric Gass, "Using the *Frye* Rule to Control Expert Testimony Abuse," *For the Defense*, February 1987, p. 23.
9. Federal Rules of Evidence. Rule 501, which provides for a blend between federal statutory law, federal common law, and state law reference.
10. Federal Rules of Evidence, Rule 602.

- Use the same materials that were involved in the event under study
- Meticulously track your tests or experimental steps
- Record the tests or experimental event carefully
- Make your demonstrations substantially similar to the actual events in issue
- Make your models to precise scale
- Detail all findings, both positive and negative
- Do sufficient research to establish that the test or experimental procedure is scientifically and technically recognized as authoritative[11]
- Consult with counsel to ensure the best posture for tendered admissibility

Refer to Chapter 8, where alternative methods of presentation of test and experimental data are enumerated. Consult texts which present various methods of graphic presentation.[12] Efforts to enhance effective presentation of your tests and demonstrations will pay big dividends at trial.

CONCLUSION

Many areas of testing constitute part of your forensic presentation. Conduct of tests must be carefully monitored. Destructive testing raises difficult problems because of the risk entailed in destruction of real evidence. Trial demonstrations and experiments in the presence of the factfinder must be carefully validated and checked for proper operation.

Test results, while not always dramatic, often determine the outcome of a case. Unless the test or demonstration is adequately founded, you may encounter serious problems concerning admissibility. Always take careful steps to ensure adequate foundation for tests, demonstrations, or models. A passing understanding of evidence rules also helps the expert prepare scientific, technical, and professional testimony.

---

11. In *State* v. *Miller*, 429 N.W.2d 26 (S.D. 1988), an effort to time-date a death failed due to lack of scientific verification. In an attempt to correlate the age of insects in the deceased's body, an anthropologist placed corpses in various unburied locations. The court rejected the effort because of absence of proof that the method had any scientific validity. Defendant was nevertheless convicted on other admitted evidence. See *Scientific Sleuthing #1*, Vol. 13, Winter 1989, p. 7.

12. Filter. *The Demonstrative Evidence Sourcebook*, (Staffort Hart Publishing, 1985). Appendix O is the index to that text.

12

HOW TO COMMUNICATE WITH ATTORNEYS: YOUR FINAL REPORT

INTRODUCTION

The title of this chapter may suggest the ultimate oxymoron: some people think it is impossible to communicate with attorneys. However, you must communicate with the attorney who engaged your services, with opposing counsel, and with judges and administrative hearing officers.

Forensic assignments are divided into several milestones: engagement, investigation, preliminary report, final report, discovery, trial, and file closing. All except the last require communication with attorneys.

One of the fundamental difficulties in communicating with attorneys involves the fact that they sometimes use a different language than the rest of the world. Contrary to popular belief, that language is not used to delay, deceive, or confuse. As in any profession, particular terms have specific meaning. All that is necessary is to be able to translate. A glossary of frequently used terms, most of a legal nature, is included at the end of this book to demystify conversations, correspondence, and pleadings.

Dr. Robert M. Hutchinson, professor of geology at the Colorado School of Mines and geological consultant, in responding to the survey, has this to say about communications between attorneys and experts:

> It is my personal feeling . . . as an expert witness . . . that the onus lies on the attorney to be able to understand and translate into usable courtroom evidence the . . . findings of the expert witness. Getting the expert witness to translate . . . findings into usable form is, of course, the direct responsibility of the attorney in charge. Expert witnesses must realize this. . . .

The experts who responded to the survey isolated seven problems in communicating with attorneys. In order of priority they were:

- Lawyers are too busy to have time to discuss the case.

- They do not know technical language.
- They do not listen to experts.
- They are too aggressive and adversarial.
- It is hard to get them to return phone calls.
- They oversimplify complex issues; they require "yes" or "no" answers.
- They contact the expert at the last minute.

The experts suggested the following ways in which attorneys could improve the situation:

- Give the expert more time
- Plan and organize better
- Attend technical seminars
- Be more professionally competent

Thirteen percent of the experts do not think anything can be done to improve the problems.

Communication between you and the attorney carries dual responsibility. You must translate technical terms and concepts for the attorney. The attorney must translate the legal vocabulary for you. A clear understanding of objectives and goals given to you by counsel will sharpen your focus. Development of one or more working hypotheses will enhance mutual understanding. To improve communication, you and the lawyer must focus together on what is to be accomplished.

TECHNIQUES TO IMPROVE COMMUNICATION

Most technical, professional, and scientific fields boast a text or series of books which constitute "the Bible" for that field. Experienced trial lawyers will regularly ask you for such texts. Failing that request, take the initiative and make that material available to the attorney. The attorney should make available to you enough information about the judicial process and your role in it for you to function effectively.

The discovery product in a case may reveal articles which will further enhance your ability to support, guide, and advise the lawyer. Make sure counsel knows of your desire to have access to all material which has been produced, either by the client or the opposition. You could be held responsible for knowledge of an authoritative text or article without having endorsed the publication as "authoritative." The rules of evidence state that if any expert recognizes a text as authoritative, you may be examined or cross-examined concerning it.[1]

---

1. Federal Rules of Evidence, Rule 803(18).

Timeliness of communication is almost as important as clarity. Your verbal or written report will be due at a certain time. Fulfill at deadline. If the attorney does not set interim dates for the accomplishment of various steps, you should do so (see Chapter 9). Serious professional experts respond promptly to requests for information and progress reports. Obviously, your professional reputation will be enhanced by excellent professional service. Therefore, do not take on more work than you can adequately and promptly handle.

The main points during an assignment about which you will communicate with counsel are:

- Engagement
- Understanding the overall assignment
- Getting to know each other's literature and vocabulary
- Preliminary report of initial findings
- Drafting of interrogatories, requests for production, and deposition questions
- Preparation for deposition, both yours and the opposition
- Preparation of a final report
- Preparation for trial
- Development of direct examination questions
- Assistance in preparation of cross-examination
- Trial testimony
- Other trial assistance

At each of these points, confirm with counsel your understanding of what is being said to you, either verbally or in writing. Ask counsel to do the same for you. Repeating communications is an excellent way to ensure accurate understanding. The following cases demonstrate good communication between expert and attorney.

Case No. 1. The suit was brought by the parents of a three-year-old child who had been burned about the head, shoulder, upper torso, and leg when a pot of boiling water fell on him at a daycare center. Visual projection of the burn trauma was necessary to present the case for trial. The plastic surgeon explained to the attorney all biological and anatomical features of the skin when burned, as well as treatment and the healing process. Expert and lawyer exchanged detailed drawings and explanations of burn treatment and healing in preparation for delivery of that explanation to the jury.

Case No. 2. In commercial litigation involving alleged rule violation in the commodities trading industry, the expert made the leading text on the commodities industry available to counsel. The attorney and expert conferred regularly to develop hypotheses for why the loss occurred and what custom and usage practices were violated. The expert created a chronological table of moment-by-moment events and analyzed telephone tapes between the broker and the exchange. The interchange allowed counsel and the expert to communicate clearly and effectively with the court about the practices that were followed and rules of the exchange which were violated.

YOUR FINAL REPORT

Your final report should demonstrate organization, clarity, and neatness. Its contents will depend on the scope of your assignment. The following recommended list of items for inclusion is intended to suggest possible areas to consider:

- Your qualifications (you may incorporate in your report your full current resume or curriculum vitae)
- The name and address of the client and any corporate, business, or official title
- The name and address of the client's attorney and the law firm, agency, or business affiliation
- General description of the item, event, or activity which is the subject of your assignment
- The stated objective of your assignment
- Your general methodology
- Your summary, conclusions, diagnosis or prognosis, and final opinion
- Specific dates, times, and places of investigatory activities: title, description, make, model, serial number, date, time, place, and operative facts of the event
- Photographs, samples, drawings, schedules, maps, charts, and summaries
- Investigative reports incorporated into your report
- Test examinations, calculations, computations or other procedures which you followed
- Consultation with other experts, particularly those that are ordinary, customary, and expected for persons in your field
- A statement of various hypotheses under investigation
- Areas of investigation still open due to unavailability of data or incomplete test or evaluation results
- Findings on physical examination: all normal physical findings, negative findings, and objective findings and observations
- Treatment, remedies, or corrective action: what was done, dates of treatment, remedy or corrective action, methods followed

- Limiting conditions, exclusions and disclaimers: you may wish to qualify your opinion or leave the conclusion somewhat open, subject to later determined facts

In preparing your report, use standard internal quality assurance and final check procedures. Recheck all calculations; make sure technical terms are used correctly. Review the report for typographical errors, grammar and syntax, and clarity. The sequence of pages, exhibits, and attachments should be verified. Make sure you have covered the who, what, where, why, and when areas. Finally, make sure your report is distributed only to the proper recipients.

The final report submitted is an excellent occasion to make sure your charges for professional services are current.

CONCLUSION

Your final report is an excellent opportunity to exercise your communication skills and to demonstrate your competence. The techniques you use to communicate with attorneys are the same ones you will use for testimony to the trier of fact in court or administrative hearing. That process will be examined in Chapter 20 in great depth, where the subject of effective testimony is explored. Reference to the glossary of terms should enhance your communication ability.

13 CONFIDENTIALITY BETWEEN EXPERT, ATTORNEY, AND CLIENT

INTRODUCTION

In the best of all worlds, communications between you and the attorney or client should be confidential, if not absolutely privileged. Whatever you say to the attorney or client would seem to be confidential. Their communication to you should also be protected. However, those are not the facts of life.

Certain communications are, by law, not subject to disclosure. Effort is often made to bring attorney, client and expert communication within that protection. Good reason exists to justify attempts to restrict access to your preliminary work. Effort you render as a consultant is distinguishable from that generated as a testifying witness in the setting of confidentiality.

There are some precautionary steps to take to avoid disclosure. Ethical considerations also must be examined when dealing with these concepts. The discovery process is the setting in which disclosure most often arises.

PRIVILEGES

Statutory privileges exist in many jurisdictions for limited classes of communication. Communications between doctors and patients, attorneys and clients, and lawful religious leaders and their parishioners are privileged. Husband–wife communications, with certain limitations, are privileged. In some jurisdictions, client communications with certified public accountants are protected. That about exhausts the list of statutory and common-law privileged communications.

Certain privileges or confidentiality rules exist for consultants but not for examining, active, or testifying experts. Courts have recognized an expert consultant's role as subject to technical advisor privilege.[1] Attorney work product, what the attorney's thoughts are during preparations for trial, are privileged and cannot be reached by opposing counsel.[2] The courts have refined the work-product privilege to include the lawyer's refinement of information, sifting of data, legal theories, and strategy plans. These products are not reachable by discovery. However, no such privilege attends your thought processes for trial preparation.

In general, the presence of a third party at a conference which would otherwise be privileged breaks the privilege. The issue is whether the presence of you, the expert, will destroy the privilege. The fine line seems to be between your role as a consultant, in which case privilege may well still obtain, and your role as an active investigating or testifying expert, in which case it probably will not. Your task is to maximize the possibility that your communication will be subject to the attorney work product or other privilege to avoid it being reached by opposing counsel during discovery.

Why worry about privilege? Why are there things you do not want the opposition to know? The reasons are the same as those which attend other confidential communications. Your work may involve delicate or personal matters which have no bearing on your assignment in the current case. You may be exploring various hypotheses, some of which will be discarded along the way. You may be correcting a fault or flaw in a product. Sound public policy dictates that such corrective action proceed smoothly. So there are good reasons for privileged communication. In addition modern rules of discovery usually flush out all relevant information about your current inquiry.

The survey attempted to determine how frequently the opposition sees an expert's entire file. Figure 13.1 charts the frequency with which the opposition actually obtains files of the responding experts.

THE BASIC RULES

Recent case decisions and rules of evidence generally provide that the information on which you rely to help you form opinions may be inquired into through the discovery process. That means that any communication with the attorney, client, witnesses, or other experts, or any part of your investigative field process which in any way formulates a basis for your opinion can be viewed and inquired into by the opposition.

---

1. Wigmore, *Wigmore on Evidence*, §2301 at 583 (1961); *People* v. *Lines*, 13 Cal.3rd 500, 119 Cal. Rptr. 224, 531 P.2d 793 (1975); see also Criminal Justice Mental Health Standards §7-3.3(b) (1984).

2. *Hickman* v. *Taylor*, 329 U.S. 495, 91 L.Ed. 451, 67 S. Ct. 385.

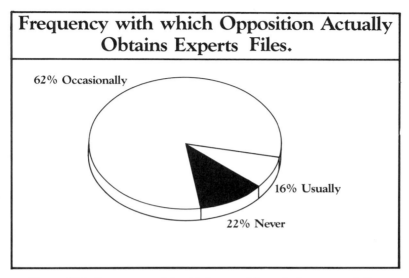

Figure 13.1 Frequency with which opposition obtains experts' files.

While you may start out as a treating or consulting expert, if your role changes to that of testifying or investigative witness, everything in your files will be produced. If at any time your client puts medical, legal, accounting, or similar issues into issue, that will take down the privilege barrier for any communications you have in those areas. The following case illustrates this.

Case No. 1. In a case involving failure to diagnose and treat cancer, the patient's entire medical history was determined relevant by the trial judge. Every medical file and every doctor–patient communication available to plaintiff's expert was deemed available for discovery.

In a situation such as this the court had to balance the utility of opening up all manner of unnecessary medical files against the opportunity for the defense to prove other indications of cancer had existed and should have been the subject of diagnosis by prior doctors.

Case No. 2. In a lender liability action, plaintiff claimed the bank's conduct was the cause of his financial demise. The entire accounting, financial income, and expense history of claimant in possession of his accounting expert was subject to discovery. All tax returns and internal financial statements for more than ten years were ordered available to defense experts for purposes of testing the defendant's financial condition before the bank breached its loan agreement and caused the foreclosure and bankruptcy proceedings of which plaintiff complained.

ATTEMPT TO STAY CONFIDENTIAL

There are some things you can do to help maintain a fighting chance for confidentiality or privilege:

- Limit distribution of written communications.
- Hold written communications to an absolute minimum.
- Mark written communications "Confidential" or "Attorney Work Product" if that is really the case.
- Attempt to keep the attorney involved in the communication so it is indeed the attorney's thought process and work product which is being discussed.
- Have the attorney give you summaries of data rather than basic data which would otherwise be confidential. That may make the item attorney work product.
- Segregate confidential and privileged communications in your file rather than merging them with your general materials.
- Make sure your communication with the attorney responds to attorney's request for information.
- Experts may protect as confidential trade secrets or patent information.
- If the information involves competitive information, obtain a protective order to suppress it and make it unavailable for any purpose other than that of the subject litigation.
- Attempt to show that production of documents or other items is too burdensome or constitutes an act of harassment.

Prepare all materials as if they may be subject to discovery production. Test everything you write as if it were going to be used against you in open court. Determine whether you could explain or justify the contents of the memorandum, note, report, or technical observation.

HOW DISCOVERY WORKS

Before your testimony or deposition is begun, make sure the lawyer for whom you are acting gets a chance to review your file. If the lawyer does not have time to do this, you must do so. Items which are clearly privileged should be removed. Note each item removed by date, subject, and recipients and deliver the list to the attorney who hired you, for forwarding to opposing counsel. It is then up to the other side to determine whether any of the items removed should be subject to further discovery proceedings and possible orders for production.

Orders for production occur in a typical order:

- Your expert file is reviewed before deposition or trial.
- Various items are removed; they are identified for benefit of opposing counsel.
- Opposing counsel then seeks a show-cause order or order for production.[3]
- The documents in issue are submitted to the court by the attorney for whom you are acting in a sealed envelope for an *in camera* (in chambers) examination.
- The court or tribunal examines the documents in issue against the legal arguments tendered without allowing opposing counsel to see them.
- Orders are entered as to whether the items are privileged.

REMOVAL OF DOCUMENTS FROM YOUR FILE

It is unethical for an attorney or witness, when faced with a formal request for production of file documents, to remove items from a file without making a disclosure of that removal to opposing counsel. Do not continue to work for an attorney or client if improper removal has occurred.

If a formal request for production has been made and the attorney recommends that you improperly remove items from your file, you have several choices of action:

- You should ask the attorney why the items were removed without disclosure.
- If you are satisfied with the explanation, ask the attorney to replace the items in your file.
- In lieu of putting the items back in the file, ask the attorney to provide an itemized list of the items removed from your file to opposing counsel.
- If necessary discuss the matter with the attorney and client, setting forth your reasons for requesting the disclosure to opposing counsel.
- Recommend consulting with another attorney, possibly your own, on the subject of propriety of the removal.
- As a final alternative, demand that the list of documents be revealed to opposing counsel; if it is not, withdraw your services.

---

3. See, for example, Federal Rules of Civil Procedure, Rule 37.

If your file is examined before trial or deposition as part of careful preparation, no formal request for production of documents is made, and documents are properly removed, several scenarios are possible:

- No questions will be asked of you as to what was removed. In that event, there is no duty to disclose, unless the removed material somehow formed a basis for your opinion, in which case disclosure or a description of the item is required.
- A question may be asked of you as to what was removed. In that event, there must be an honest disclosure of the information, either by producing the item or by describing it generically for an *in camera* examination.

There are no hard-and-fast rules in some of these areas. Legal research and attorney consultation is often required. Snap judgments should be avoided. Take a thoughtful and deliberate approach to these issues.

Why all the fuss? In a criminal case, the intentional withholding of evidence could itself be considered a criminal act. In a civil case, willful withholding of evidence could be the subject of severe sanctions, both monetary and punitive. But most important, your own integrity as an expert is at stake. To countenance illegal or improper procedures concerning your work effort and files not only demeans you as an individual but also casts an adverse reflection on the entire process.

TRIAL VERSUS CONSULTATION EXPERTS

An article in the *American Bar Association Journal* comparing trial and consultation experts suggests that the expert and attorney should confer, keeping in mind the rules of liberal discovery, before placing in the expert's hands a sensitive document or revealing to the expert what could be potentially damaging information.[4]

Under Rule 26(b)(4) of the Federal Rules of Civil Procedure, a critical distinction is made between experts who do not testify — those who are merely consultants — and those who are employed for litigation purposes. Trial experts are generally subject to full discovery, whereas consultants are usually immune from that obligation.[5] Facts and information should not be given to an expert unless there is some specific reason for doing so. Always consider how a skillful cross-examiner might use a piece of information.[6]

---

4. Daniels, "Protecting Your Expert During Discovery," *ABA Journal*, Vol. 71, September 1985, p. 50.
5. Daniels, "Managing Litigation Experts," *ABA Journal*, Vol. 70, December 1984, p. 64.
6. Daniels, "Managing," p. 66.

There is no question that experts are generally not protected by any attorney–client or work-product privilege. The expert's opinion, even in conjunction with the attorney's litigation strategy, does not fall within a work-product privilege.[7] Under Federal Rules of Civil Procedure, Rule 26(b)(4), only experts retained for trial and trial preparation can be the subject of discovery. If you are retained only as a consultant, not in anticipation of trial testimony, your work on the case is probably not discoverable.

In one case, the court considered four factors in determining whether the expert was a retained witness for trial purposes or an informally consulted expert:[8]

- The manner in which the consultation was initiated
- The nature, type, and extent of information and material provided to the expert
- The duration and intensity of the consultation relationship
- The terms of the consultation, such as items of payment and like considerations

There is also an exception in the discovery rules involving the testimony of an expert who is retained in anticipation of litigation but who is not expected to testify at trial. Normally, that witness's files and opinions are not subject to the usual rules of discovery.

If a party can show that exceptional circumstances exist—that the information being sought is not otherwise available—some courts will carve out an exception and allow discovery for a nontestifying expert. In such cases, the opposition usually has to show the following:

- The expert has information about an item that has been destroyed or changed.
- The party seeking discovery cannot otherwise obtain an expert.
- Few experts exist.
- All other available experts have been retained by the opposition.[9]

WAIVER OF PRIVILEGE

Assuming that some limited privileges attend your files and testimony, that privilege may be waived by the attorney or client. Privilege can be waived in the following ways:

---

7. Mueller, "Protecting Expert Consulting Teams From Discovery," *For the Defense*, July 1987, p. 14.

8. Mueller, p. 17, citing *Ager* v. *Jane C. Stormont Hospital and Training School for Nurses*, 622 F.2d 496–501, 502 (10th Cir. 1980).

9. Mueller, p. 18.

- The material is inadvertently produced for the opposing side without a claim of privilege.
- A third party is present at the time of the privileged communication.
- Work done as attorney work product is later used by the expert to help formulate expert opinion.
- Court or statutory tests for existence of the privilege have not been met.
- The subject matter of the privileged communication is placed at issue by the client or attorney.

CONCLUSION

To protect yourself in the event of discovery, insist on receiving all materials relevant to your investigation, not just those that support your opinion. Avoid highlighting or annotating written materials until you have formed an opinion on the case. Discuss your reports with counsel before you commit your opinion to writing.[10] Remember that in most cases both your file and your opinions will be subject to discovery. That being the case, test everything you write, note, report, or say against the probability that it may fall to the opposition or may be introduced at trial.

---

10. Vernon, "Protecting Your Expert from Discovery," *For the Defense*, June 1989, pp. 16–21.

14 SEEKING THE ASSISTANCE OF OTHER PROFESSIONALS

INTRODUCTION

In the ordinary course of your professional experience, you frequently consult with other experts, either in your own field or in related areas. This is one of the ways professionals stimulate their thinking, generate ideas, and develop hypotheses.

Because such consultation is so routine, the rules of evidence, in certain circumstances, permit usual and customary consultations, themselves inadmissible, to support your expert opinion. Typically, Federal Rules of Evidence, Rule 703, provides that if experts are using sources usually and reasonably relied on in a particular field to form the basis for opinions, they may use such sources for litigation investigation reference. That has been taken to include professional consultations.

The dispute-resolution process is designed to solve problems. Consultation with other experts assists that process. Logic, and good judgment suggest the consultation process should be readily undertaken.

Figure 14.1 shows frequency of consultation by the experts who responded to the survey. The chart also demonstrates how often the experts reveal those consultations in their written reports.

THE EVIDENCE PROBLEM

If you use consultations to help form your opinions, how can the basis of your opinions be explored by investigation or cross-examination in deposition or trial? You should consider the investigation process as if it occurs in real life.

Your usual process should be followed. If in an ordinary case, you would rely on the services of some one or more consultants, you should not hesitate to use the same procedures in a forensic context.

Examples of such routine consultation include: radiology reports used by orthopedic surgeons, voluminous computations adopted by tax accountants and field measurements relied on by engineers and architects.

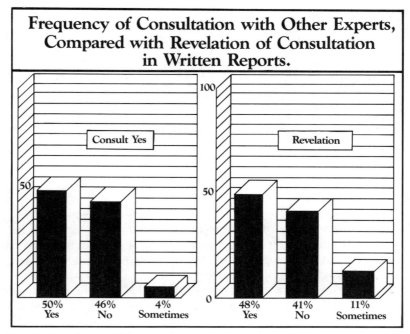

Figure 14.1 Frequency of consultation with other experts, compared with revelation of consultation in written reports.

Routine preservation of the relied-upon data in your file should solve the evidence and testimony problem.

MULTIDISCIPLINARY CASES

Another type of consultation frequently practiced is the interdisciplinary or multidisciplinary approach to a forensic problem. The following cases show how a team of experts can work together on complicated cases.

Case No. 1. In a case involving a gas explosion, thirteen specialized fields were involved in the investigation: explosion dynamics, gas chromatography, environmental law violation, toxicology, building and structure matters, LP gas regulator function, general surgery problems, dermatologist/burn specialization, psychological/psychiatric problems, economic loss analysis, rehabilitation, prosthesis use and availability, and real property damage. The case was unique because the controversy was resolved short of trial due to the high degree of expert cooperation and thoroughness of investigation, reports, and depositions.

Case No. 2. An automobile crash resulted in a victim with herniated cervical discs at C4 and C5, necessitating cervical laminectomy. The team of experts included eight fields: accident investigation and reconstruction, automobile repair specialist, metal frame and strength technician, orthopedist, neurologist, oncologist (the claimant was a recent colostomy patient), economist, and home care specialist/practical nurse.

The cooperation among the experts resulted in a successful courtroom result for the seriously injured plaintiff. All expert groups should become successfully welded into a smoothly functioning organization.

Case No. 3. In a case involving inverse condemnation of a motel, the team of experts included four experts: a real estate appraiser, a motel appraiser, the client's accountant, and a contractor/architect. Their task was to evaluate damage to the property caused by construction of an elevated road. The property was evaluated from a structural, financial, business, and real property value standpoint, each of the experts approaching the valuation from a slightly different perspective. All the experts conferred during their investigations. Because of condemnation law requirements, all evidence which bore on damage to the value of real property became a part of the lead real estate appraiser's report. However, all supporting experts testified about their own area of expertise to sustain the summary testimony of the real estate appraiser.

The blend of expert testimony created a seamless fabric for courtroom projection. All the expert testimony was admitted.

However, not every consultation results in a satisfactory outcome in multidisciplinary cases. The following case exemplifies such problems.

Case No. 4. A claimant sustained breast cancer some ten years prior to the current onset of right shoulder pain. The internist referred the patient to a radiologist. The radiology technician, under supervision of the radiologist, placed the x-ray plate in the machine in reverse position, with the indicating notch on the left rather than the right side. The radiologist, reading the x-ray, concluded that the patient's left shoulder should be the site of a biopsy, whereas the patient was sustaining pain and discomfort on the right side. Despite the patient's repeated and frequent protestations, a needle biopsy was performed, attempting to reach a suspected growth on the left side. Not only was the wrong side invaded, but the process was further complicated by a resulting pneumothorax. Expert reports served to resolve the case well short of trial.

CALL ANOTHER EXPERT

A unique area of expert consultation arises when you are presented with a case beyond your expertise. It is gratifying to both client and attorney to meet a forensic witness who, because of maturity and self-confidence, knows the limits of competence and refuses to step over that line.

Select experts carefully. Examine credentials. In most cases suggestion of three possible experts is indicated. The attorney and client should make the selection.

CONCLUSION

Consultations are usual in professional and specialized fields. Use them in your forensic assignments when appropriate. Administrative panels, arbitration boards and courts generally welcome forensic cooperation to aid in the dispute-resolution process, as long as the process remains fundamentally fair. The perfect blend of expert testimony creates a solid case for trial.

15 WHAT IS DISCOVERY?

INTRODUCTION

Discovery has been defined as: "the pre-trial devices that can be used by one party to obtain facts and information about the case from the other party in order to assist the party's preparation for trial."[1] Under most rules of civil procedure, discovery tools include depositions on oral or written questions, written interrogatories, production of tangible items, property, physical and mental examinations, and requests for admission. Civil discovery is usually governed by procedures such as the Federal Rules of Civil Procedure Rules 26–37. Discovery and inspection in federal criminal cases is generally governed by Federal Rules of Civil Procedure 15 and 16, or state, civil, or criminal rules of similar nature.

In layman's terms, discovery is the sometimes laborious process you go through to learn the underlying facts surrounding a matter in dispute. Certain devices are available by rules of procedure or practice in the various jurisdictions to help uncover underlying facts. Some lawyers think that discovery is the key to really getting to the fact basis for litigation. Others consider discovery the bane of their existence and the weight which is driving the dispute-resolution process to unfathomable depths.

All procedural rules must be liberally construed to secure just, speedy, and inexpensive dispute resolution.[2] The idea behind the rules of discovery is best stated in the rules themselves. According to Rule 26 of the Federal Rules of Civil Procedure:

(1) *In General.* Parties may obtain discovery regarding any matter, not privileged, which is relevant to the subject matter involved in the pending action, whether it relates to the claim or defense of the party seeking discovery or to

---

1. *Black's Law Dictionary* (West Publishing, 1983), p. 243.
2. Federal Rules of Civil Procedure, Rule 1(a).

the claim or defense of any other party, including the existence, description, nature, custody, condition and location of any books, documents, or other tangible things and the identity and location of persons having knowledge of any discoverable matter. It is not ground for objection that the information sought will be inadmissible at the trial if the information sought appears reasonably calculated to lead to the discovery of admissible evidence.

The rules typically should be construed to secure simplicity, fairness, and the elimination of unjustifiable expense and delay.[3]

Over 85 percent of the experts surveyed claim to understand the main purposes of discovery. Specific examples submitted by the experts generally support such basic understanding. Additional explanation of the process may serve to sharpen your grasp of why discovery is undertaken and what makes it so important.

Discovery affects you in two distinct ways. First, you can be an important source of information to your client in gathering data to support the case. Second, your work, investigation, and opinion may be the subject of discovery effort by opposing counsel.

THE DISCOVERY COMPONENTS

Under the rules of civil discovery that attend most court proceedings, the following general devices make up the discovery arsenal:

- Written interrogatories, or questions to an opposing party or witness
- Verbal deposition, or the informal process of taking sworn testimony from witnesses before trial
- Requests for production of documents, items, samples, property, and specimens
- Physical and mental examination of parties and examination of premises
- Requests for admission, designed to eliminate issues from trial

The rules of civil discovery differ from rules of criminal discovery. The constitutional guarantee against self-incrimination limits discovery from defendants in criminal cases. This is based on the fifth amendment to the Constitution, which holds that defendants in a criminal case cannot be forced to testify against themselves or give evidence against their own interest.

The Republic's founders were concerned about forced confessions, so much so that protection from self-incrimination is deeply ingrained in

---

3. Federal Rules of Civil Procedure, Rule 2.

our criminal law practice. Because of the fear of forced self-incrimination, the prosecution in a criminal case has limited access to the files, records, documents, and projected testimony of a criminal defendant prior to trial.

Certain identifying items, such as blood, hair, urine, handwriting, breath, fingerprints, footprints or voice exemplars have been carved out as acceptable prosecution discovery products. Search warrant power "on good cause shown" allows government officers access to the files and premises of a criminal suspect or defendant.

Defendants under the Federal Rules of Criminal Procedure are allowed a number of remedies in order to probe government files in preparation for trial. The Federal Rules of Criminal Evidence typically allow some discovery by defendants through the prosecution's case preparation files. The practice of many states parallels the federal practice.

Under the Federal Rules of Criminal Procedure, for example, the government must disclose statements of the defendant, the defendant's prior criminal record, documents, other objects which are intended to be evidence at trial, and reports of examinations and tests. The government does not have to disclose internal government documents, inspections, or reports in connection with an investigation or prosecution of criminal case, or statements made by government witnesses or prospective government witnesses, except as provided by detailed statutory exceptions.[4]

Under the Federal Rules of Criminal Procedure, a defendant must provide copies of documents which are intended to be used at trial, if the defendant has asked for production from the government. The same is true for reports of examination and tests. Defense memos or documents created in connection with the investigation or defense of the case by the defendant, the defendant's attorney, or their agents, which include experts, need not be produced.

Typical is Rule 15 of the Federal Rules of Criminal Procedure. It holds that depositions may be taken if exceptional circumstances are shown and specifies what objects the defendant may obtain under criminal procedures disclosure rules:

- Police arrest and crime or offense reports
- Statements of witnesses
- Statements of the accused
- Grand jury transcripts (in some jurisdictions)
- Tangible evidence

---

4. 18 U.S.C. §3500.

- Results of physical, mental, and scientific tests
- Results of experiments or comparisons
- Books, papers, documents, photographs, or other tangible things which will be evidence in the case
- Record of prior criminal convictions of the accused or co-defendant
- Tape and transcripts of electronic surveillance

In addition, the following materials may be produced only by court order:

- Material in possession of other governmental agencies
- Defendant's expert reports or statements
- Physical or mental examination of defendant or other witnesses
- Scientific experiments or comparisons

Almost all rules of discovery, civil and criminal, make mandatory a continuing duty on the part of a responding party to update responses based on additional or newly discovered information. All discovery rules, both civil and criminal, typically have sanction provisions by which the court can enforce its orders and require compliance. Current trends in the area show that the courts are using a heavier hand in imposing sanctions for violation of both the letter and spirit of discovery rules. As a responding person, you should be aware of these trends.

A major distinction between civil and criminal discovery is that civil discovery is generally activated by the attorneys. In the criminal setting, almost everything must be initiated either by agreement or on appropriate court order. The reason for the distinction is the Constitution's protection of the rights of the accused in a criminal setting.

Both criminal and civil discovery must be distinguished from the administrative law processes. Administrative hearings often involve modified discovery. For the most part, discovery is governed by the administrative board and is not subject to self-activation by the parties or their attorneys. In the arbitration process, discovery is minimally allowed, subject to express approval of the arbitration panel. Arbitration is likely to involve a panel of one or more experts, whose field is the same as that of some of the testifying witnesses. As a result, discovery is often less necessary in that setting.

YOU AND THE DISCOVERY PROCESS

With knowledge of these rules, you enter as a consulting or testifying expert. Your initial attitude may be, "Well, discovery is nice for the attorneys and the litigants, but it doesn't have anything to do with me.

I'm a scientist. I'll do my fieldwork and research the way I've always done it, without cumbersome rules of procedure that require continuous jumping through ever-diminishing hoops."

However, the rules do indeed apply to you. For example, if you are a state-employed toxicologist taking blood samples from a suspected drug or alcohol abuser, and you do not perform the procedures in the correct fashion, your test results will never see the light of day. As a forensic expert in a civil case, if you have not had the benefit of complete discovery through the opponent's files, your database will be inadequate. That could result in an unreliable conclusion and opinion.

DISCOVERY FAILURES

Some examples of experts who attempt to reach valid conclusions in civil, administrative, and criminal cases without adequate discovery will serve to illustrate the point.

Case No. 1. In a civil suit involving sexual assault, the defense obtained a court order authorizing the psychiatric and psychological evaluation and examination of the alleged victim. The psychiatrist requested the defense attorney use whatever discovery processes were necessary to obtain the claimant's entire medical history.

The complainant responded to the request for discovery by indicating that she had no prior psychiatric, emotional, or psychological medical history. As a result, the defense psychiatrist concluded that her severe emotional and psychiatric distress were caused by the sexual assault.

It was not until cross-examination of the plaintiff's physician during trial that the fact of prior hospitalization for psychiatric and emotional distress surfaced. Examination of records were ordered during trial. The records revealed numerous occasions of false charges of sexual assault and extensive treatment for that syndrome. The case was ultimately dismissed when the plaintiff's attorney concluded in good faith that proceeding with the matter would violate rules of procedure and ethical standards.

That case stands for the proposition that discovery can be better late than never. However, a pretrial deposition of the plaintiff's doctor might well have uncovered the key medical history earlier in the suit.

Case No. 2. In a case involving substantial damage to a semitrailer load of dressed beef, it was claimed that a truck-mounted refrigeration unit was defective, allowing the meat to warm during transcontinental shipment. The product was putrefied when the sealed semitrailer was opened at its destination.

Later examination of the refrigeration unit by the plaintiff's expert revealed equipment in good working order and capable of refrigerating the thousands of pounds of meat in the trailer during shipment. As a result, the plaintiff's expert reported that the refrigeration unit was apparently functional and the meat deteriorated because of its defective condition when placed in the trailer.

Many months later, during the discovery phase of the case, it was learned that the refrigeration unit on the truck was repaired shortly after the defective shipment was completed. The expert's attempt to obtain repair orders and work tickets on the unit had been unsuccessful. Not until appropriate court orders had been entered as part of the discovery process was the shipper required to produce its equipment history files, which revealed not only the repairs but also reports which established the unit's defective condition during the applicable time period.

In this case, the plaintiff's expert had done everything good engineering practice required. Unfortunately, the expert was not armed with the muscle of discovery and the power of sanctions, which ultimately resulted in revelation of the underlying facts. The plaintiff's counsel and the expert, working as a team, produced a result neither could have accomplished alone.

Case No. 3. A young girl sustained severe and disabling lacerations to her right arm and shoulder when a power boat she was operating turned sharply and went out of control. She was thrown into the water. The boat circled back over her, causing the injuries.

The issue in the case, from a scientific standpoint, was the malfunction of the boat's kill switch. The manufacturer of the component, in response to discovery requests, reported no prior incidents of malfunction of the switch.

Through the use of a claimant's network, the plaintiff's attorney learned of other events of malfunction and injury stemming directly from failure of that switch to operate when the boat operator was no longer holding the throttle. Appropriate court orders were obtained, and a substantial settlement followed.

It is important to distinguish the discovery process from your usual professional or technical information gathering procedures. Your professional information gathering can complement discovery.

Your fact-gathering tasks are undertaken based upon an organized plan of investigation and inquiry. Your use of investigative protocol, case plans, and action plans creates a process for getting your work done. The steps you follow to complete your investigation enable you to gather, in an orderly and logical way, the facts and information on which you will base your expert opinion. You follow customary and routine courses of testing and investigation and consult with others to gather the facts you need.

Discovery, on the other hand, is structured and driven by the time deadlines imposed by court or procedural rules. Each item of discovery is undertaken in a set manner, with or without court intervention, by attorneys representing the disputing parties. The fundamental distinction between the discovery process and your inquiry is that the discovery process is ultimately subject to supervision of the court or administrative tribunal.

BLENDING DISCOVERY WITH YOUR INVESTIGATION

What discovery and standard expert investigation have in common is that, in each case, facts are gathered which ultimately will shape your opinion and hence the dispute outcome. Professional investigation and inquiry can blend with and be enhanced by the discovery process. Two cases, one criminal and one civil, illustrate the complimentary nature of independent investigation and court based discovery.

Criminal Case

A unique burglary ring was discovered in a suburban community. The leader of the gang was a young mother of two. The woman was a cult leader who conducted bizarre rituals in the basement of her modest home. Actively working in the burglary operation for her under her direction and supervision were her husband, her husband's brother, and a societal dropout who had recently joined the group.

The focal point of the ritual activity of the group was a satin-lined casket, which was the first item they had stolen. Criminal charges against them included many counts of burglary. In addition, the three adults were charged with contributing to the delinquency of the fourth member of the ring, who was a minor. According to the investigative reports, the cult leader motivated her followers by dispensing drugs and sexual favors, sometimes in group settings.

Each defendant was tried separately from the others. An investigator-criminalist engaged by counsel for the brother-in-law discovered the existence of statements in the district attorney's files from other defendants. Appropriate motions were made under the rules of criminal procedure to require the district attorney to produce the statements for examination prior to trial.

The investigator also discovered that numerous items of stolen property were to be used as exhibits at the trial. Again a motion made to the court required the district attorney to allow the defense counsel to inspect the items before trial.

In addition, the client advised the investigator and counsel that all the accused persons had made statements to the investigating and arresting officers. Those statements had not been transcribed, although the investigator determined that one of the arresting officers had made extensive notes of conversations with the accused. Again, motion to the trial court required the officer to reveal those notes to defense counsel prior to trial.

On the prosecution side, a number of stolen items carried fingerprints which matched prints taken from various crime scenes. When booking the accused, the police obtained fingerprints from each to compare with those on the items of stolen property and at the crime scenes. Some of the items of stolen property had been recovered from a garage some distance from the cult leader's home. Police had taken custody of items in that garage without a search warrant and without any showing of probable cause. Appropriate motions were made, and the evidence was suppressed by court order following a discovery hearing.

This case shows the blending of effort between formal discovery and the expert's informal steps. Similar cooperation and blending of effort is found in the civil arena.

Civil Case

A number of years ago, a soldier at Fort Dix, New Jersey, became ill. His illness was tentatively diagnosed as swine flu. From that one case, never actually confirmed, the full power of the United States Public Health Service swung into action.

The entire government was mobilized. Private contractors were authorized to manufacture millions of doses of swine flu vaccine. The government indemnified the manufacturers, because vaccine testing procedures were abrogated due to the perceived threat to the public health.

There was some evidence that the government concluded it had no place to store the vaccine. It was determined to literally "warehouse" the vaccine in the bodies of the people of the United States rather than incur the expense of physical storage. Testing procedures had not yet been completed.

The press, radio, and television carried warnings of the dangers of swine flu and urged mass inoculation. The Surgeon General of the United States made pleas. As a result, millions of persons were inoculated.

Then epidemiologists started to note cases of a disease called Guillain-Barré syndrome, a neurologic impediment which had from mild to fatal effects on its victims. Not much was known about Guillain-Barré syndrome except that it affected the central nervous system and resulted in paralysis or weakness of various parts of the body. The attacks were unpredictable, and treatment was not well established. Massive amounts of physical therapy and drugs were prescribed for the sufferers; some never recovered.

The victims of Guillain-Barré were correlated with persons who had received swine flu vaccine. It became obvious that the swine flu vaccine was the cause of the Guillain-Barré outbreak. Tort litigation was commenced in many federal districts against the United States government and the vaccine manufacturers. The government admitted causal connection for a certain group of victims, and Congress passed a law making the government fully responsible for the claims and further indemnifying the drug manufacturers.

A multidistrict litigation panel of the federal court system was convened. Judge Gerhard Gesell of the United States District Court in Washington, D.C., was the supervising jurist of all swine flu vaccine cases. A claimants' committee undertook a first wave of discovery against the drug manufacturers and the government.

Many experts were engaged to track the relationship between the swine flu vaccine and the onset of Guillain-Barré syndrome. National forensic experts worked closely with a plaintiffs' steering committee to frame the discovery questions which were asked of the Federal government and the drug manufacturers. Some discovery areas included:

- Diagnosis of swine flu
- Actual cases of swine flu
- Components of the swine flu vaccine
- Vaccine test procedures followed
- Test procedures which were known to be applicable but which were not used
- "Warehousing" by inoculation of the vaccine without adequate testing

A number of physicians, primarily neurologists, engaged by victims throughout the country further guided the discovery process against both the drug manufacturers and the federal government. After extensive research into the disease process as compared with the vaccine components, they testified as to epidemiologic information, time relationship between inoculation and symptom onset, uniform treatment procedures, morbidity, and available physical and drug therapy.

Depositions, interrogatory responses, and requests for production of documents, as generated by the attorneys and guided by experts, allowed many patients to reach maximum recovery. In addition, the victims won substantial damages based on trial and settlement.

CONCLUSION

Discovery is the general term for the ways in which information is formally gathered to support and supplement your fact investigation.

An understanding of just what the discovery process entails will help you work more effectively with the legal system. Civil and criminal discovery have certain distinct differences. But in either setting, constant digging and pressure is necessary to obtain relevant information. Cooperative effort, blending your investigative activity with formal discovery, is likely to yield the best result for your client.

16 YOUR ROLE IN THE DISCOVERY PROCESS

INTRODUCTION

The expert becomes involved in formal discovery in three ways: as a generator of questions for the opposition, as an advisor in responding to the opposition's questions, and as the person responding to written and verbal questions prior to trial. To assist in formal discovery in a meaningful way, you must be:

- Professionally and technically competent
- Knowledgeable about the real world
- Conversant with current literature, practice, and procedure
- Familiar with the facts of the case
- Close to reaching a preliminary opinion
- Innovative in digging out information from the opposition
- Well-schooled in the art of brevity
- Informed about ethical guidelines which attend the discovery process

The survey produced dramatic data comparing engagements with depositions and actual trial testimony. Figure 16.1, displaying averages of the sample, contrasts those three elements. The results show that reports of experts resolve most cases, although about 20 percent of cases require deposition testimony and about 12 percent require actual trial testimony.

The survey also showed how often expert consultation about discovery is sought where the expert is not asked to formulate an ultimate opinion. Figure 16.2 shows that this happens infrequently.

YOUR SPECIFIC TASKS

There is a fundamental rule in discovery matters which you probably already know. Your client may not win the case during discovery, but the case could well be lost at that time. Talking too much in discovery,

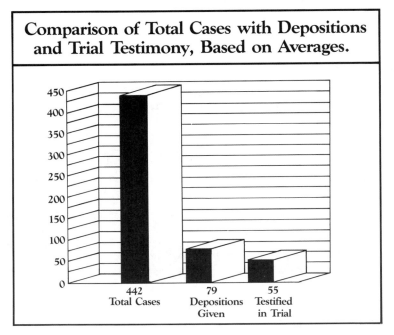

Figure 16.1 Comparison of total cases with deposition and trial testimony.

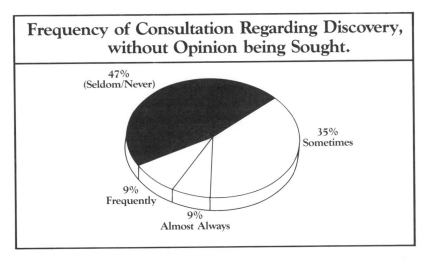

Figure 16.2 Frequency of consultation regarding discovery, without opinion being sought (17% of respondents did not answer the question).

revealing more than is required, waxing eloquent or acting egotistical, telling all you know about the entire subject: all can be detrimental to the case.

You may be called on as an expert to assist in discovery in a number of ways. You might be asked to draft written questions that the opposing party must answer fully and under oath. Another task might be to prepare lists of documents and other tangible things the opposing party has in its possession that will help you reach a final opinion. You may be called on to outline areas of inquiry and construct specific questions for use during deposition of the opposing party or their witnesses or experts.

You may also conduct experiments, tests, inspections, observations, or record or photograph operative events, with or without the opposition being present. You may assist the attorney in responding to written interrogatories tendered to your client by the opposition, or to frame responses to requests for production of documents or other items.

During the deposition stage, you may give your own deposition to opposing counsel or be present during the examination of the opposing parties' expert witnesses. You may be called on to review requests for admission for accuracy and completeness. You must be aware of the rules of privilege and confidential communications which might attend items sought by the opposition.

Finally, you should be familiar with the rules of ethical conduct required of experts and attorneys. You must be in compliance with those rules at all times.

Before you undertake a role in the discovery process, you must know about the case. Review Appendix J for a moment. You should have at least as much information as is needed for a preliminary report and have worked through the investigative process to that point before you can be of help in the discovery effort. You should have done as much fact gathering as is available to you from all sources but the opposing party. If you have prepared your case plan and action plan and followed your professionally prescribed investigative process, you will be in a good position to render meaningful assistance at this stage.

DEVELOPMENT OF A CASE THEME

Before discovery, you, the client, and the attorney should meet to frame objectives. Various hypotheses should be discussed in depth. At this stage, development of a case theme, a one-line summation of the case, helps keep you and the discovery effort pointed in the right direction.

The case theme is the common thread or focal point for the case which will guide your entire effort. You cannot put a case theme forward early in the engagement. Sometimes it takes considerable grinding of facts and law, examination of witnesses, a run at preliminary discovery, and a lot of thought. Suddenly the theme starts to emerge. Some typical themes are as follows:

- The defendant was not at the crime scene.
- The defendant didn't do it.
- The plaintiff caused the injury himself.
- The product was basically safe.
- The accident was unavoidable.
- The cause was an act of God.
- The events were caused by third parties.
- The event was triggered by a sudden emergency.
- It was a short-term marriage, hence no maintenance should be granted.
- This is a case of mistaken identity.

From the beginning of the case, everyone involved must focus on that aspect of the case which is most believable, credible, and persuasive. By continual repetition of the theme, in varied forms, the message is ultimately delivered to the decision maker.

SOME EXAMPLES OF EXPERT INPUT

Some examples of what you can do for the discovery process will demonstrate the kind of assistance you will be expected to render. This list is by no means exhaustive.

Case No. 1. In a product-liability case involving an item of allegedly defective machinery, the lead forensic expert noted certain areas of discovery:

- Obtain the product design file, including all requests for engineering action (REA).
- Obtain the OSHA and NTSB compliance files.
- Investigate the product bulletin drafts.
- Have the specification sheet and all predecessors produced.
- Obtain the notice-of-injury file the manufacturer maintained for the product.

With the expert's assistance, it was determined that a safety switch which was not installed on this equipment had not been a state-of-the-art option at the time the machine was built. However, engineering action was underway within the manufacturer's company to make the safety switch optional. Several injuries similar to that sustained by the plaintiff had occurred. Had this switch been in place, the injury would probably have been avoided.

Case No. 2. The case involved multiple murders by one family member. The issue was which of the parents was the last to die, for purposes of allocating life insurance proceeds. A criminalist whose experience included twelve similar cases in which multiple parties had been stabbed to death guided the discovery. This expert suggested specific items to be obtained. Response to the discovery indicated a substantial probability that one of the parents survived longer than the other. This paved the way for a resolution short of trial. In this case, initial expert witness information was requested from the opposition by written interrogatory questions, guided by plaintiff's expert.

A typical set of those interrogatory questions is set out at Appendix K. You may be asked to help draft questions of this kind. You will certainly be asked to help respond to similar questions. Appendix K is a good outline of the things you will need to do to help prepare any case for trial.

Case No. 3. The defendant in a criminal prosecution was charged with soliciting an unnatural sex act in a public restroom. The investigator/criminalist, after preliminary investigation, inspection of the crime scene, and talking with the accused, concluded it was impossible for the arresting officers to have seen the acts and gestures the accused was supposed to have performed.

Further inspections of the premises revealed a peephole near the ceiling of the men's room. After obtaining appropriate court orders for inspection, the investigator inspected the observation post. Photographs taken through the peephole conclusively established that the officers could not have seen what they said they saw from their observation post.

As a result of the investigator's work, not only was the criminal charge dropped, but the wrongly accused suspect received a letter of apology from the city and police. The defendant chose not to pursue remedies for abuse of process and false arrest, though the expert's effort unquestionably established good basis for such claims.

OPPOSITION DEPOSITION

The following are some preparatory steps you should take to maximize your value at deposition of the opposite expert or adverse party:

- Survey applicable literature.
- Examine available reports of the event.

- Confer with examining counsel concerning a summary of legal principals involved.
- Visit the scene of the event.
- Complete your preliminary examination.
- Find out the attorney's objective for the deposition.
- Outline areas of inquiry you think the attorney should follow.
- Examine your preliminary report to see which areas are still open and how the deposition responses could help provide answers.
- Learn as much as you can about the opposing expert.

Skilled investigators use depositions to do several things, only one of which is to gather new information. Another is to determine credibility of the witness. Witness statements can be taken to convey to the witness that you are totally informed about the case. This will help keep the witness's recollections honest and accurate.

If you are present at the deposition of the opposing party or their expert, you can help your client's attorney in a number of ways. Keep the following guidelines in mind at such times:

- Observe all the attorney's admonitions.
- Maintain a noncommittal posture and a poker face.
- Take notes unobtrusively.
- Don't confer with the attorney during examination; wait for an appropriate break.
- Carefully observe the witness's demeanor and make appropriate notes.
- Observe what items are kept available to refresh the witness's recollection.
- Note possible area of further inquiry.
- Try to determine the outline being followed by the examining attorney.
- Sense the examiner's effort at developing a theme, and determine the theme if possible.
- Shortly after the deposition, write a summary memo of all of your notes while your impressions are fresh.
- From your observation of the witness, make up your mind how you would have testified.
- Use the deposition as a tool to help you become a better witness. Your ability to respond to questions will be improved by your observations of the opposing expert.

CONCLUSION

Your assistance in the discovery process is critical to overall case preparation. The purpose of discovery is to learn as much as you can and tell as little as you must. Help the attorney develop a theme for the case. Recognize that your input as an expert will be vital to case preparation and trial. Your assistance during deposition of opposing parties, witnesses, and experts can expose weaknesses and support your own fact-gathering process.

17 YOUR DEPOSITION: CHALLENGE AND OPPORTUNITY

INTRODUCTION

Chinese philosophy recognizes that each challenge carries with it a commensurate opportunity. Your deposition is not only a challenge to your professional excellence but also an opportunity to materially assist in the dispute-resolution process.

BASIC PREPARATION

Getting ready for deposition is in many respects a mini-preparation for trial. You can be expected to go through some of the same training steps for both events. It is helpful, in approaching the deposition, to know the opposition's objectives. In general, these include:

- To gather additional information
- To attempt to impeach you
- To lock you into a position or story which will be difficult for you to maintain at trial
- To assess your demeanor as a witness
- To demonstrate to your client and attorney the extent of knowledge and expertise the opposition possesses

It is valuable to practice giving deposition on videotape. The attorney can ask you some drill questions. You can have the benefit of observing your physical mannerisms and your method of answering questions for purposes of self-improvement. Certainly not every case warrants video-taped deposition preparation. But for cases that do, the results of rehearsal are dramatic.

Do not attend a deposition without substantial preparation. Guidelines for trial and deposition testimony are found in Appendix L. Study that list before giving testimony. Following is a checklist of things to do before and during your deposition:

- Review your entire file.
- Carefully check the accuracy of your final report (or preliminary report, if that is the stage at which you are being deposed).
- Sanitize your file for work product memos or correspondence which should properly be removed.
- Visit the scene of the event or inspect the item or object in question.
- Confer with attorney and client.
- Dress in conservative clothing for the deposition.
- Get a good night's sleep before the deposition.
- Review guidelines for testimony that have been made available to you.
- Practice the following techniques in everyday conversation:
  - Take a breath before answering each question.
  - Maintain an alert posture: arms on the table, no slouching or chewing gum.
  - Keep your eyes on the examining attorney at all times. Maintain eye contact whenever possible.

HOW TO ANSWER QUESTIONS

Some examples of good and bad answers to deposition questions will help you prepare. First, the bad answers.

QUESTION: Mr. Witness, please state your name.

ANSWER: My name is Harvey Doright. I live at 1224 Main. My phone number is (707) 333-8811. My consulting company is known as Doright Consulting.

COMMENT.   Obviously, Mr. Doright has not done right in this instance. He has violated a cardinal rule of deposition examination: He gave more information than was actually requested. See what that technique does for Mr. Doright later.

QUESTION: Did you inspect the parking lot?

ANSWER: I did and I will tell you there is no way that the parking lot complies with the Uniform Building Code, the architect's design or the National Safety Council requirements.

COMMENT.   The correct answer would have been "Yes." Mr. Doright's answer opens up a whole series of questions about items which Mr. Doright may have examined. In his desire to be the consummate expert, Mr. Doright tries to tell all he knows. If he had not disclosed the three items on which he relied, examining counsel might never have asked about them. It might turn out that the three items do not support Mr. Doright's conclusion, and some back-pedaling would then be required at trial.

QUESTION: Mr. Doright, do you have an opinion as to why Mrs. Undastad fell in the parking lot?

ANSWER: Yes, I do. She fell because the concrete parking bumper she tripped over was not painted the required color. It was dark between the cars, she had her arms full of groceries; she followed her daughter into the parking lot; the daughter stepped over the parking bumper. Mrs. Undastad failed to see the concrete bumper, tripped, and fell. There is absolutely no question in my mind that failure of the store to paint the parking bumper yellow was the direct cause of the fall.

COMMENT. Here Mr. Doright has done quite a number of things wrong. First, instead of just answering the question with a simple "yes," he proceeded to explain everything he knew about the subject. Each piece of information he volunteered constitutes a trail for the skillful examiner to follow.

The next thing he did wrong was to state his opinion in absolute terms. He forgot that anything is possible. He also forgot that all he has to state is his opinion based upon a probable, not an absolute, basis. He also opened up the defense of contributory or comparative negligence, by noting that his client failed to see what her daughter clearly saw.

QUESTION: Is it possible, Mr. Doright, that you've made a mistake in your opinion?

ANSWER: Absolutely not, and I resent you even suggesting that idea. I did my work. I made my measurements. I studied everything there was to study. I've been in this field for thirty-five years. Young lawyers don't know anything. I don't know why I have to stand for these insulting and insidious innuendoes.

COMMENT. Now, Mr. Doright has violated several more rules of good testimony procedure. He has gotten angry with the attorney, insulted him, and suggested his own infallibility. In all respects, he has done no service to himself or his client.

After proper schooling and some video practice, Mr. Doright becomes a much improved witness.

QUESTION: Mr. Doright, do you have an opinion as to why Mrs. Undastad fell?

ANSWER: Yes.

QUESTION: On what do you base your opinion?

ANSWER: Could you clarify that question?

QUESTION: What is the basis for your opinion?

ANSWER: My investigation of the case.

COMMENT. At this point, examining counsel has a choice. The answer can either be accepted or probed further. A good examiner would probe further, but if it is getting late and the witness seems to be in control of the examination, the attorney may move on to something else. That would be beneficial to Mr. Doright's client and his position as a testifying expert. He can tell all he knows at trial, not at deposition.

QUESTION: Mr. Doright, in light of all the circumstances of this case and with a view toward your testimony at the time of trial, just what is it that you are saying and how do you explain your position at this time?

ANSWER: I don't understand your question; it is really two questions.

QUESTION: Which part did you not understand?

ANSWER: If you could break the question down into separate questions, I'll try to answer each one as accurately as I can.

COMMENT. This shows Mr. Doright's understanding of the process of complex and compound questions. Numerous questions, some of which were vague and unclear, were built into the attorney's long and rambling question. Doright did right by politely asking the attorney to break the question down into separate parts.

QUESTION: Mr. Doright, did you talk with anyone before coming into this deposition room today about your testimony?

ANSWER: Yes.

QUESTION: Who did you talk to?

ANSWER: I talked to the attorney who engaged my services.

QUESTION: What did he tell you to say?

ANSWER: He told me to be truthful with you in all respects.

COMMENT. The attorney can make little response to this question-and-answer series. He should move on to something else. From that response Mr. Doright has done right again and has been truthful and honest in his answer.

QUESTION: Mr. Doright, what do you think could have been done to remedy this parking lot situation?

ANSWER: Are you asking for my opinion?

QUESTION: I want to know what you think.

ANSWER: My opinion is that in all probability standard lighting and painting would have avoided the situation.

COMMENT. The attorney is trying to obtain a guess or speculation. Mr. Doright, sensing that trap, persists in rendering his opinion. In trial, that opinion will be enhanced and embellished based on reasonable scientific and technical probability.

QUESTION: Mr. Doright, are you absolutely certain the parking bumper was not painted yellow at the time of Mrs. Undastad's fall?

ANSWER: I'm reasonably certain that was the situation.

QUESTION: Isn't it possible that the paint wore off between the time of her fall and the time of your inspection?

ANSWER: Many things are possible, sir, but in my opinion, that did not occur here.

COMMENT. The attorney is attempting to lock Mr. Doright into an absolute position, knowing that given the rules of human conduct there are few absolutes. But because the witness framed the answer in terms of his investigation and reasonable probability, he avoids the trap.

QUESTION: Is it not true, Mr. Doright, that part of the responsibility for this fall must be squarely placed on Mrs. Undastad for not having watched her step?

ANSWER: If I am not mistaken, that decision is not for me to make.

COMMENT. Here Mr. Doright has shown his careful preparation of the case and his recognition of the legal principals involved. His field of expertise and technical examination does not extend to the ultimate weighing of comparative fault or contributory negligence. He knows that matters of claimant's contributory or comparative negligence are jury questions, not for determination by the design-and-construction expert.

QUESTION: Is it correct that the amount of light available at the site of Mrs. Undastad's fall is measured by your guesstimate?

ANSWER: No, that is not correct.

QUESTION: Well, how is the light measured?

ANSWER: By use of standard test equipment which measures light intensity in terms of candlepower.

COMMENT.   At this point, Mr. Doright is tempted to but did not go into techniques of measurement, description of standardization equipment, recognized scientific procedures, methods by which lighting was tested, and precautions which he took to make sure the test was done at the same time of day Mrs. Undastad fell. If examining counsel wishes to go into those items, he will. If not, the matter is best left for sponsoring counsel to explore at trial.

OTHER AVENUES OF CROSS-EXAMINATION

Your deposition may be preceded by a required written report and a series of written interrogatories. A typical set of written interrogatories taken under Rule 26(b)(4) is found in Appendix K. Review that appendix to prepare for your verbal deposition as well, because you should be ready to answer the same questions in writing or verbally. Examining counsel has the right to select any reasonable means of discovery. Written interrogatories may be used.

There are six areas you should be aware of as you prepare for deposition:[1]

- Conversations conducted to prepare you for deposition may be discoverable.
- The lawyer who attends the deposition with you may not be able to instruct you as to whether you can or cannot answer questions.
- What items to volunteer in your answers must be carefully reviewed with counsel.
- If you have published or testified to something inconsistent with your position, discuss this with counsel in advance.
- Be open to suggestions from counsel about your behavior, attitude, and posture during testimony.
- Prior drafts of your reports may be required to be produced, in some jurisdictions.

---

1. Daniels, "Protecting Your Expert During Discovery," *ABA Journal*, Vol. 71, September 1985, pp. 50, 52.

TECHNIQUE FOR EFFECTIVENESS

Your deposition examination will probably follow the general content of Appendix K and M. This format is not applicable in every case, but the following general guidelines are:

- Your overall air of quiet confidence and control will be immediately apparent. You may also wish to select a seat which requires others in the room to shift their position, or sit with your back toward the glare of outside windows.
- The papers and materials you use to refresh your memory during or before testifying, may be ordered produced. If you have not been subpoenaed to produce documents, it may be best to reveal these documents one at a time. Of course, if you have done a report that has been provided to the other side, that is the best memory refresher to use.
- Do not hesitate to ask for a recess if you are tired or if the questions appear to be coming too fast and furious.
- Remember that any discussions you have with counsel during the recess may be inquired into by the examining attorney. So if there is a smoking gun, do not discuss it during recess consultation.
- Under most procedures, the examining side must pay your fees for the preparation, deposition, and review of deposition following testimony. That compensation agreement should be clearly spelled out at the outset of your deposition. An agreement should be stated on the record, if not before.
- It may be appropriate and proper for you to have your own attorney attend your deposition, in case confidential matters involving other clients are inquired into which you are prohibited from disclosing.
- The deposition room represents a full court press. There should be no off-the-record or informal discussions with counsel. They are a trap for the unwary and inexperienced expert. When the deposition is concluded, do not ask the attorney who hired you how you did. You will learn soon enough.
- Size up the method and manner of approach of the examining attorney. Is the approach aggressive and tenacious, or does he try to "nice guy" you to death? Your early analysis will be important, both for deposition and trial. The attorney might vary his style to throw you off base. Be alert to changes in demeanor.
- Treat everyone at the deposition politely. Jokes or flippant comments are inappropriate. Maintain your professional demeanor at all times, but do not appear cold.

Part of your effectiveness will be measured by your ability to anticipate what the cross-examination may entail. Appendix M is an outline
of possible areas of cross-examination.

THE DEPOSITION DRAMA

Now you are ready for the moment of truth. No one else can really live
through the agitation and anxiety of the deposition except you. The
entire case may ride on your testimony.

You walk into the deposition room. The lawyers, parties, and other
experts may be present. The court reporter is poised to take down your
every word. You will be nervous, but that is not all bad. Nervousness
will stimulate your performance and cause you to rise to the occasion.

You have reviewed your facts and file. You are comfortable with your
subject matter. You know more about the case than anyone else in the
room. You display an air of competence and composure, no matter how
you feel internally. Your demeanor should be that of a person who is
familiar with the spotlight and sufficiently accustomed to it to be comfortable there.

Your posture will tell a great deal about how you approach the task,
so walk into the room standing tall. Avoid fraternizing with anyone in
the room. Seat yourself at the designated place or pick your own spot if
possible. Sit erect, maintain eye contact, be alert.

Your dress should say you are an organized and efficient person,
without being ostentatious. Your manner, attitude, clothing, and behavior should reflect competence and pride in your accomplishments.

Now the questions start. This lawyer is not so bad. A very polite
person, friendly. He seems to want to help you get through this. The
beginning questions are relatively simple. This is a snap, you think.
Then comes a line-by-line verification of your curriculum vitae. Every
detail is checked. Now you may have a doubt or two. Is everything on
that resume true and accurate? If not, you and your client may be in for
a long afternoon.

Now begins the serious examination. Who hired you? When were you
hired? What are you being paid? How many hours have you devoted to
the project? What have you done? Who have you seen? What tests have
you performed? What do they show? What did the attorney tell you
about the case? Produce every communication you have had with the
lawyer. What other experts have you consulted? What did they say?
What texts or periodicals did you review? Which are authoritative, in
your opinion?

Your skillful yet limited answers will keep the examination on track and going your way. If you start volunteering information, you will know it at once, because the tide will turn against you.

It is time for your conclusions and opinions: "Do you have an opinion as to the source of the poison in the children's chocolate milk?" "What was the chemical composition of the poison substance?" "Do you have an opinion as to who placed the substance in the milk?" "State each and every fact on which you base each of those conclusions." "How are the facts related to your opinion?"

During the deposition, do not look to the attorney who engaged your services for assistance. The primary reason for this is that your eyes must be focused on the examining attorney, no one else. Second, what will the opposition think of you as a witness if you have to keep looking to counsel for aid? The other side will know that, come the time of trial, you will not be able to stand up to the rigors of examination.

Some of the questions will appear almost harassing. Others will seem irrelevant. Some questioning will look like a fishing expedition. But you should be cool under fire and not ruffled by seemingly needless questions.

If you sense that the questioning is not going well, here are a few reminders to get you back on track:

- Ask for a recess or comfort break. Use the time to regroup.
- Use the technique of abdominal breathing with slow nasal exhale to calm you down.
- Readjust your positive posture.
- Do not attempt to search your file and answer questions at the same time.
- Go back to giving only "yes" or "no" answers.
- Slow the pace.
- Block any mistakes you may have made from your mind.
- If necessary, correct previous misstatements.

Now the deposition is concluded. You feel comfortably tired knowing you have done a good job. You were well prepared, and you answered truthfully and honestly. Gather your papers and say polite goodbyes to everyone in the deposition room. You will have ample opportunity to confer with counsel and client later. Your self-confident, calm behavior should prevail to the instant you leave the room.

Some days or weeks after the deposition, a transcribed copy will be made available for your review. Examine it to correct typographical errors, not to make substantive changes you have thought of since the deposition. Make the minimum number of corrections or changes possible, because the changes you make can become the basis of cross-examination at trial. An important "yes" when you should have said "no" will be hammered hard at trial.

Always consult with counsel concerning changes you make in your transcribed deposition testimony for a full explanation of the implications of change. After you examine the transcript, you will be asked to sign an affidavit which approves the transcription as made or with modifications. If you do not examine the transcript, then most local rules provide that the deposition may be filed without your signature, with approval being assumed. Therefore,always review the transcription for transmission or typographical errors.

CONCLUSION

Your deposition presents a challenge and an opportunity. The challenge will become less severe in direct proportion to the degree of your preparation. The opportunity is to display your ability as a witness, not to display all the knowledge you have amassed on the subject of this or any other case. Your calm, cool, demeanor and confident professionalism should permeate the entire deposition experience.

18 FINAL TRIAL PREPARATION CONFERENCE

INTRODUCTION

As a rough stone starts to take on luster during the final polishing, so does a litigated matter start to take on clarity during final trial preparation. This is true whether the case is to be tried for a day or a month. The clarity is heightened by the final status conference between you, all other experts, the attorney, and your client.

The survey results indicate that experts sometimes meet with other experts prior to trial. Figure 18.1 shows the degree of frequency. More formal pretrial expert conferences are held with more or less frequency. Figure 18.2 shows that the responding experts participate in such conferences for about half their cases.

BENEFITS OF THE FINAL STATUS CONFERENCES

The following major benefits attend a final status conference between experts, attorney, and client:

- It allows you to meet the other experts.
- It allows all experts to review their findings together to be sure their conclusions do not conflict.
- It exposes any inconsistency in findings, conclusions, or methodology.
- It reassures the client during the anxious period just before the trial.
- It allows each expert to explain or practice use of courtroom charts, drawings, models, and demonstrations.
- It develops a team spirit.

Counsel usually sets the time and place for the final status conference. If the attorney does not suggest a conference, you may do so. Such conferences should take place in person, rather than by telephone. Every effort should be made to have all experts, attorneys, and clients present.

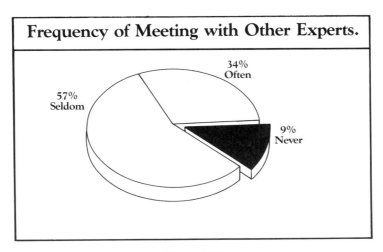

Figure 18.1

The conference allows each expert to encapsulate his or her trial presentation. By summarizing your assignment, processes, and conclusions, you test your effort and integrate it with that of other professionals. Therefore, approach this session with an open mind and a thick skin. Perhaps you have made some mistakes. It is better for them to be exposed at the final status conference than in the courtroom. If errors in your process or methodology are found, admit them and correct your

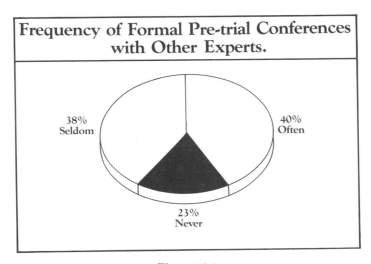

Figure 18.2

work. Expert witnesses are human and subject to error. A mistake in your process is not the end of the world, but stubborn retention of an untenable position is inexcusable.

All prior considerations and observations about confidentiality apply to this meeting. While the discovery phase is probably over by the time of the conference, the opposition may attempt to probe for disclosures made at the meeting. In order to enhance confidentiality, everything about the meeting should be labeled as attorney work product if appropriate. Whenever possible, all the information at the conference should be couched in terms of the attorney's thought processes in preparation for trial. Any memoranda generated for the use of experts should certainly be so labeled.

The final status conference is an exercise for the benefit of experts and for testing the attorney's thought processes and trial preparation effort. There are some precautionary steps to follow, on the assumption matters discussed at the final status conference might be discoverable during trial or through subsequent discovery:

- Test whatever you are about to say for courtroom disclosure.
- Ask yourself whether your statement would sound appropriate if it were disclosed while you are on the witness stand.
- Determine whether the assistance you might get at the status conference from other experts is of the type normally utilized by experts such as yourself in your usual and ordinary investigative processes.

In other words, if you get help from other experts at the final status conference, couch your request in customary terms of professional, technical or scientific consultation. In that way, under the rules of evidence, there is a possibility your inquiry will be treated as proper and you may not have to disclose the information obtained. If disclosed, the data would be a professionally proper consultation.

The interdisciplinary team members, with their demonstrative charts, graphs, drawings, diagrams, and visual aids can be examined by the assembled gathering with a jaundiced eye. You may need help eliminating apparent errors or inconsistencies in your evidence. You can help other experts in doing the same.

It may be beneficial for you to exchange reports with other experts, under the attorney's supervision. This exchange is designed to achieve common goals. It can improve the accuracy and quality of your presentation.

It is not absolutely necessary for the attorney to be present at the final briefing conference, although it is certainly recommended. In some cases, an informal gathering of the experts will accomplish many of the conference objectives.

THE STATUS CONFERENCE IN ACTION

One case example will serve to demonstrate how effective the final status conference can be.

Case No. 1. Public health authorities had charged a massive grocery store with health code violations. The list of alleged oversights was lengthy, and the store was threatened with closure. Among the charges were contaminated food, chemicals stored adjacent to consumables, evidence of rodent infestation, lack of sanitary practices for food handlers, improper lighting and ventilation, and lack of overall sanitation and cleanliness.

To meet the charges, which probably had been prompted by a private vendetta between the public health officer and the store manager, market officials responded with a public health team of its own. Included were a bacteriologist, an entomologist, a retired public health official, and a professional maintenance service manager. Prior to the hearing before the public health board, the team investigated the store premises extensively.

The experts meticulously compared the regulations with the charges of health code violations. Each was assigned an appropriate group of violations to study. At an informal meeting, the experts united all their testimony into a smooth and persuasive presentation. The retired public health official served as team leader in coordinating the defense effort. The trial result was satisfactory.

At the status conference, the team can anticipate opponent's strategy and cross-examination direction. The input of other professionals is particularly valuable in helping you infer the kinds of questions that might be asked of you on the witness stand. A few examples of possible cross-examination questions that have been suggested at these conferences demonstrate the point:

- "Were all chemical reagents of sufficient strength?"
- "Was the photograph taken at an angle to improperly reflect the distance?"
- "Were there witnesses you could have interviewed but did not?"
- "Have you preserved all specimens which you analyzed?"
- "Was the number of tests you performed in conformity with established standards?"
- "Was your sample statistically adequate?"
- "Is the process you followed recognized in the scientific community?"
- "What literature did you study before undertaking your field investigation?"
- "Have you ever read literature that contradicts your conclusion?"

If the conference suggests a problem with your report, correct it at once. Consult counsel; consider an addendum or errata to your report; notify the other side. Do not assume that the problem will go away or the opposition will overlook it.

PROCEEDING TO TRIAL WITHOUT THE FINAL STATUS CONFERENCE

What if the case is not substantial enough to warrant a final status conference? You can accomplish final trial preparation without the formal conference:

- Review your file, eliminating attorney work-product communications. Make your file orderly, organized, and helpful. Strip superfluous notes, calculations, and comments from the file.
- Have graphic displays, models, drawings, charts, and diagrams in order and complete. Make sure all are self-explanatory without any testimonial discourse.
- Make sure your report is complete and accurate. Check it for incorrect calculation, typographical errors, or omissions. All attachments should be in place. Every page should be legible.
- Explain your assignment, your process, and your conclusion to someone who is unfamiliar with the case. Encourage your listener to ask questions. Can you explain, describe, and demonstrate everything you were asked to do, how you did it, and what you found in the process?
- Present your findings and conclusions to your work organization, either peers or staff. It will be easier for you to tell your story in court if you have already told it to an audience. Timing, pacing, rhythm, clarity of statement and documentation are all enhanced by such a practice session. Be especially receptive to the comments of your captive audience.

OTHER SOURCES OF HELP

Some other sources available to you at this juncture include those listed in the bibliography of this text. Other steps you can take to become a more effective expert witness include:

- Visit your mentor—a former college professor, senior partner, first employer—someone who has assisted you in developing your career. Describe the case and discuss possible strategies.
- Talk to others in your field about possible troublesome areas.

CONCLUSION

Final trial preparation help can come from other experts and the attorneys who engaged you. The final status conference can be a positive event. Other professionals and your own observation and reading should answer most questions about final preparation for trial.

19 PREPARING FOR TRIAL ON YOUR OWN

INTRODUCTION

It will sometimes be necessary for you to prepare to go to trial without meeting or working with the attorney who engaged your services. Because the process works so much better with attorney-expert consultation, it is unfortunate that some cases proceed to trial without it. Nevertheless, if that does happen, you can be ready.

THE STEPS TO SELF-PREPARATION

There are twenty-three steps to follow if you are heading for trial or hearing without an opportunity to confer with counsel, client, or other experts. Beginning these steps presupposes that you have done everything right to that point. Engagement, investigation, preliminary report, discovery, and final report have been accomplished. Only final trial preparation and trial remain. The remainder of this chapter discusses these steps.

1. Develop a Trial Theme. Developing a theme does not require further digging into the facts, interviewing witnesses, or doing calculations. After you have run through your work product, stand back. See what the case is all about and how your role fits into it. Decide which of your findings will be most helpful to the client and the cause. In Chapter 16 ten typical themes are suggested. Study the case facts to develop the theme for your testimony. A theme will give you a point of focus and a common thread for your testimony.

2. Order of Proof. Consider how you will present your study and report. Usually, identifying questions will come first: who you are, what your assignment was, what you did, and how you did it. Your observations and tests will come next, and finally, your opinions and reasoning. Decide when you will use visual aids and models to illustrate your testimony for maximum effectiveness.

3. Refining Your Testimony into Three Concise Sentences. If you cannot tell your tale in three brief sentences, you do not know the material. Spend time encapsulating your study, findings, conclusions, and opinion into three brief statements. Practice delivering those three statements to neighbors, friends, and family members. Do they understand? Are they persuaded? If they do not understand or are not persuaded, refine further.

4. Examining Exhibits and the Scene. If the case involves a place or tangible object reasonably accessible to you, inspect it one last time before trial. If you have access to the opposition's visual aids or expert reports, review them. If necessary, contact the attorney who has engaged your service for assistance in obtaining access to these items.

5. Obtaining Advance Approval of Demonstration Items. You may need counsel's assistance to obtain advance approval to use demonstrations. These items should be the subject of disclosure to opposing counsel before trial. If that requires contacting the attorney who engaged you, do so.

6. Staging Your Testimony. Become familiar with the trial setting. If possible, visit the place where your testimony will be taken. In particular, determine the location of electric outlets and walls or screens for projection. Determine how your visual aids will be projected. Make sure they can be seen from important positions in the room. Check equipment and prepare for emergencies such as power failure or bulb burnout. Review Appendixes C and L.

7. Reviewing the Discovery. You have probably been provided with copies of interrogatories you helped answer or draft. Review them prior to trial. Review tests, examinations, and pretrial preparation which was the subject of formal discovery response. Take particular time with the transcript of your deposition and those of concurring and contravening experts. Study all these documents for strong and weak points. This will help you anticipate cross-examination.

8. Anticipating Evidence Problems. Take a look at the documents or tangible things you expect to sponsor as an expert. Are they technically trustworthy? Do they need only minimal explanation to be understood? Who prepared them? If they were prepared by others, will they be admissible in the ordinary course of your professional experience? Are they reliable? Develop an alternative plan if the items you expect to offer into evidence are rejected. The attorney by whom you were engaged will appreciate your observations about motions to limit or accept evidence.

9. Checking Technical Terminology. Consider use of a glossary if your testimony will require use of technical terms. This will build your credibility, assist the teaching process, and enhance your position as a reliable and believable expert. Clear your use of the glossary with all counsel in advance. If you are denied permission to use it, you can still write out definitions on a flip chart or chalkboard during your testimony. Do not be afraid to suggest such a solution.

10. Structuring and Organizing Your Testimony. Outline the main divisions of your testimony, building from the initial strong points to the weaker points in the middle and then to a strong finish.

Whether you appear well-organized on the witness stand will tell the trier of fact a great deal about your confidence, competence, and credibility. Having all your materials in neatly arranged notebooks, tabbed and well-organized, will give you an aura of professionalism and competence. The notebook should include your report, a summary of the data you relied on, answers to interrogatories which relate to your testimony, your discovery deposition, and the subpoena which commanded your appearance at trial.

11. Preparing Your Exhibits and Demonstrations. Whatever documents you need as exhibits should be ready. They must be orderly and easily accessible. They should be filed by date, witness or party, and subject matter and cross-indexed. If necessary, use computer-assisted filing and search.

Decide which of your exhibits are to be enlarged or set up for slide or overhead projection. Have them ready. If you will sponsor a number of documents, prepare an exhibit list. Make enough copies of all exhibits you intend to rely on for yourself as a witness, the court or hearing officer, and each of the parties represented at trial. Make absolutely certain your experiments and demonstrations work every time. Leave nothing to chance. Practice.

12. Considering the Trier of Fact and the Forum. If you are testifying at a jury trial, decide what type of person would be most receptive to your information, knowledge, experience, and opinions. Scan the jury for such a person and direct your testimony to that person.

If the matter is being tried before a judge or administrative panel, obtain information about attitudes, points of departure, and prior rulings in similar cases. It will sharpen your testimony and help target it to the factfinder.

Question the court clerk, bailiff, or reporter, and other expert witnesses about the idiosyncrasies of judges, hearing officers, and other tribunals. The best way to determine local behavior and preference is to observe a trial or hearing. See if there are local problems in the geographic area. For example, if you are a company witness, is the company liked or disliked by the community?

13. Meeting with Other Experts. The benefits of consultation with other experts involved in the case have been discussed. A meeting of experts should be held only with approval of counsel. Check with the attorney. It would be beneficial for you to participate in such a meeting with or without the presence of counsel.

14. Obtaining Instructions Which Bear on Your Testimony. If the matter is to be tried before a jury or commission which is subject to law instructions, review the instructions as they relate to your testimony. By knowing what legal instructions the factfinder will receive, you can focus your testimony to meet those legal tests or requirements. Consult with the attorney who has engaged your services to obtain those instructions.

15. Suggesting Questions and Remarks to Counsel. Your input into *voir dire* (questions to potential jurors) and opening and closing statements could potentially be very helpful. This is particularly true if there are unique items in your testimony to which a jury should be alerted. Your comments about counsel's opening and closing statement should not be seen as presumptuous. Rather, they are your effort to be a part of the litigation team. Your attitude and demeanor in making suggestions to counsel will set the tone for current and possibly future forensic engagements.

Here are two examples of possible *voir dire* questions or argument comments prepared by experts:

There will be testimony in this case about biopsy, mammograms, and ultrasound diagnostic procedures. Dr. Smith will explain those procedures as part of his expert testimony.

You will be asked to decide whether tests performed on the operating lever established fatigue or impact fracture. Fatigue is caused by metal coming apart due to defective casting and mixing of hot metal. Impact fractures are caused by a heavy object coming into contact with metal so that it literally breaks due to the added force being exerted.

16. Scheduling Problems. You need to know when you will testify. Trials and hearings are sometimes delayed by sickness, unavailability of witnesses, or emergencies. If the attorney has not informed you of whether and when you will testify, telephone the forum clerk or secretary to determine the schedule.

Prepare a schedule of what will happen. Include these items:

- When your materials will arrive
- How they will get there
- When you will arrive
- When you might be called to testify
- How long you will testify on direct examination
- How long cross-examination may last

Finally, determine whether your presence is needed before or after your testimony.

17. Being Subpoenaed to Appear. It is beneficial for you to be under subpoena rather than voluntarily appear for trial. Your independence and credibility are enhanced if you have been subpoenaed. Usually a phone call to the attorney will accomplish this. Try to establish by testimony the fact that you are under subpoena.

18. Choosing Clothing. Dress conservatively. Avoid flashy jewelry, accent handkerchiefs or scarfs, dark sunglasses, and obviously expensive clothing. Dress for serious business.

19. Transporting Your Materials. On a complicated case, your materials may consist of numerous files, boxes, experiments, models, mockups, drawings, and other bulky items. Plan your move to the hearing room well. Determine in advance who is to move your materials and how and when it is to be done.

20. Anticipating the Opposition's Plan. Do your best to gather information about the facts, law, and positions the other side is relying on. Analyze their strategy. Figure out how you would cross-examine yourself on the facts and evidence of the case.

21. Damaging Cross-examination. When faced with a damaging cross-examination question, you may wish to premise your answer with: "As you have refreshed my recollection, the answer is…"

22. Charts. These are best done black on white with no dark borders using yellow highlighter for emphasis.

23. Four key concepts. Remember the four concepts of credibility, teaching, demonstration and simplicity, which underlie all expert testimony.

CONCLUSION

This chapter enumerated the steps necessary for you to prepare yourself for testimony at a hearing or trial. Following these steps will ready you for trial, even if you have not had the opportunity to be prepared with counsel's assistance.

20 ENHANCING CREDIBILITY THROUGH DIRECT EXAMINATION

INTRODUCTION

The primary objective of effective expert testimony is to present yourself as a well-organized, interesting and memorable person. The fact-finders need not become amature experts because of your testimony. They only need to be convinced you are a believable person with something important to say, who will materially assist them in doing the job of deciding the case.[1] Whether the case is decided in support of your position is not the true measure of the effectiveness of your testimony, though it is always preferable to win than to lose. The true test of testimonial excellence is whether you were credible, and the best opportunity you have to establish that trait is through direct examination.

You must be professionally competent and have done a thorough job of analysis, investigation and reporting. Your individual style and demeanor must be developed. You should display enthusiasm without advocating. Pattern yourself after your best teachers, and be prepared to illustrate your testimony graphically or with demonstrations.

Prior to actually testifying, mentally visualize your best possible performance as a witness. Use of the word "performance" is intentional, because in a way you are performing a key role in a real-life drama. Your credibility will be established by effective use of teaching skills.

In responding to a question asking them to define "credibility," half the experts stated that credibility was made up of three factors: believability, integrity, and being respected. Twenty-six percent of the responding experts stated that credibility consists of expertise, credentials, ability, and experience. Other important factors reflecting credibility include honesty, sincerity, and truthfulness; ability to demonstrate and convince; effective preparation and presentation; ability to be neutral, objective, truthful and open; and consistency in performance. Accord-

---

1. Malone, "Direct Examination of Experts," *Trial*, April, 1988 pp. 42–49.

ing to responding experts, a witness enhances his or her credibility by being knowledgeable, having up-to-date information, and demonstrating professional practice and diligence.

There are several ways to present and enhance all of these factors including positive and open body language, repetition of key points, getting your main points established early, repeating the main points at the conclusion of your testimony, and recognizing the need for common sense explanations.

The survey results generated five significant responses to the question: "What is the single most important admonition you have ever received about the testimonial [or deposition] process?" The experts responded:

- Answer only the question asked; do not volunteer information.
- Be factual, truthful, and concrete.
- Stick to the point and be brief.
- Do not argue with counsel, the court or tribunal.
- Keep cool and never display irritation.

These traits, characteristics, factors, and techniques will be explored and developed in this chapter. Emphasis will be placed on those things to remember which will enhance your credibility during the process of direct examination.

SOME IMPORTANT POINTS TO REMEMBER

The essence of trial competence centers around projecting an image of credibility from beginning to end. Accuracy of citation, precision in factual presentation, articulate organization of graphic materials, and an organized presentation of testimony and documentary evidence are all required.

As part of that credibility effort, you must project an ambiance of honesty, integrity, and believability. Given the fact both sides in a dispute tend to present their own conflicting views of the real world, you must stand forth as a beacon of believability.

This comment and others are noted by Robert Wells, consultant to the Kansas Trial Lawyers Association and the Kansas College of Advocacy.[2] Expertness, according to Wells, is the extent to which the witness appears to be competent, intelligent, authoritative, trained, experienced, skilled, informed, professional, and the source of valid information.[3]

---

2. Wells, "Lawyer Credibility: How the Jury Perceives It," *Trial Magazine*, July 1985, p. 69.
   3. Wells, p. 69.

Additional traits which are beneficial to an expert witness include being honest, open-minded, friendly, well-mannered, warm, fair, polite, dynamic, and positive. You must be a good listener and project yourself as a reliable source of information.[4]

One national authority on the subject of forensic engineering, Marvin M. Specter, founding president of the National Academy of Forensic Engineers, suggests how these factors, traits, characteristics, and techniques can be projected in the testimonial process,[5] initially displayable on direct examination.

- Convey the fact that you are a professional, dedicated to accurate and detailed work.
- Avoid any impression that you are a hired gun, by not being drawn into biased or exaggerated statements.
- Emphasize the specialized task you performed in the case, and that your testimony represents professional investigation and careful analysis.
- Be ready to bolster your opinion with recognized technical publications.
- Do not be afraid to expose the weakness of your case to counsel and your client. Sometimes that can lead to a graceful settlement.
- Remember that the courtroom is a serious place; your task is of utmost significance.

OFTEN OVERLOOKED POINTERS

There are some points that only experience teaches. They are enumerated here to telescope mistakes and observations of experienced expert witnesses and trial attorneys. Just knowing about these seemingly minor admonitions will further serve your goal of increased credibility projection during direct examination. A descriptive vignette will illustrate salient suggestions.

As you walk into the testimonial location, display common courtesy to all with whom you come in contact. You never know who is a juror, hearing officer, arbitrator or judge. You will do well not to discuss who you are and certainly not why you are present with persons you do not know. Contact with opposing experts, regardless of your degree of friendship with them, should be minimal; a casual greeting will suffice. Potential fact-finders will observe hallway demeanor.

---

4. Wells, p. 70.
5. Specter, "What Does It Take to be a Good Expert Witness?" *ASTM Standardization News*, February 1988, pp. 38–40. Copyright ASTM. Reprinted with permission.

Now, you are called to testify. How you carry yourself will transmit subtle messages to the audience, so walk in looking good, feeling confident. Make sure your voice, on the occasion of your first "I do" when asked if you will tell the truth, comes across loud and clear. Use your voice tone, volume and modulation to maintain interest, vary the presentation, and keep everyone awake. Conversational normalcy is the order of the day, but make sure you can be heard throughout the room. Your illustrative drawings and charts should stand alone and be self-explanatory. If called on to draw or write on a board or chart, keep your handwriting legible, and as a good performer, never turn your back on the audience. When asked to examine a document, you stop talking, because you know you can't read and talk at the same time. During any recess, maintain your distance from everyone. If you need to confer with counsel, do so out of sight of fact-finder and opposition. And be particularly cautious of casual conversation in hallways, restrooms and dining areas. Throughout your testimony you have been conscious of proper breath control, upright posture and elimination of distracting or nervous mannerisms such as facial grimace, inappropriate smile, or hand tremors. Other hearing room behavior suggestions include the avoidance of note-passing to counsel during any part of the proceedings, not sitting at counsel table, and leaving the hearing room on completion of your testimony. These final observations are directed to maintaining your appearance and position of independence and non-advocacy.

TESTIMONY EXAMPLES CONTRASTED

It may help to explore the performance of some of the best and some of the worst experts. First a good example:

Case No 1. At issue was whether a landlord had installed heating, ventilating, and air-conditioning equipment (HVAC) equal in value to a lease-required rent increase. If the equipment installation was equal in value to the rent increase, the plaintiff, a real estate broker, was entitled to a substantial renewal commission. If the equipment was not equal to the rent increase, then no renewal commission was due.

The tenant was a nationally-known personality. The landlord was a seventy-year-old, gray-haired widow. It seemed that the two had made an effort to utilize the HVAC installation in lieu of a rent increase and thereby defeat the real estate broker's claim for a renewal commission. The expert chosen by the brokerage firm was not an experienced forensic expert, but a technical representative in the HVAC industry.

Without formal forensic training, this expert brought to the witness stand twenty-five years of experience in designing and installing HVAC equipment. His demeanor was calm yet enthusiastic. His factual data were thorough and impeccable. His pretrial calculations were clearly presented on a hand-made chart.

The expert was intentionally not informed as to the compensation issue of the case, but merely asked to give his opinion as to the HVAC installation cost. The witness combined all features of the ideal expert, yet he had never before testified. He knew his field. His preparation was meticulous. His manner was certain. His dress was conservative. His delivery was forthright and direct. The jury believed him and as a result found in favor of the broker.

Not all expert testimony results in a positive performance.

Case No. 2. The case involved a toxic spill. The witness was an executive of the defendant company. He slouched, frequently covered his mouth with his hand, fidgeted with his clothing, paper, and pencils, and failed to make eye contact with the jury. As the testimony wore on and the witness became more tired, he began to answer questions flippantly.

The witness's disdain of the claimant's position was manifest through his tone of voice and superiority of attitude. It became clear that this executive, who lived thousands of miles away from the scene of the toxic tort, was unconcerned about the victims, whose lives had been disrupted by a traumatic event caused by his company. His testimony triggered the jury's development of an attitude contrary to the defendant's interests and might have determined the adverse outcome of this complex case.

A JUDGE'S VIEW OF EFFECTIVE DIRECT EXAMINATION

Attorneys, witnesses, and jurors are often consulted as to what makes a believable, credible, and persuasive expert witness. It is not often that we have the opportunity to gain insight into that subject from a veteran trial judge. In 1986, Judge Alvin D. Lichtenstein, an experienced litigator, public defender, and trial jurist, summarized qualities which to him characterized the performance of expert witnesses on direct examination which were most effective with courts and juries.[6]

At the outset, presentation of credentials deals only with the true highlights; minute detail is omitted. Hypothetical questions are stated with clarity, when used. All opinions are clearly stated as such, and are based on "a reasonable degree of (scientific, technical, or professional) probability." The persuasive expert is prepared to explain reasons for the conclusion, and testifies using non-technical terms that can be understood by everyone. Weakness of opinion or testimony is exposed

---

6. Lichtenstein, "Garbled Communications with, by, and to Medical, Expert Witnesses." *Trial Talk*, April 1986, p. 100.

during direct examination, such as frequency of examination or testimony, compensation paid by the retaining side, or possible disagreement with other experts. Because outstanding expert witnesses are practiced in responding to examination questions, they are poised and self-assured.

DIRECT EXAMINATION ENHANCERS

Experts and attorneys agree that certain elements can tip the scales in favor of one expert as opposed to another. Those elements include the ability to coordinate verbal testimony with documentation, conveyance of a sense of caring about the outcome, without advocacy, supporting opinions with admitted evidence, absorption of opposing views to support your opinions, and lastly, participation in some hands-on way with a solution to the underlying problem, if a solution is possible.

Coordination: This involves a smooth blend of verbal testimony with charts, drawings, exhibits, and other tangible items to exemplify the spoken word.

Caring: Sometimes a blasé witness comes across as just too remote and dispassionate. The better blend is suggested for you to portray a caring, considerate person who is concerned about the ultimate result of the situation, particularly if your testimony surrounds a patient or client whom you have actually helped in some way.

Admitted Evidence: If your opinion is based on facts already admitted into evidence, or which will be admitted, the power of your conclusion is greatly enhanced. It is a building block philosophy "Since A, B, and C are already established, D must be true."

Absorption: If prior adverse expert testimony has established certain facts or conclusions, the more of those facts and conclusions which you can use to bolster your opinions the stronger your opinion will appear.

Hands-On Solution: In a case involving a cure or need for correction or treatment, if you actually participated in solving the problem or making the patient well, you will be seen as more effective and involved. For example treating doctors are always viewed with more credence than those who are merely called to examine a patient in preparation for trial.

Two additional examples of outstanding trial performance will help you visualize how these qualities work in practice.

Case No. 3. The scientific issue in a case centered around a combustible mixture of ambient air with 5–15 percent methane gas to create an explosion potential. The consulting forensic witness, a chemist, was given the task of demonstrating the molecular change which takes place in an explosion of methane and air.

The chemist, a frequent university lecturer, used three styrofoam molecular models to bring alive his chalkboard formula of conversion from methane — CH_4 — to one part carbon and four parts hydrogen. By use of the models, the chalkboard formula, and a friendly, enthusiastic teaching style, the witness explained a complex chemical process in an interesting way.

Case No. 4. In testimony involving a person's use of four different names to conduct various banking activities, a forensic examiner compared over fifty handwriting specimens and six exemplars, including five specimens obtained during the discovery process. The discovery-produced exemplars were displayed on three-by-four-foot enlargements.

The expert then identified seven unique writing characteristics revealed by the specimens. Next, he placed enlargements of suspected signatures, also three-by-four enlargements, next to the exemplars. Using a pointer and moving back and forth between the suspected handwriting and the exemplars, the witness condensed weeks of work, painstaking and laborious microscopic examination, and volumes of data into a concise, informative, persuasive half-hour presentation. The witness was then cross-examined briefly.

QUESTION: Sir, isn't it true that you have not always been 100 percent correct in your expert testimony concerning questioned documents?

ANSWER: I believe I have always been correct in my analysis. However, two juries in over 1,000 cases have disagreed with me.

The witness was able to convey his high degree of personal conviction in his conclusions and at the same time indicate that his conclusions were not accepted by the factfinder in a small number of cases. His ability to convey that skillfully and openly, without appearing egotistical, is a skill born only of many years of courtroom testimonial experience.

DO'S AND DON'TS

From Lustberg's *Testifying with Impact* comes a list of testifying do's and don'ts.[7]

DO	DON'T
Communicate ideas	Read words
Be interesting	Be dull and lifeless

---

7. Lustberg, *Testifying with Impact* (Association Department, U.S. Chamber of Commerce, 1982).

Consider testifying as an opportunity	Consider testifying as a chore
Be pleasant	Be intimidated
Grab audience attention	Put listeners to sleep
Make the audience pleased to listen to you	Make your audience wish it were somewhere else
Practice breathing and relaxation exercises	Ignore the importance of breathing and relaxation
Learn to relax	Get tense and stay that way
Smile when appropriate	Frown continually
Communicate attitudes and feelings	Rely purely on logic
Vary the pitch and rate of your speech	Use more volume than you need to be heard
Gesture for emphasis when appropriate	Tie up your hands or wave them in the air
Say what you mean and mean what you say	Merely recite words from a page
Prepare	Trust to luck
Practice vocal and facial exercises	Assume you will be animated under stress
Concentrate on the material	Think only about yourself
Talk, chat, or converse	Read, preach, or orate
Deliver a verbal summary	Present a detailed wordy recitation

Detailed guidelines for testimony, designed to make you a more effective witness on direct and cross-examination are included at Appendix L. Consult those guidelines now and before every time you testify.

SHARPENING YOUR SKILLS FOR DIRECT EXAMINATION

You become a better expert witness by observing others. Watch, listen, and read. Visualize yourself as a witness and observe your testimonial performance on film or video tape. Review your own depositions with an eye toward improving the sharpness of your answers. Undertake forensic engagements which allow you to sharpen your skills, your style, and your technique.

The goal of all this work is to become a more competent, persuasive, and believable witness and a more reliable resource for the dispute-resolution process. Better testimonial skill is but one aspect of that effort. That skill is first displayed on direct examination.

An overwhelming 89 percent of responding experts are positive and enthusiastic about using demonstrative materials to enhance their effectiveness as witnesses. They suggest four ways of improving the effectiveness of visual aids:

- Keep them simple.
- Make the items large, clear, and visible.
- Have them prepared professionally.
- Develop them with counsel's assistance.

The experts found no real problem with the question-and-answer format. However, they noted the usual limitations of restriction of information exchange, loaded questions, and mandatory yes/no answers. The responding experts suggested that the system could be improved in the following ways:

- Afford more pretrial preparation.
- Make questions simpler and more direct.
- Allow the expert to have input in constructing the questions.
- Make the process less formal.
- Eliminate trick questions, loaded questions, and questions that tend to intimidate witnesses or distort the facts.
- Allow narrative explanation answers.

As a final observation, almost 34 percent of experts believed their preparation would be enhanced if they were not called in at the last minute. The attorney must give you enough time to do your work. Nineteen percent of the experts also believed their preparation would be enhanced if they were given better information on which to base their expert opinions.

TEACHING SKILL IS FUNDAMENTAL FOR DIRECT EXAMINATION

If the essence of your forensic skill is the ability to teach, then an analysis of what it takes to become a good teacher is instructive.

Some qualities of persuasive and effective teaching are transmutable to the forensic arena. Good teachers are well-informed, enthusiastic, provocative, and questioning. They use examples and illustrations. They have a sense of humor and are dedicated to their work.

Years ago the United States Navy developed a standard teaching format, represented by the acronym "TOM I. PASTA," which included nine main parts.

- Title
- Objective
- Materials
- Introduction
- Presentation
- Application
- Study
- Testing
- Assignment

You can use this format when you take the witness stand for direct examination to teach what you have learned about a case to the judge, jury, or hearing panel. The following cases show how this works.

Case No. 5. An elderly woman who was physically and intellectually disabled, received conveyance of corporate stock from a grown child. It was asserted that the conveyance was a device to delay creditors. For other purposes, the child sought the signature of the mother to convey the stock on to other family members. In a court proceeding, the issue was whether the mother was physically and mentally capable of understanding the nature of her act and the extent of her property when she conveyed away the stock.

The expert witness, an internist who had treated the woman for many years, was consulted for an opinion concerning the woman's competence. Specifically, he was asked whether the elderly woman understood the nature of her act in conveying the corporate stock. That was part of a longer question as to whether the woman understood the nature of her property and was able to care for herself and the things she owned.

Applying the Navy teaching outline to these facts, an outline of the expert's testimony was developed.

Title: Was the elderly woman competent to understand the nature and extent of her property and to care for herself and her property?

Objective: To convince the court the woman was not competent.

Materials: Medical history of the patient, current hospital records, and recent clinical examinations.

Introduction: The physician professional qualifications and long-term care and treatment of the woman were described.

Presentation: The attorney and witness conveyed to the court the information necessary for the court to reach a conclusion as to the woman's competency and her ability to care for herself and her property.

Application: The court applied the expert testimony to determine whether the woman was competent.

Study: The court examined the medical history, hospital records, clinical tests, and courtroom testimony.

Testing: The trial court's decision might be "tested" on appeal. And the dispute-resolution process is continuously put to the test of public criticism, comment, and evaluation.

Assignment: The expert in this case had no further assignment other than to treat the patient, as he had done for a number of years.

You can prepare to testify by using the TOM I. PASTA outline to organize your thoughts and materials and sharpen your skills as a trial teacher.

Case No. 6. Defendant was charged with criminal possession of controlled substances. He had two similar previous arrests, with dismissal of the charges on technical grounds. The third arrest was based on probable cause and execution of a warrant search of the defendant's home. The accused was a twenty-year-old who had suffered some previous emotional problems. An expert psychologist was engaged to evaluate defendant's qualifications to participate in a federal drug rehabilitation program, rather than serving a prison sentence. The testimonial outline followed the TOM I. PASTA format.

Title: What is the defendant's potential for rehabilitation in a drug rehabilitation program?

Objective: To establish that the defendant did have rehabilitation potential.

Materials: Clinical test results and psychologist's notes of interviews, together with defendant's school and work record, and detailed personal background investigation conducted by the psychologist.

Introduction: Psychologist's curriculum vitae and opportunity to meet with, observe, and test the defendant.

Presentation: The expert testified that in his opinion, the defendant should be selected for the program. Testimony was based on tests and evaluations, family support, absence of severe past problems with the law, and defendant's stated willingness to participate in the rehabilitation program.

Application: The sentencing applied the expert's opinion in light of two prior arrests for drug offenses, neither of which had resulted in a conviction.

Study: The court took under advisement the reports and hearing information.

Testing: In the strict sense of the word, the test was the criminal justice system itself.

Assignment: The court sentenced the defendant to two years with the federal drug rehabilitation program.

AN EXAMPLE OF DOING IT WRONG ON DIRECT

In the effort to become more competent, it is sometimes helpful to examine cases where less competence was displayed. By analyzing one of those situations and seeing what was done wrong, you can avoid like problems in the future.

Case No. 7. In a child molestation, sexual assault, and kidnapping case, defendant's appeal ended in the United States Supreme Court. The primary issue was whether the police criminalist had failed to preserve semen specimens and clothing samples from the victim and thus had violated the defendant's right to due process. The items were not refrigerated and hence were not available for defendant's pathology tests, as was admitted on direct examination.

The United States Supreme Court held the police did not have a constitutional duty to perform any particular tests and that unless a criminal defendant can show bad faith on the part of the police, failure to preserve potentially exculpative evidence does not constitute a denial of due process. The defendant's conviction was affirmed, notwithstanding the apparent error by the police lab.[8] This case is an example of obvious mishandling of forensic evidence. The pathologist's failure to plan ahead was the root of the problem. In all probability a standard protocol was violated in handling the samples and specimens. Direct examination requires careful attention to every detail.

SIMPLIFYING THE COMPLEX ON DIRECT EXAM

Statistical data and expert testimony have been shown to be difficult for juries, judges, and hearing panels to understand. The reason is simple: the presentation is boring!

The presentation of statistics does not have to be uninteresting if you take certain precautions. Studies have shown that lengthy statistical data can be vitalized by a single hypothetical case example.[9]

For instance, if a statistical chart demonstrates a particular conclusion, that drab numerical summary can be brought to life by use of factitious example. If the summary chart of 1000 events suggests a particular incidence of drug reaction, the expert on direct could proceed as follows:

---

8. *Arizona* v. *Youngblood*, 102 L.Ed.2d 281, 109 S. Ct. 333 (1988).
9. Goodman, Greene, and Loftus. "What Confuses Jurors in Complex Cases: Judges and Jurors Outline the Problems." *Trial*, November 1985, pp. 65–73.

QUESTION: Doctor, you have examined the chart, Exhibit A, isn't that correct?

ANSWER: Yes, I prepared it for purposes of this trial.

QUESTION: What does a chart like that really mean?

ANSWER: It means that if I see 1000 patients, only 1.2 or say a maximum of two, will ever experience the drug reaction that occurred in this case. It really says the chance of this adverse reaction occurring is quite remote.

To present statistics clearly, you must explain how the statistics were gathered and that each part of the statistical analysis is made up of many real-life cases. Explain how information from each case is compiled to give scientific or technical credibility to a proposition by numeric probability. Illustrate your presentation with lively, clear, and persuasive visual aids. Finally, relate the statistics to the facts of the case being tried. The example shown does that by humanizing the result, and making it applicable to the subject case.

A simple, well-organized graphic display can convey vast amounts of information in support of your verbal testimony. Figure 20.1 is a particularly effective demonstrative chart summarizing voluminous information in well-organized, understandable form. Here are some other suggestions for presenting statistical data on direct examination in a positive and understandable way.[10]

- Use simple, familiar presentations.
- Present details in your spoken testimony and add and interrelate information with overlays from chart to chart.
- Graphic software programs do not present well visually. If you use them, stick to solid colors like red, green, and blue.
- Use charts and graphs to show the clearest contrast between your position and that of the opposition.
- Avoid visual distortions by always using a zero-based axis.
- Use slides to present graphic information, which can be discussed during direct examination.
- Simple poster boards and flip charts sometimes are more effective for a small audience.
- Employ the services of a graphic artist or technician.
- Explain complex financial, statistical, or technical data by use of simple analogy.

---

10. Phillips, "Presenting Financial Damages," *ABA Journal*, January 1989, pp. 68–70.

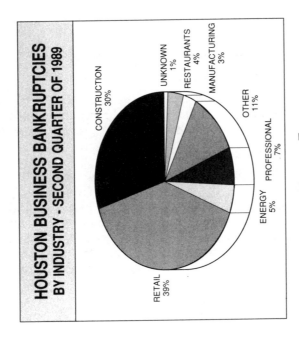

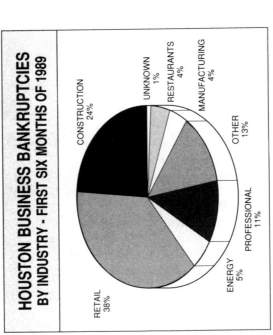

Figure 20.1 Summary chart. Courtesy Price Waterhouse Litigation Services, Houston, Texas.

CONCLUSION

Repeatedly visualize your own outstanding direct examination testimonial achievement. Become the star that you know you can be. Teach and persuade, using all available body language and verbal and demonstrative techniques. Recognize the good feeling you will experience when you are congratulated on your direct testimony. Enjoy the satisfaction you will experience when you are recognized as a credible forensic witness on direct examination.

As a forensic witness, you become a teacher to the factfinder, particularly on direct examination. Therefore, teaching devices serve that process well, including an overall outline of your teaching testimony and visual aids. Even the most complex, dull material can be made interesting and informative by innovative use of demonstrative materials and vital performance. However, the world's best chart still has no vitality unless a single personal example is used to explain the complex statistical compilation.

21 THE CHALLENGE OF CROSS-EXAMINATION

INTRODUCTION

There are some specific things you can do to prepare yourself for cross-examination. Most obvious are those which have been previously discussed in this text. All those devices and ideas serve to enhance your credibility as an expert witness. As your credibility is enhanced, cross-examination threats are diminished.

BECOME LESS VULNERABLE

There are specific things you can do to make yourself more ready and less vulnerable to cross-examination.

Put Your House In Order. Your resume must accurately reflect what you have actually accomplished, not what you wish you had done. Do not exceed the bounds of your own expertise. In taking on assignments and in answering questions, do not venture beyond the areas in which you are professionally qualified. The temptation is great to move into areas in which you are not qualified. Your image and credibility will be enhanced by sticking to your field of knowledge, training, and experience.

Your Preparation Must Be Complete. Whatever investigative steps you have taken must be completed and fully documented. The thoroughness of your preparation to testify will be exemplified by your direct examination. Accurate investigation creates a dense fabric of fact which becomes difficult to penetrate on cross-examination.

Make Your Direct Examination Persuasive. If you are believable and you have done your homework, your persuasive abilities will be obvious. Psychological persuasion conveyed by body language, repetition of theme, dress, and demeanor all add to your positive posture.

The smooth, solid presentation you made on direct examination must be maintained throughout cross-examination. When the examiner asks a potentially damaging question, use the same air of certainty that you evidenced on direct examination. Say, "Yes that is correct, but let me explain." This does two things. First, you have told the attorney who hired you to come back and ask you to explain. Second, you have shown your credibility in a forthright, nonapologetic manner.

Witnesses who are certain of their own effort and preparation are questioned cautiously on cross-examination. The cross-examining attorney quickly senses your truthful and positive answers.

Exercise Your Ability to Teach.   Part of the stimulation of a classroom setting is the ability to field questions from students. The skill with which those questions are responded to is often the mark of a great teacher. Your function as a dispute-resolution teacher is merely an extension of that exercise. The cross-examiner who probes your qualifications, preparation, conclusions, and opinions will press you for answers.

Know What You Have Previously Written or Said.   During your professional career, you might have written articles, books, or reports. In addition, you might have testified in deposition or at trial on prior occasions. Your personal library should include reprints of every article you have ever published and every deposition or court transcript of your testimony.

One of the major opportunities of cross-examination is to find prior statements, either in your writings or testimony, which contravene the opinions you are tendering in the current case. You may be asked to produce some of those inconsistent statements during the discovery phase.

The attorney and client for whom you are working are entitled to know about your prior opinions. Therefore, you should index your prior writings in such a way that you can find relevant items before taking on new assignments. In addition to alerting you and the parties for whom you act to areas of cross-examination, your prior writings and testimony can supply positive support or rebuttal material for cross-examination.

If you have written or testified contrary to the position you are now taking in the current case, be aware of the potential problem. The basic premise that supported your testimony in the former case may be different from that of the current matter. Your past opinions might have intended to be general rather than specific. Understanding the rationale and principles upon which you based prior writings or testimony and distinguishing those of the current case can blunt cross-examination and in some situations solidify your direct testimony.

Seventy-eight percent of those responding to the forensic expert questionnaire indicated they do retain copies of prior writings and testimony; 54 percent use some indexing system.

KNOW THE EXAMINER'S GOALS

Professor James W. McElhaney suggests eight fundamental techniques used to cross-examine an expert witness:[1]

- Make the expert your witness; turn the testimony to support the opposite position.
- Attack the field of expertise; show lack of recognition of the professional field.
- Attack the witness's qualifications; establish gaps in the professional resume.
- Expose the witness's bias; give reasons why testimony is slanted.
- Attack the witness's fact basis; investigation was inadequate.
- Change the hypothetical used on direct; vary the facts to support the opposition if use of the hypothetical question is the basis for expert opinion.
- Impeach the witness with learned treatises and journals; any recognized text, authoritative in nature, can be used to cross-examine.
- Attack the witness head-on.

The following cases show how opposing counsel attempts to achieve these goals during cross-examination.

Case No. 1. In an action involving construction of a golf course in a residential neighborhood, the applicant's expert testified that, in his opinion, perimeter fence around the golf course would not be unsightly. He based his conclusion on the fact that other fences at nearby golf courses, which he had photographed, did not appear to disturb neighborhood aesthetics. Cross-examination was designed to make the witness support the opposition.

QUESTION: Do you agree, Mr. Witness, that the fence will be at least forty feet high?

ANSWER: Yes.

QUESTION: It will be supported by telephone pole-size support columns?

ANSWER: That's true.

QUESTION: The fence is to be made of chicken wire, is that correct?

ANSWER: That's correct.

---

1. McElhaney, "Expert Witnesses," *ABA Journal*, March 1989, pp. 98–99.

QUESTION: And the fence will border residential property for approximately 300 yards, is that also correct?

ANSWER: Yes.

QUESTION: Do you agree the chicken wire and telephone pole structure will be twice as high as any of the residences in the neighborhood?

ANSWER: I can't say for sure.

QUESTION: Well, the houses are all one-story houses, are they not?

ANSWER: Yes.

QUESTION: Is there any other structure like the one you have described anywhere in the neighborhood at this time?

ANSWER: No.

QUESTION: And the homes have been there for years, isn't that true?

ANSWER: Yes, many years.

The objective of the questioning was to emphasize that the fence was out of character with the residential homes in the neighborhood. In effect the witness, through the cross-examination, supported the opponents. The adverse effect could have been avoided if other tall structures in the area could have been identified.

In attacking your field of expertise, the effort is to show there is no scientific, technical, professional or other recognized basis to support your testimony.

QUESTION: Dr. Jones, your field of expert testimony is environmental epidemiology, is that correct?

ANSWER: That's correct.

QUESTION: Is it true, doctor, that there is no college or university in the United States that now offers a degree in environmental epidemiology?

ANSWER: That's correct.

QUESTION: As a matter of fact, doctor, isn't it true there is no college or university in the world that offers a degree in environmental epidemiology?

ANSWER: That's correct.

QUESTION: Isn't it correct, doctor, that there are no national boards, associations, or professional societies which deal exclusively with the subject of environmental epidemiology?

ANSWER: That is correct.

The fact that there is no degree in the subject and no professional association dealing exclusively with the area of expertise does not disqualify you to state opinions. However, question has now been raised as to whether there is such a specialty field as environmental epidemiology. The sting should have been anticipated and brought out during direct examination, not left for a cross-exam bombshell.

An attack on the witness's qualifications can cover many aspects of the resume.

QUESTION: Mr. Smith, it appears from your professional resume you attended the University of Wisconsin. It that correct?

ANSWER: Yes, that's correct.

QUESTION: Mr. Smith, in your resume it doesn't say what degree you received from the University of Wisconsin. Is that because you did not receive a degree?

ANSWER: The work toward my undergraduate degree was almost completed when I left the university.

QUESTION: Mr. Smith, isn't it correct that you did not receive a degree from the University of Wisconsin?

ANSWER: Yes.

QUESTION: As a matter of fact, Mr. Smith, isn't it correct that you never received a degree from any college or university in the United States?

ANSWER: Yes, that's correct.

QUESTION: And isn't it also correct that you have been practicing as a professional engineer without being licensed in any state of the United States to practice that profession?

ANSWER: Yes.

While the witness did not attempt to conceal the absence of professional qualifications in his resume, the cross-examiner is making him seem unqualified to the jury. If the problem had been explored on direct examination, the thunder would have been taken from the cross-examiner.

Bias or prejudice are relatively easy to show, particularly if you had a personal or professional relationship with either the counsel or client by whom you were engaged.

QUESTION: Isn't it correct that you have testified in seven cases like this on behalf of Attorney Smith?

ANSWER: Yes.

QUESTION: Isn't is also correct that in each of those seven cases Mr. Smith was representing claimants such as plaintiff in this case?

ANSWER: Yes.

QUESTION: And isn't it correct that you were compensated in each of those other seven cases for your services?

ANSWER: Yes.

QUESTION: And of course you're being compensated for your testimony in this case?

ANSWER: Yes.

QUESTION: Do you believe that the prior cases you worked on with Mr. Smith would cause you to have any predisposition in favor of Mr. Smith's client now?

The series of questions establishes that the attorney and expert have a long-standing professional relationship. Again, direct examination exposure of prior relationships would blunt the problem.

In an effort to attack the factual basis of testimony, the examiner could attempt to show any of the following:

- You are not familiar with the scene of the events.
- You have not examined the actual product in question.
- You made no measurements.
- You carried out no tests.
- You were not in a position to observe the events.
- Your opinion is based on second-hand information.

Such attacks go nowhere if you have done your homework.

Use of hypothetical questions is still a valid method of examination. In preparation for direct examination, you and counsel will prepare a list of hypothetical questions which encompasses all facts which have been established. The technique on cross-examination is to insert into a hypothetical question facts which could lead you to reach a conclusion opposite to that tendered on direct examination.

Case No. 2. In an action involving an alleged defective setting of a ski binding which failed to release, a technician rendered an opinion that the binding had been too tight for the weight and ability of the claimant. On cross-examination, the defense attempted to establish that the claimant had lied about his skiing ability and his weight. The following exchange occurred:

QUESTION: Isn't it correct, Mr. Technician, that unless you are advised accurately as to the skier's ability and the skier's weight, you can't make the proper adjustment on the ski binding?

ANSWER: That's correct.

QUESTION: If, instead of being an intermediate skier, the claimant was only a beginner, would that make a difference to the installing technician?

ANSWER: Yes.

QUESTION: If the skier said he weighed 150 pounds when in fact he weighed 175 pounds, would that make any substantial difference in the adjustment?

ANSWER: Of course.

QUESTION: For the sake of my examination, Mr. Technician, I want you to assume that the plaintiff told the ski binding technician he was an intermediate skier when in fact he was a beginning skier. I want you to further assume that the claimant stated he weighed 150 pounds when in fact he weighed 175. Now with that information, what would the proper binding setting have been, assuming those facts?

The objective of the questioning was to create a set of facts which accorded with the defense view of plaintiff's conduct. One way to counter the adverse insertion of contrary facts is to observe: "I'll make those assumptions, but my investigation does not support those facts."

Attacking you by use of an authoritative publication is one of the most effective devices in the cross-examiner's tool kit.

Case No. 3. In a case involving dissolution of a marriage, a rehabilitation counselor testified for the wife concerning her alleged inability to return to the job market because of the psychological trauma she had sustained from the divorce proceeding. A series of quotes was read from a text to the testifying witness which suggested the type of trauma being used to support the testimony was not supportable.

After four quotes had been read, the witness asked the examining attorney the name of the publication. To the witness's surprise, the cross-examining attorney told the witness that the quotes had been extracted from his own technical writing published within the preceding year. The court found the wife able to return to the job market. The lesson is obvious: know what you have written previously, and be aware of what is authoritative.

Rule 803(18) of the Federal Rules of Evidence states that you as an expert do not have to recognize a learned treatise as authoritative to be cross-examined about it. At least in the federal courts, if any expert witness testifies that a particular treatise is authoritative, you, as a testifying witness, may be examined about it. This rule makes you responsible for mastering vast amounts of information.

A direct attack on your position is difficult to undertake, yet the effort will be made in a proper case. On occasion, you may be tempted to maintain a position of absolute certainty even in the face of overwhelming contradications. That dogged adherence to a position can destroy your credibility.

Case No. 4. In a case involving valuation of real property, the expert stated that his task was to place himself "on the piece of property ten years prior" and attempt to determine value in that hypothetical stance. Cross-examination and other evidence revealed that the expert had not contacted the actual buyer, another appraiser, or the zoning official, all of whom dealt with the property ten years before. All three of those individuals testified that the expert's opinion of value was substantially incorrect.

Nevertheless, in the face of that overwhelming contravening testimony, the expert stood fast. He maintained that he was in a better position to value the property ten years after the fact than the three knowledgeable persons had been at the time. Steadfast adherence to an untenable position served to erode the witness's credibility.

TESTING THE ENTIRE FIELD

The question whether you will be allowed to testify may not come up until trial. Under the Federal Rules of Evidence, the trial judge determines the qualifications of witnesses.[2] The test may be whether the scientific principles you rely on are considered reliable enough to support expert opinion. Attacks on your field of scientific expertise should

---

2. Federal Rules of Evidence, Rule 104(a); *McCormick on Evidence* 2nd ed., §53, (West Publishing Company, 1972), p. 121.

not be overlooked by you as you prepare to testify, if the area of testimony has not yet reached scientific or professional acceptance or recognition.[3]

REDUCING VULNERABILITY TO CROSS-EXAMINATION

Certain areas of weakness attend some expert testimony. Those areas will certainly be the grounds for attack by a cross-examining attorney. Knowing the areas of jeopardy will help you prepare in advance for the cross-examination.

1. Is your opinion based in whole or in part on judgment as opposed to measurable fact? It is always proper for cross-examination to probe the basis for your well-established conclusions. If that basis is technical and scientific testing, you will not be vulnerable. However, if subjective judgment and opinion are the sole basis for your opinion, you are vulnerable. Consider two examples.

a. A chemical test involves mixing a compound and then adding a measured number of drops of reagent to turn the compound from pink to blue. The exact number of drops necessary to cause the color change constitutes a specific scientific measurement. No judgment or opinion attends this test. The results can be documented with laboratory protocol and photographs.

b. Valuation of motor vehicles requires an orderly examination of each vehicle against a fifty-point checklist. Each item on the checklist is graded from one to ten. Each of the fifty items requires judgment based upon observation. True, an expert's observation is more valid than that of the average person. However, "judgment" is the key word. This valuation would be considered a major area for cross-examination.

2. Is your opinion based upon input from others? You are to testify as an orthopedic surgeon. The issue is the extent of a fracture sustained in a fall. The radiologist's report suggests to you a compound comminuted fracture with thirty bone fragments at the fracture site. You testify to that effect. However, by cross-examination it is established your testimony is based on the radiology report. As an orthopedist, you may not be able to identify thirty bone fragments from the x-ray, but ordinary practice allows you to rely on the radiologist's report. You must be ready to defend your reliance as customary in your field.

3. Have you made prior inconsistent statements? The questioner will ask about whatever you have written and testified to in the past. Aggres-

---

3. Sapp, "Pretrial Challenges to Expert Testimony in Toxic Tort Cases," *For The Defense*, June 1989, pp. 22–28.

sive cross-examining counsel will comb those written materials for inconsistency.

4. Does your behavior suggest insecurity? The skillful cross-examining attorney will observe you carefully. If you have your hand near your mouth or face, you may be withholding information, according to the attorney's way of thinking. If you flush or your hand trembles, you may feel insecure. If you hesitate and stammer or fumble through papers and files, you may feel a lack of confidence in your own ability. Skillful examining attorneys sense a weak, inadequately prepared, or unsure witness. When that sixth sense is activated, they will move in for the kill.

5. Are you in control? The basic tenet of cross-examination for the attorney is control of the witness. Therefore, you must stay in control. You must attempt to avoid being led by the cross-examiner. A pattern of yes/no questions and answers should warn you that the examining attorney is attempting to control the situation.[4] But you have another option besides a "yes" or "no" answer.

QUESTION: Mr. Expert, isn't it correct that traffic lights sequence green to yellow to red?

The easy answer to the question is "Yes," but the better answer is "Yes, in most cases, unless there is a malfunction." In this way, you have avoided the trap of a yes/no answer.

6. Have you generated all the help you can?

a. Have you tested your opinion. Does it make sense? If it does not, go back to the drawing board.

b. Have you made sure your language is understandable and that you translate technical terms.

c. After you have told the trier of fact what needs to be known, stop! Do not tell all you know about the subject.

d. Be sensitive to client-attorney confidentiality. If possible, have the attorney prepare summaries of relevant facts and documents rather than providing the documents or client statements.

e. Develop a list of projected cross-examination questions. Your careful preparation will allow you to guide the examination.

f. Make sure the theories on which you rely rest on reliable foundation, are based on scientifically valid principles and are relevant to the case.

---

4. Bridgers, "The Selection, Preparation, and Direct Examination of Expert Witnesses," *The Docket*, Vol. 2, No. 4, Fall 1987, p. 7.

CONCLUSION

Be alert to the eight fundamental goals of cross-examination. By knowing the objectives of cross-examination, you can use the questioning process to solidify your position.

Objectives of cross-examination include use of your testimony as a springboard for the cross-examiner's own expert. The cross-examination may seek to use your testimony to contradict other experts on your side or to obtain information beneficial to the cross-examiner's case.[5] However, your preparation, credibility and positive demeanor will blunt the challenge afforded by cross-examination.

The usual admonition for cross-examining counsel is to stop when you're ahead, use restraint, and not overplay. These same admonitions are equally true for you as the expert witness undergoing cross-examination. Do not overplay the expert role. Do not overemphasize your superior knowledge. Be accurate with the facts. Be firm without being an advocate. Maintain control of the situation.

---

5. Goldberg, "Courting the Jury to Reduce Damages," *For the Defense*, April 1987, pp. 10–19.

22 ETHICAL AND INTERPROFESSIONAL PROBLEMS AND SOLUTIONS

INTRODUCTION

Four categories of ethical problems plague the use of expert witnesses in the dispute-resolution process. The first has to do with unethical conduct of forensic witnesses. The second relates to admissibility of expert testimony. The third addresses negligent performance of expert service. The fourth area concerns interprofessional relations. Examination of problems and solutions provides you with guidance for future conduct, keeping in mind always that objectivity is for the expert and advocacy is for the attorney.

UNETHICAL CONDUCT

The expert survey probed experience with dishonest expert testimony. Some of the comments, in many cases guarded, reveal instances of dishonesty:

- "A lab rewrote a report. The actual data was thereby hidden. Both reports were finally produced through discovery." You should never be a party to willful alteration of a report which is designed to mislead.
- "Expert testimony was tendered by a witness who did not actually do the work, assuming that the testimony would be accepted based upon the reputation of the witness alone." One act of bluff can destroy a lifetime of dedicated performance.
- "I have seen exhibits created using forgeries and alterations. These powerful exhibits, once exposed, worked dramatically against the perpetrator." To fabricate is to defraud a court and possibly commit criminal perjury.
- "I've actually seen witnesses testify falsely under oath; the sad part is that even with dishonest testimony and a resulting loss to their client, these experts still collected very substantial fees for them-

selves." False testimony is usually discovered by the cross-examination.

- "The most frequent example of dishonest testimony has been evidenced by experts willfully ignoring factual data." If you chose to exclude data, say so and explain why.
- "I have experienced occasions when experts attempted to recant prior testimony because it did not fit the particular client's theory of the case." Prior testimony should be explored prior to taking a new assignment.
- "While I know of no person who has deliberately falsified data or wrongfully altered or modified reports, I am aware of experts who have furnished erroneous opinions because of lack of knowledge or attention to detail."
- "You can't teach or preach competence. If a case is beyond you pass it."

Unfortunately, the survey revealed a number of efforts by counsel to influence the decision-making process or the opinion of the responding experts. Almost 15 percent of the experts were distressed because counsel had suppressed information. Another 9 percent were concerned about loaded or irrelevant questions; 19 percent about trick cross-examination questions, quotations out of context, and distortion. In 4 percent of the responses, criticism was leveled at the bar because of biased information provided by the lawyer.

In a particular case, two acts by forensic witnesses justified exclusion of testimony at trial.[1] One expert witness, who demonstrated no scientific basis for his opinions, had actually sought out the plaintiff and volunteered his service as an expert. Another of the plaintiff's experts had reached a conclusion as to causation before doing any testing. Their testimony was excluded on the grounds that it lacked probative weight or value.

In a recent federal court case, the United States District Court was presented with an unusual testimonial dilemma.[2] A plaintiff involved in a claim against the Ford Motor Company had modified a vehicle and then obtained expert testimony that the modification had not occurred. The expert witness was aware of the deception but did not disclose it. He was involved in incomplete, dishonest, and misleading reports and testimony. The Federal judge handed down a severe censure, resulting in the permanent banning of the expert as a witness in the United States District Court.

---

1. Socha, "Excluding Plaintiff's Expert Testimony," *For The Defense*, September 1987, p. 24.

2. *Schimdt* v. *Ford Motor Company*, 112 F.R.D. 216 (D. Colo. 1986).

SCIENTIFIC ACCEPTANCE NO LONGER REQUIRED

There is concern in the forensic and legal community that scientists have gained unprecedented power over the outcome of civil and criminal cases, a power that can be abused.[3] Scientific evidence, transferred from the laboratory to the courtroom, can be distorted for a more liberal application of the "general acceptance" *Frey* test, combined with other relaxed evidentiary standards.[4] However, the expert can help avoid these dangers:

> A conscientious scientist can ask questions of his own –
> can determine, for example, what the lawyer hopes to
> establish, what other experts (the lawyer) plans to call
> as witnesses, and how (the lawyer) plans to divide the
> labor among them. The scientist can also introduce the
> lawyer to the nature and limits of his specialty, making
> clear that he is qualified to address certain issues, but
> less qualified than another expert, or not qualified at all,
> to address others.

Some new areas of scientific testimony come under attack. For example DNA "fingerprinting," a recent scientific advance now widely accepted in court, was under some question in several jurisdictions.[5] Its reliability had been attacked; recommendation for a National Academy of Sciences certification had been disregarded.[6]

A few recent cases hold that if no scientific data support an expert's opinion, the conclusion will be disallowed by the trial court.[7] However, the current trend is to allow expert opinion based on scientifically valid principles, relevancy and reliability, without requiring "scientific acceptance".

THE EXPERT'S LIABILITY FOR NEGLIGENCE

It is not only scientists who are concerned with unsupportable, inadequate, negligent, or false expert testimony. Case law has imposed legal liability on forensic witnesses for negligence, if the expert deviates from accepted standards of professional competence. In *Levine v. Wiss & Co.*, [8] accountants valued a business in a divorce case. Generally ac-

---

3. Imwinkelried, "Science Takes the Stand: The Growing Misuse of Expert Testimony, *The Sciences*, November-December 1986, p. 20.

4. Imwinkelried, p. 25. But see *Daubert v. Merrell Dow, supra.*

5. Lander, DNA Fingerprinting on Trial, *Nature*, Vol. 339, June 1989, pp. 501-505.

6. Lander, p. 505.

7. *Brock v. Merrell Dow Pharmaceuticals*, 874 F.2d 307 (5th Cir. 1989); *Daubert v. Merrell Dow Pharmaceuticals Inc.*, 951 F2d 1128 (9th Cir. 1991), *rev'd*, _____ U.S. _____, 113 S. Ct. 2786, 125 L. Ed. 2d 469 (1993).

8. *Levine v. Wiss & Co.*, 478 A.2d 397 (NJ 1984).

cepted accounting practice (GAAP), the professional standard, was not followed in the evaluation. The plaintiff was forced to accept a compromise in the case based on improper evaluation. Following settlement of the divorce case, the plaintiff sued the accountants. The basis for the claim was that the accountants, even though court-appointed experts, undertook to render services in the practice of their profession and in doing so were required to exercise that degree of skill and knowledge normally possessed by members of their profession in similar communities. The appellate decision remanded the matter for trial.

A number of situations can be envisioned where, because of unsupported or negligent expert testimony, a particular result occurs in the dispute resolution process. In such circumstances, the forensic expert is subject to judicial scrutiny, just like any other professional in a contested setting.[9]

INTERPROFESSIONAL RELATIONSHIPS

Several proposed codes of conduct for attorneys who deal with expert witnesses are in the drafting stages. One such code, found in Appendix N, encompasses twelve major points to assist in the attorney–expert witness relationship. While the code has not been adopted by either legal or forensic groups, members of both professions feel that the level of performance, conduct, and ethical relationships must be raised.

The tendered code states that attorneys shall not knowingly proffer an expert with fraudulent credentials. Such conduct would certainly subject an attorney to severe sanctions, if not criminal penalties.

In 1980, the American Bar Association published *Standards for Criminal Justice*. That publication included prosecution and defense standards for dealing with experts. It emphasizes the expert's independence and need for impartiality.

The National Society of Professional Engineers in 1987 published an extensive code of ethics for engineers. While that code does not deal with the subject of forensic testimony specifically, it sets high standards for general professional excellence.

Typical of the effort to ease the relationship between attorney and forensic witness is the development of interprofessional guides for expert witnesses and lawyers by various states. The purposes of these guides are to promote an understanding between lawyers and expert

---

9. See for example, Restatement (Second) Torts, §299 A (1965); *Bruce* v. *Byrne-Stevens & Associates*, 51 Wash. App. 199, 752 p.2d 949 (1988), *rev'd* 776 p.2d 666 (1989) was just such a case. The court concluded that experts are not immune from claims when they do their work in a negligent manner. The Supreme Court of Washington, in reversing the lower appellate court, based its decision on the doctrine of testimonial immunity.

witnesses, to improve communications between them, and to minimize disputes. A typical code covers following general areas.[10]

Role of the Expert Witness.   The role of the expert is that of consultant to perform experiments, tests, or analyses, prepare written reports, provide testimony at deposition and trial, and serve in an advisory capacity at trial or for litigation preparation.

Communication.   There is to be frequent communication between expert and attorney to avoid unnecessary disagreements.

Prior Contacts Precluding Retention.   If information of a confidential nature is provided to an expert, the expert should keep records of that consultation. Disclosure could serve to disqualify the expert from future assignments in the same case.

Written Retainer Contract.   Agreements, including fee estimates, scope of services, and the expert's qualifications, if necessary, are to be part of a written retention agreement. Payment responsibilities regarding fees, deadlines, advance payment, and cancellation requirements should also be included.

Fee Guidelines.   Four factors are to be considered in setting fees for forensic assignments: time spent on the case, degree of knowledge and skill required, amount of effort expended, impact on other income and commitments of the expert's practice.

Itemized Billing.   Itemized billings are to be provided on a regular basis to expedite payment.

Retaining Lawyer Is Not the Expert's Lawyer.   Experts often have to hire their own counsel when certain ethical or procedural matters present themselves. It would be improper for the client's attorney to serve as the expert's attorney. The expert may need his own attorney for matters of production of documents, production of prior studies, and guidance for deposition or trial testimony.

Disclosure and Discovery Guidelines.   Four issues are covered here: confidentiality and privilege; formal methods of disclosure and discovery, including the procedure by which answers are to be given; informal contacts with third parties, including opposition experts; and releases to authorize disclosure. By far the most troublesome area is the matter of informal contacts by third parties. The guide provides that the retaining lawyer shall be contacted if third parties attempt to discuss a case with a retained expert. This precaution usually suffices to protect the interests of the client and the attorney work product, which might be exposed by such contacts.

---

10. *Interprofessional Guide for Expert Witnesses*, approved by the Interprofessional Committee of the Denver and Colorado Bar Associations, July 1984, presently being redrafted. Reprinted by permission of *The Colorado Lawyer*, Colorado Bar Association.

Subpoenas and Scheduling of Testimony.   The attorney should respect the expert's time. Every effort should be made to have the expert available to testify at a certain time and not to have the expert wait an inordinate length of time to testify.

Deposition Testimony and the Obligation of Payment.   The party taking deposition of an expert shall be obligated, under the rules, to pay for the costs of preparation, the taking time, and review of the deposition transcript.

Mutual Understanding of Roles in Preparation For Testimony.   Five points are covered:

- The manner in which reports, records, documentary evidence, and exhibits are to be prepared, filed, and maintained.
- The types of information on which expert opinion can be based, keeping in mind the evidentiary rules that might apply.
- The importance of answering questions asked by opposing counsel in a forthright manner, using simple and understandable language.
- Scheduling requirements and other areas requiring cooperation of the lawyer and the expert.
- Preparation of an updated resume or curriculum vitae by the expert at any time major changes in the expert's credentials occur.

Dispute-Resolution Procedure.   An interprofessional committee composed of experts and lawyers is established for resolution of any dispute which arises between forensic experts and attorneys. Both parties are urged to utilize the interprofessional committee, rather than court processes, to resolve disputes.

CONCLUSION

There is some dissatisfaction in the scientific and legal communities with the demands being placed on forensic experts, particularly in new areas where scientific and technical literature and studies do not necessarily support the expert's stated opinion. Also troublesome is the witness's liability for negligence, which is a growing and fertile area for new claims against expert witnesses. The legal and forensic professions are working to develop codes of ethical conduct and interrelationship guides to help solve interprofessional problems. There is growing support for the development and use of these codes for forensic witnesses and lawyers.

23 GETTING IN THE WAY OF ADDITIONAL PROFESSIONAL ASSIGNMENTS

INTRODUCTION

A number of devices are available to forensic witnesses who wish to increase their forensic practice. These devices will enable you to expand the breadth of your forensic work in a professionally proper and ethical way. The forensic expert survey revealed that 63 percent of the experts responding were interested in expanding their forensic testimony practice. When asked how the field of forensic testimony could be made more rewarding, the experts suggested generating more revenue, establishing more respect as a professional, receiving better case assignments, more effective use of the expert as a witness, and more time to perform the work assigned.

The experts responding to survey questions see six opportunities for increasing their professional undertakings:

- Active exposure at professional associations
- Listings in telephone directories and professional journals; direct-mail advertising
- Professional prominence and fame
- Word of mouth, networking, and referrals
- Group seminars and presentations for attorneys
- Expanding services available and improving qualifications

Do the Best Job Possible Each Time Out

The famed criminal defense attorney Jake Ehrlich emphasized the theme that constituted the mark of his brilliant trial career.[1] Success is guaranteed if, each time you are presented a litigation opportunity, you perform in an outstanding fashion. That same theme is applicable to the expert who seeks to expand his or her activity as a forensic witness. By

---

1. John W. Noble, *Never Plead Guilty: The Life of Jake Ehrlich* (Farrar, Straus & Cudahy, 1955).

exhibiting outstanding and tireless effort and a constant striving for excellence on each case, you will develop a reputation that will guarantee future assignments.

That does not mean coasting on your reputation. Your reputation may get you the assignment in the first place, but it will not garner further assignments without excellent performance.

TRADITIONAL PRACTICE-BUILDING DEVICES

In almost all fields, certain activities have long been recognized as enhancing professional visibility. These traditional strategies constitute a strong foundation for some of the more innovative suggestions in the next section. The first step to practice building, however, is careful self-analysis. Study your own strengths and weaknesses. Consider opportunities and impediments. Develop a marketing plan to guide your practice-building efforts. Then try some of these proven techniques.

Word-of-Mouth Reference

The most traditional and still the most effective device for enhancing professional assignments is the personal, word-of-mouth reference. This kind of reference indicates satisfaction with your work. Most forensic experts who are well-known in their fields became known first by personal referral.

Professional Societies and Associations

Membership in technical, professional, and scientific societies and associations is just that — mere membership. It does little to enhance professional image. The contrary, however, is true when you display leadership and accomplishment within those organizations. Such leadership roles are reflective of the high esteem in which you are held by your peers. Undertake committee assignments as a way of developing an area of expertise.

Writing, Teaching, and Lecturing

To enhance your professional image, your articles in print and your name on professional programs does a great deal. Pay particular attention to selecting the groups before whom you speak. The more prestigious the group, the more significant an addition to your professional reputation. Although there are dangers of attribution which come from extensive writing and publication, professional reputations are expanded by these activities.

Professionally Appropriate Advertising

Not all advertising is professionally proper and tastefully done. Obtain professional guidance concerning the format and content of advertisements you contemplate. Such elements as clear message, layout, placement, color tone, and target publications are best decided for you by a professional.

NONTRADITIONAL DEVICES

We now turn to more unusual ways of enhancing professional availability. These devices require substantial commitment of energy and funds, but your benefits will be in direct proportion to your efforts.

Information Columns in General or Professional Publications

There is a need for information columns about technical fields in both the general press and in scientific and trade publications. Those columns make your name recognized as a source of specific information in your field. The general press addresses audiences quite different from those of professional journals on the one hand and trade publications on the other. Remember that meeting regular publication deadlines is not an easy task. However, columnists and regular contributors to professional and technical publications develop reputation for expertise.

Becoming a Vendor at Professional Gatherings

Exhibiting at a conference is usually a useful way to get your name out there and to develop contacts. As with lectures and publications, the more prestigious the gathering, the more beneficial the exposure. The vendor booth not only affords you an opportunity to meet potential employers but also showcases your skills if your area of expertise generates a demonstrative or graphic product available for display.

Listings in Professional Journals and Publications

The publication most widely used by lawyers to locate expert witnesses is probably *The Lawyers Desk Reference*. This source lists expert witnesses by professional field. To find out how to be listed, contact the publisher. Other similar listings, such as that published by TASA® (Appendix B), constitute sources of professional assignments. There are also many specialty organizations and publications that afford the forensic expert with listing opportunities.

Publicizing Your Name

There are a number of ways to get and keep your name in the public eye. Here are some of them.

- Make sure your firm or personal name, address, and telephone number appear on all handout, outline, and lecture materials, as well as on your written reports.
- Use a distinctive logo or letterhead on your business cards, correspondence, lecture materials, brochures, and professional reports.
- Make sure that journalists who cover your trial testimony spell your name correctly.
- Send out frequent announcements of events in your organization.
- Hold social gatherings. Maximize these exposures with handouts, brochures, professional calling cards, articles, or other tangible reminders of the event.

Desktop Publishing

With the advent of computers, opportunities for desktop publishing of bulletins, articles, and newsletters abound. For example, some experts now regularly publish informative technical bulletins in their specialty areas. Their professional reputations are enhanced by these readable, informative publications.

GENERAL MARKETING IDEAS

In addition to these specific ideas, marketing concepts will help you increase your exposure and opportunity for forensic assignments.

Be Innovative

Do new things in different ways. A few examples of innovative demonstration devices prove the point. Computerized animation and graphic enhancement, video portrayal of microscopic analysis, video display of deposition testimony, and dramatic courtroom demonstrations of chemical and electrical reactions are but a few of the innovative devices that have been used to enhance the professional reputation of forensic experts.

Advance New Ideas

Developing a new scientific process may allow you to carve out a special niche for yourself as a forensic witness. For example, the two firms that do most of the nation's DNA fingerprinting have established a niche for themselves in the field of forensic testimony. New techniques established by recognized scientific research and study can be applied to the dispute resolution process. Those who first undertake that application become the recognized experts.

THIRTY THRIFTY IDEAS

This list will serve to stimulate your thinking as to possible devices to enhance your professional exposure.[2]

- Make sure your premises are orderly, businesslike, presentable and reflect professional competence.
- Use the best, most modern equipment available.
- Use standard forms and checklists whenever possible.
- Conduct your forensic activities in a businesslike way.
- Use written engagement letters, regular monthly statements of charges, and informative time and billing records.
- Maintain an effective internal data retrieval system.
- Be generous with gratuitous advice or information.
- Introduce your staff and associates to clients and counsel at every opportunity.
- Analyze where your new clients come from to determine patterns of regular referral.
- Sponsor or co-sponsor informative community events.
- Host regular breakfast, lunch, or dinner meetings with existing or prospective clients.
- Maintain a high profile at community charity functions.
- Prepare specialty information pamphlets, audio- or video tapes for education and information purposes.
- Network with attorneys, clients, and agencies.
- Package your reports attractively.
- Send thank-you letters to those who refer new assignments to you.
- Periodically send a service-evaluation questionnaire to your clients.
- Project enjoyment of what you are doing (if you are not enjoying it, do not do it).
- Assume a role of leadership in community, civic, and church activities.

---

2. These ideas are adapted from Feder, "Successfully Marketing the Small Firm," *Legal Economics News*, March 1989, pp. 49–51. By permission of *Legal Economics News*. Special acknowledgement also to Jay Foonberg and Milton Zwicker for their continued creativity in this area.

- Do not hesitate to do a personal favor for a potential client or friend.
- Never publicly badmouth your employees, partners, professional associates, or opposing experts.
- Make sure your staff projects your enthusiasm to clients and visitors.
- Greet clients personally in a pleasant, efficient, knowledgeable and enthusiastic manner.
- Make your billing statements clear and fair.
- Develop and maintain a master mailing list of clients, attorneys, friends, and professional associates who regularly refer assignments to you.
- Join in referral networks with other forensic witnesses.
- When working with client or counsel, give the conference 100 percent of your attention.
- Do not be afraid to work nights and weekends on your clients' matters, and let them know you are doing so.
- Mail reprints of your published articles to appropriate persons on your mailing list.
- Dress for success and behave in a professional way.

CONCLUSION

This chapter focused on the progression between advertising, sales, and marketing. Advertising makes it known you are interested in receiving forensic assignments. Sales involves attempts to obtain that work. Marketing is determining what your target audience wants and providing it to them. When you develop an advertising, sales, and marketing program, stick with it. Determine your promotional goals and objectives. Develop the professional image you wish to project. Carry out your marketing devices regularly.

24 FOR ATTORNEYS ONLY

INTRODUCTION

This text was originally planned for use by attorneys and experts. However much literature is available for attorneys on the subject of expert testimony, but little for experts. Therefore, this book was created for the use and benefit of the forensic witness.

However, everything in the text applies to attorneys who work with experts. It is valuable for trial attorneys to know how experts can better assist in trial presentation and how experts can improve their function in that role. Therefore, this final chapter consists of the frank views of a nationally known expert witness who has seen the process in operation and observed its growth for more than twenty years.

A VIEW FROM THE WITNESS STAND

Marvin L. Stone is a certified public accountant who was a partner in Coopers & Lybrand until 1982, when he withdrew to continue practice as a forensic witness. He has been a consultant to the Comptroller General of the United States and has served as an expert witness more than 200 times. He has testified on over one hundred occasions and has appeared in courts and dispute resolution forums in twelve states. His fields include auditing, accounting, taxation, antitrust, computation of damages, valuation, and many related subjects. He has been a frequent lecturer at law schools, universities, tax institutes, and professional seminars and a regular contributor to professional journals.

Mr. Stone is a past president of the American Institute of Certified Public Accountants (AICPA) and has served on many of its councils and committees. He is past president and director of the Colorado Society of Certified Public Accountants. He has served on numerous boards and is actively involved as a financial consultant and forensic witness today.

With that background, Mr. Stone presented at Hastings College of

Law, San Francisco, California, a paper entitled "A View From the Witness Stand." The paper was later expanded and has served as the basis for a number of in-house presentations to large law firms throughout the United States.

Mr. Stone's views are significant and articulate. He brings to the topic pointed, helpful, and sharp comments for the benefit of an attorney dealing with any forensic witness. His points of departure include engagement, pretrial discovery, deposition, direct testimony, cross-examination, and visual aids.

When Engaging an Expert, Attorneys Should:

- Investigate credentials and inquire if the expert's background contains any potentially damaging material (e.g., felony convictions, prior contrary testimony or writings).
- Engage the expert sufficiently in advance of the date that witnesses must be disclosed to opposing parties, so the expert's opinion can be elicited before deciding whether the expert is to be called as a witness.
- Explain to experts that they are engaged initially only as consultants (to attempt to preserve confidentiality at that point).
- Insist that experts express their candid opinions on the issues upon which testimony might be sought, and their willingness to so testify, before certifying them as witnesses.
- Spell out the rules relating to discoverability of experts' work papers and written communications in the event they are named witnesses.
- Inform experts of all actual and potential opposing parties (e.g., cross-claims and third-party defendants), whose names should be checked for conflict of interest.
- Provide experts with sufficient material to permit them to form an opinion.

Before a Deposition of the Expert, the Attorney Should:

- Review the expert's files and work papers.
- Inform the expert of the purpose of the deposition.
- Instruct the expert to answer honestly and concisely but not to volunteer information.
- Inform the expert of the meaning of objections raised during the deposition and the importance of the instructions and suggestions the lawyer may make to the expert during the deposition.
- Reach agreement with opposing counsel as to who is to compensate the expert for time spent in preparation, actual deposition, review of transcript, and travel.

- Inform the expert of the importance of a careful review and correction of the deposition transcript before signing it.

Prior to a Deposition of an Opposing Expert, the Attorney Should:

- Subpoena all documents in the expert's possession relating to the matter at hand.
- Obtain copies of such documents far enough in advance of deposition to permit review by the lawyer and consultants.
- Obtain a biographical sketch of the expert and check its accuracy.
- Prepare an outline to be used as a guide during deposition.

During Deposition of an Opposing Expert, the Attorney Should:

- Strive to maintain a noncombative atmosphere in order to maximize results.
- Restrain the normal cross-examination approach in order to improve knowledge without unduly educating the expert and opposing counsel.

Prior to the Expert's Direct Testimony, the Attorney Should:

- Rehearse testimony and expected cross-examination with the expert.
- Remind the expert to reread the deposition transcript and review all work done by staff members as part of the pretrial preparation.
- Brief the expert about how to behave in court and the likely reactions of the judge and opposing counsel.
- Give the expert biographical information about the jurors.
- Instruct the expert in appropriate conduct in or near the courtroom:
  - Avoid contact with the lawyer when the jury is present.
  - Avoid comments that might be overhead and misinterpreted by a juror or other witnesses or parties.
  - The experts should remember that they are being observed at all times.
- Inform experts that they should appear to be dispassionate professionals, not an advocate; avoid overreaching.
- Tell experts what materials to bring to court and to the witness stand.
- View all exhibits and examples experts expect to use during testimony.
- Understand the expert's opinions and their basis; otherwise, rehabilitation during redirect testimony is impossible.
- Instruct the expert to direct answers to the judge, jury, or hearing panel, not the examiner.

- Inform the expert of prior testimony by other witnesses that bears on the subject matter of expert's testimony; provide expert with pertinent deposition transcripts or portions of daily trial transcript.
- Provide copies of the expert's exhibits to opposing counsel in a timely manner.
- Make sure that all information upon which the expert's opinion relies has been admitted in evidence.
- Recommend that the expert link testimony wherever possible to data in evidence.
- Inform the expert of the technical meaning of such words as "speculative."
- Instruct the expert to avoid eye contact with you during crossexamination.
- Maintain control of the form and content of the expert's proposed testimony.

During the Expert's Direct Testimony, the Attorney Should:

- Give sufficient time and thought to the qualifications of the expert.
- Refuse opposing counsel's offer to stipulate that the witness is an expert.
- Disclose information about the expert's fee (hourly rate, total fee, nondependence on outcome).
- Listen attentively to the expert's responses.
- Request amplification of points that are unclear or require emphasis.
- Avoid lengthy hypothetical questions.

During the Opposing Expert's Cross-Examination, the Attorney Should:

- Avoid excessive reviewing of the expert's exhibits by the jury.
- Keep the expert witness sitting in the witness chair as much as possible, rather than moving about the room.
- Avoid questions that request or permit the witness to express an opinion.
- Thoroughly understand the importance of their own questions and the likely responses to permit appropriate follow-up.
- Listen carefully to the witness' responses rather than slavishly following notes.
- Be brief.
- Sit down when the desired responses have been obtained.

Points to Remember About Visual Aids:

- Numerous media are available (chalkboard, overhead projector, flipchart, photographic blowups).
- Dim the lights sparingly, if at all.
- While copies of exhibits can be given to jurors, use of a large blowup is preferable.
- Leave blowups on view after testimony is finished. Long exposure makes a more lasting impression on the jury.
- Be sure the visual aid is clear and legible to the trier of fact.
- Writing the chart before the jury's eyes gains attention and fosters better understanding, but it requires advance preparation.
- If transparencies are used, provide the court with hard copy.
- Make sure the information shown is relevant and supports your expert's opinions.
- Visit the courtroom before testifying to see its layout.
- Using visual aids allows the witness to walk around, which helps to hold the jury's attention.
- Visual aids should be simple and clear; they should make sense; and they should be easy to remember.
- Clear plexiglass or flexible acetate overlays can be used to display trends in related areas.
- Placing a clear overlay on the opposing expert's exhibit is an effective means of "correcting" the exhibit to reflect your expert's opinions.

To Optimize the Effectiveness of Charts:

- Illustrate only information that furthers your line of argument; avoid extraneous information that only derails jury's thinking.
- Keep each chart simple for maximum clarity.
- If you use interrelated charts, display them side-by-side to illustrate their relationship.
- Use overlays to illustrate relationships and heighten dramatic effect.
- Place labels next to plots in charts rather than in legend.
- Make axis numbers large and readable, labels horizontal and adjacent to or within the bar, line, or slice.
- Use white background and black print.
- Use scales that fairly illustrate trends.
- Use different thicknesses or colors to distinguish lines from one another; use dashed lines for projections or omissions.
- Stack colors or shades within bars from darkest at bottom to lightest at top.

CONCLUSION

This experienced forensic expert's view of the attorney's function is incisive. Attorneys should give particular consideration to Mr. Stone's knowledgeable and thoughtful comments in the areas of engagement, pretrial discovery, deposition, direct testimony, cross-examination, and visual aids.

APPENDIXES

Appendix A
Things To Do List

THINGS TO DO
(I VOW TO STAY ORGANIZED)

Circle One: This Week   This Month   This Year   In My Lifetime

It is suggested you maintain four "To Do" lists at all times, one for each time period.

Priority	Places To Go		Priority	People To See		
	Location	Reason		Name	Subject	Location

	Documents To Draft			Phone Calls		
	Description	Subject		Number	Person	Subject

	Correspondence				Miscellaneous
	Name	Address	In Re:		
				1	Mental/Physical Health Activity

Appendix B

Technical Advisory Service for Attorneys$_{SM}$ (TASA$_®$) Listing of Expert Witness Categories

TASA'S computer contains 8000 experts in 3000 categories. Here is a partial list:

Accident Reconstruction	Deck Machinery	Industrial Hygiene	Office Equipment	Stock Market
Accounting	Demographics	Information Science	Offshore Oil Operations	Structural Engineering
Acoustics	Demolition	Infrared Technology	Oil & Gas Reserves	Suicidology
Actuaries	Dentistry	Inland Waterways	Oil Burners	Surveying
Adhesives & Glues	Disaster Planning	Instrument Design	Oil Drilling & Exploration	Swimming
Advertising	Diving	Insulation	Oil Spills	Tank Trucks
Aerial Charts & Surveys	Document Examination	Insurance	Operations Research	Tape Analysis
Aeronautical	Drafting	International Arbitration	Optics	Television & Radio
Aerosol Cans	Dredging	Irrigation	Ordnance	Terrorism
Affirmative Action	Drugs & Alcohol	Jails & Prisons	Ornithology	Textiles
Agricultural Machine Safety	Dust Explosions	Janitorial Operations	OSHA	Thermography
Agriculture	DWI	Jet Aircraft Noise	Outboard Motors	Tires
Agronomy	Earning Capacity	Jet Engines	Ovens	Tools
Air & Water Pollution	Earth Handling Equipment	Jewelry	Overhead Cranes	Toxicology
Air Conditioning	Ecology	Job Analysis	Packaging & Containers	Toys
Airports	Econometrics	Journalism	Pain & Suffering	Traffic Engineering
Alarms	Economics	Judo	Paints & Coatings	Transportation
Alcohol & Drugs	Electrical Engineering	Jury Selection	Parachutes	Trucks & Buses
Amusement Rides	Electricity	Juvenile Delinquency	Patents	Typewriter Identification
Animal Husbandry	Electric Line Maintenance	Karate	Pesticides	Ultrasonics
Appliances	Electronic Surveillance	Kayaking & Canoeing	Petroleum	Ultraviolet Detection
Appraising	Electron Microscopy	Kegs	Pharmacology	Underground Storage
Archeology	Elevators & Escalators	Kerosene	Physical Training	Underground Technology
Architecture	Energy & Fuels	Ketones	Physics	Underwater Photography
Arson	Entertainment Industry	Kilns	Pilots	Underwater Technology
Asbestos	Environmental Engineering	Kinetics	Plastics	Uranium Mining
Astronomy	Equal Opportunity	Kitchen Equipment	Plumbing	Urban Affairs
Athletics	Explosions	Knives	Police Procedures	Urban Planning
Audio	Explosives	Knots	Pollution	Urban Transit Systems
Automation	Failure Analysis	Labeling	Polygraph	Utilities
Automotive	Farm Equipment	Labor Relations	Printing	Vaccines
Aviation	Fasteners & Couplings	Ladders & Scaffolding	Property Taxes	Vacuum Engineering
Bacteriology	Finance	Landscaping	Prosthetic Devices	Value Analysis
Ballistics	Fingerprint Analysis	Languages	Protective Equipment	Value Engineering
Banking	Firearms	Lasers	Psychology	Valves
Batteries	Fire Investigation	Law Enforcement	Public Utilities	Vans
Bicycles	Fishing & Fisheries	Lawn & Garden Equipment	Qualitative Analysis	Vapor Barriers
Biochemistry	Flammability	Libel	Quality Control	Vehicle Safety
Bioengineering	Fleet Maintenance	Lighting	Quantitative Analysis	Ventilation

Biology
Blasting
Bleachers Design
Boating & Boat Safety
Boilers
Botany
Bottling
Brakes
Bridges
Building Design
Building Management
Bulldozers
Buses
Cable Television
Campus Safety
Carcinogens
Cargo Handling
Cartography
Cement & Concrete
Ceramics
Chain Saws
Chemical Engineering
Chemistry
Child Abuse
Civil Engineering
Coal Mining
Communications
Computer Science
Condemnation
Construction
Consumer Behavior
Containers
Contaminants
Controls
Conveyors
Copyright Infringement
Corrosion
Cranes & Hoists
Crashworthiness
Criminology
Crossings
Crowd Control
Cutting Machines
Dairy Operations
Dams
Data Processing

Flooding
Food & Food Processing
Food Chemistry
Forestry
Fork Lifts
Formaldehyde
Freight Handling
Fuels & Fuel Systems
Furnaces & Stoves
Gambling Devices
Gas Explosions
Gears & Transmissions
Gem Identification
Geography
Geology
Glass Fracture Analysis
Golf Course Safety
Government Contracts
Grain Explosions
Grain Handling
Graphics
Grinding Wheels
Guardrails
Gymnastics
Hand Tools
Handwriting
Harbors & Ports
Hazardous Materials
Health Care Facilities
Hearing Impairment
Heating & Air Conditioning
Helmets & Hard Hats
Highway Safety
Hoists
Home Appliances
Horsemanship
Horticulture
Hospital Safety
Hostage Negotiation
Hotels & Motels
Human Factors
Hydraulics
Hydrology
Ice Rinks
Industrial Design
Industrial Engineering

Locks
Loss Prevention
Lubricants
Lumbering
Machine Design
Maintenance
Malpractice
Manufacturing
Maritime
Marketing
Materials
Materials Handling
Mathematical Modeling
Mathematics
Mechanical Engineering
Medicine
Metallurgy
Meteorology
Mining
Mobile Homes
Mortuary Science
Motorcycles & Mopeds
Motors & Engines
Moveable Cranes
Musical Instruments
Nails & Nail Guns
Narcotics
Natural Gas
Naval Architecture
Navigation & Seamanship
Neon Lighting
Nerve Gases
Neuromuscular Control
Noise Pollution
Nonferrous Metals
Nuclear Safety
Nuclear Science
Nursing
Nursing Homes
Nutrition
Obscenity
Oceanography
Occupant Safety, Aero
Occupant Safety, Auto
Occupational Therapy
Odors

Quantum Chemistry
Quantum Mechanics
Quantum Physics
Quarrying
Quartz
Questioned Documents
Questionnaires
Quick Release Fasteners
Racing
Radar
Radiation Hazards
Radio & Television
Railroad Crossings
Railroading
Range Management
Real Estate
Recreation
Refrigeration
Regulatory Agencies
Rehabilitation
Rigging
Riot Control
Rivers & Waterways
Robots
Roofs
Rugs & Carpets
Running Shoes
Safety
Safety Belts & Restraints
Sanitary Engineering
Sawmill Operations
Scaffolding
Seamanship
Security & Alarms
Seismology
Shoe Design
Shores & Coastlines
Signal Systems
Skiing
Snowmobiles
Sociology
Soils
Solar Engineering
Space Operations
Sports & Sport Facilities
Statistics

Veterinary Medicine
Vibration
Video Engineering
Vinyl
Virology
Vision & Visual Perception
Vision Safety
Vocational Rehabilitation
Voice Identification
Wages & Hours
Warehousing
Warning Systems
Waste Treatment
Water & Air Pollution
Water Facilities & Systems
Water Safety
Weapons
Weather
Welding
Wheels & Rims
Winches
Windows
Wire Rope & Cable
Wood
Wood Shop Safety
Wood Stoves
Workmen's Compensation
Xerography
X-ray Analysis
X-ray Apparatus
X-ray Diffraction
X-ray, Radiology
X-ray Spectroscopy
X-ray Therapy
Yacht Brokerage
Yachting
Yard Craft
Yard Personnel
Yarn
Yeasts
Yokes & Couplings
Zero Gravity Environments
Zinc Mining & Technology
Zippers
Zoning
Zoology

1. Technical Advisory Service for Attorneys, 428 Pennsylvania Avenue, Ft. Washington, PA, 19034.

Appendix C
Illinois State Police Courtroom
Evaluation Rating Sheet

ILLINOIS STATE POLICE
Division of Forensic Services and Identification
Bureau of Forensic Sciences

Mock Trial/Courtroom Evlauation Rating Sheet

Name: _____

Date: _____

Rated by: _____

The goal of court testimony is to communicate the truth in a manner that is understandable and believable.

	Unsatisfactory*	Satisfactory	Comments*
Truthful	_____	_____	_____
Technically Accurate	_____	_____	_____
Understandable	_____	_____	_____
Believable	_____	_____	_____
Evidence Handling	_____	_____	_____

(getting exhibits into evidence through proper use of labeling, chain, transmittal, lab notes and reports)

* Unsatisfactory rating requires written comments.

ALL ABOVE CATEGORIES MUST BE SATISFACTORY FOR AN OVERALL SATISFACTORY RATING

CONSTRUCTIVE CRITICISM (noncritical areas for the benefit of the witness)

	Improvement Needed * 1	Satisfactory 2 3 4	No Improvement Needed 5	Comments*

Personal Impressions
1. Voice (volume, tone, fluency) _____
2. Eye contact _____
3. Posture _____
4. Facial expression _____
5. Dress _____
6. Gestures _____
7. Etiquette _____

Testimony
1. Confident (forceful, direct) _____
2. Responsive to question _____
3. Thoughtful (speed of response, limited to area of expertise) _____
4. Clear and concise _____
5. Control (answer only clear-cut questions, ask for clarification, anticipate problems, don't volunteer) _____

Preparation & Organization _____
Evidence Handling (in court)_____
Qualifying Questions _____
Visual Aids _____
Overall Rating: _____

Comments:

Appendix D
Forensic Expert Survey and Questionnaire

INTRODUCTION

Virtually nothing is known about how expert witnesses view the dispute-resolution process and their role in it. How do they perceive the legal system and their work within that framework? What are the problems and satisfactions of their service? What advice can they offer to the aspiring expert witness? How would they improve the system?

The rationale behind this survey was to allow expert witnesses to tell their own story, so that we can begin to answer these and other related questions. Unlike the standard social survey where the respondent is asked to place a checkmark next to one of a series of predetermined response categories, most of the questions in this survey are open-ended. The respondents were encouraged to put down ideas which they felt were most relevant and to elaborate on answers as they saw fit. Thus the survey allowed for open response while providing a representative sample from different parts of the country and various forensic fields.

The dangers of imposing preconceptions or biases in analyzing the results of the survey were offset by delegating this task to Mr. Martin Kretzmann, whose training and experience in survey methodology ensured a fair degree of objectivity. Kretzmann is currently completing a PhD in sociology at the University of Denver. He received training in all phases of survey research methods at the University of Akron, Ohio. He has assisted in the design and analysis of several research projects.

THE SURVEY PROTOCOL

The forensic expert questionnaire, which is part of this appendix, was mailed to approximately 160 forensic experts throughout the United States. Selection was made from an array of experts known to be active in their fields. Some had worked with the author on case assignments, but most had not.

Fifty-four responses were received, a relatively high rate of response given the length of the survey. By areas of expertise, the respondents fell into these seven categories:

Category	Number
Medical and psychiatry	9
Economics, sociology/psychology	9
Accident investigation/reconstruction	6
Construction/engineering	10
Accounting	4
Appraisal	13
Document-text interpretation/demonstrative evidence/miscellaneous	13
TOTAL	54

The averages which follow were developed by adding the total response to each question and dividing by the number of responses to the particular question. For example, for the first item, years of service as forensic expert, the aggregate number of years reported was 788. That sum was divided by 44, the number of responses to that question. In correlating the data, some significant averages emerged.

Information	Average Response
Years serving as forensic expert	14.6 years
Total number of cases investigated	442.0 cases
Depositions given	79.0 depositions
Trials which required testimony	55.5 trials
Administrative hearings requiring testimony	18.9 hearings
Depositions conducted by experts without attorney assistance	36.0 depositions
Trial testimony given without attorney assistance	15.4 trials
Cases where attorney's assistance would have been helpful	58.8 cases
Cases where attorney's assistance would not have been helpful	17.4 cases
Cases for which a written fee or engagement letter or contract was used	33.9 assignments
Cases involving fee disputes with client or attorney	2.3 situations

This forensic expert questionnaire and survey is the first known effort to obtain general information from experts themselves. While the survey might not be sufficiently broad and might not have been accomplished with all due scientific formality, some of the information elicited should stimulate further inquiry into the process surrounding expert witnesses and forensic testimony.

Following is a listing of each expert, with area of specialty, who graciously took time to participate in the survey.

Name	Address & Phone Number	Area of Expertise
John E. Bakken	2777 S. Colorado Blvd. Suite 200 Denver, CO 80222 (303) 758-8818	Business valuation, appraisal of business assets
John Bohling (MAI)	P. O. Box 5276 Wheat Ridge, CO 80033 (303) 237-9149	Real estate value
John Brady, II (Ph.D.)	615 South Main Street Milpitas, CA 95035 (408) 263-8046	Psychological evaluation
Jeff Busley	2736 Baker Street San Francisco, CA 94123 (415) 346-6908	Construction
Leonard Berk (Doctor)	850 E. Harvard Ave. Denver, CO 80210 (303) 722-0221	Orthopedic surgery
Jack Butler (MAI)	2041 E. Virginia Ave. Denver, CO 80209 (303) 698-0564	Real estate appraisal
Byron Church (MAI)	455 E. Pikes Peak Ave. Colo. Springs, CO 80903 (719) 632-1960	Real estate
Maclyn Clouse (Ph.D.)	College of Bus. Admis. University of Denver Denver, CO 80208 (303) 871-3322	Financial evaluation and valuation
Clifford Cryer (MAI)	6025 S. Quebec Street Plaza Quebec, #340 Englewood, CO 80111 (303) 741-6144	Real estate appraisal
Marvin L. Daves (Doctor)	4200 E. 9th Avenue Denver, CO 80220 (303) 270-8726	Radiology
Paul Earle (Ph.D.)	3500 E. Floyd Drive Denver, CO 80210 (303) 757-8825	Building material failure
Jack M. East (LSW/MA)	5611 Kavanaugh Blvd. Little Rock, AK 72207 (501) 666-2523	Life care planning (equipment and service projections)
Kai Erickson	115 Blake Road Hamden, CT 06517 (203) 865-1400	Sociology-response to disaaster
Kenneth R. Feder	P. O. Box 22333 Denver, CO 80222 (303) 758-3555	Mechanical malfunction, fire causation, accident reconstruction

Douglas Filter	2833 E. 16th Avenue Denver, CO 80206 (303) 355-4114	Demonstrative evidence
Vincent Gallagher	4 Longwood Court Stratford, NJ 08084 (609) 435-2744	Industrial safety
Paul Gesso	8425 W. 3rd Place Lakewood, CO 80226 (303) 237-1050	Corporate real estate
Eric Gould	6111 Montview Blvd. Denver, CO 80207 (303) 871-2706	Written texts — interpretation
Michael Graham (Doctor)	St. Louis University 3556 Caroline St. Louis, MO 63104 (314) 577-8298	Pathology
William K. Gray (MAI)	P. O. Box 7 Carbondale, CO 81623 (303) 963-1480	Real estate appraisal
Freeman Hall, Jr. (Ph.D.)	202 Ocean Street Solana Beach, CA 92075 (619) 259-2721	Visual perception, meteorology and audibility
Glyn Hanbery (CPA)	5186 S. Kenton Way Englewood, CO 80111 (303) 773-0168	Accounting and auditing
Robert E. Harner	101 W. River Rd., #6 Tucson, AZ 85704 (602) 888-7705	Safety and human factors
Clarence Hein (CPA)	717 17th Street, #1600 Denver, CO 80202 (303) 298-9600	Accounting and auditing, business valuation, securities, damages
Bryan R. Jacobs	8400 E. Prentice Ave. Suite 700 Englewood, CO 80111 (303) 793-0220	Engineering and construction
Nikki Jersin	2835 S. Monaco Parkway 1-106 Denver, CO 80237 (303) 758-2121	Appraiser of antiques and personal property
Ib Falk Jorgensen (P.E.)	134 Union Boulevard Suite 220 Denver, CO 80228-1812 (303) 989-9000	Structural engineering
E. James Judd	190 E. 9th Ave., #500 Denver, CO 80203 (303) 830-7211	Building construction

Terry R. King (AM)	P. O. Box 17328 Denver, CO 80217 (303) 777-6423	Personal property appraiser
W. Judson King (Ph.D.)	2838 Kansas Street Oviedo, FL 32765	Accident reconstruction and human factors engineering
Robert Kleeman, Jr. (CPA)	11990 Grant Street Denver, CO 80233 (303) 452-2008	Valuation of closely held business, financial damages
Jack Kunin	180 Cook St., 111E Denver, CO 80206 (303) 322-0563	Art appraiser
Mike R. Licht (CPA) (SRA)	400 E. 56th Avenue Denver, CO 80216 (303) 296-4802	Real estate appraisal and accounting
James Lincoln, Jr.	5808 S. Rapp Street #202A Littleton, CO 80120 (303) 730-8568	Economist (public and private microforecasts)
John Litvak (Doctor)	1471 Stuart Street Denver, CO (303) 825-0288	Neurosurgery
Leroy Lundgren	277 Foxcroft Road Pittsburgh, PA 15220 (412) 279-9636	Construction claims
Robert L. Lytton (P.E.)	2108 Barak Lane Bryan, TX 77802 (409) 846-5496	Soils, expansive soils, foundations, pavements, structures
Pamela McBogg (Doctor)	1056 E. 19th Avenue Denver, CO 80218 (303) 861-6630	Child development
Robert Miller (DC)	1614 Carr Street Lakewood, CO 80215 (303) 237-6582	Chiropractic, sports injuries, thermography, orthopedics
Herbert Modlin (Doctor)	P. O. Box 829 Topeka, KS 66601 (913) 273-7500	Psychiatry
Lorraine Monheiser (CPA)	26 W. Dry Creek Circle Suite 310 Littleton, CO 80120 (303) 794-5661	Business valuation, quantifying damages
John R. Morris	2309 Birch Street Denver, CO 80207 (303) 322-4203	Economic loss
Irving Morrissett	209 Boulder View Lane Boulder, CO 80304 (303) 444-1198	Economics

James O'Donnell (Doctor)	1792 Prestwick Drive Inverness, IL 60067 (312) 991-4433	Pharmacology/toxicology
Rolland Osborne	6028 Quail Court Arvada, CO 80004 (303) 431-9593	Questioned documents
Leonard Rice	2401 15th Street Suite 300 Denver, CO 80202 (303) 455-9589	Water rights, water resources, hydrology
Ira A. Rimson (P.E.)	P. O. Box 1015 Springfield, VA 22151 (703) 978-2944	Aviation safety and accident reconstruction
Jonathan Sharp	7009 W. Stetson Place Littleton, CO 80123 (303) 979-7589	Automotive and ladder safety
John Spisak	8237 Sweetwater Road Littleton, CO 80124 (303) 298-1000	Mining, milling, environmental clean-up
Lawrence Stiffman (Doctor)	5590 W. Liberty Ann Arbor, MI 48103 (313) 996-0262	Law firm economics, fee petitioning
Marvin L. Stone (CPA)	370-17th St., #3450 Denver, CO 80202 (303) 573-2882	Accounting, auditing, finance, taxation, valuation, economic loss
Robert Thompson	1971 W. 12th Avenue Denver, CO (303) 825-0777	Geotechnical and materials engineer
Stanley Weiner (Doctor)	1616 Carmel Cir. East Upland, CA 91786 (714) 981-1130	Emergency medicine
Ron Wykstra	811 Casey Key Nokomis, FL 34275 (813) 488-5334	Economic damages

FORENSIC EXPERT QUESTIONNAIRE

Name _____

Address _____

_____

Telephone _____

Area of forensic expertise _____.

Number of years you have served as a forensic expert _____.

Number of cases investigated _____.

Number of depositions given _____.

Number of court trials at which you actually testified _____.

Number of court trials for which you were called but did not testify _____.

Number of administrative hearings at which you testified _____.

Number of administrative hearings for which you were called but did not testify _____.

Number of times you went for deposition testimony without attorney preparation _____.

Number of times you went for trial testimony without attorney preparation _____.

Percentage of the times you testified that an attorney's preparation would have helped _____%.

Percentage of times you testified that an attorney's help would have made no difference _____%.

Percentage of times you had a written fee contract with a client or attorney _____%.

Percentage of times you had a fee dispute with a client or attorney _____%.

What was the most satisfying case you ever handled? Specify the facts, the result, and the role you played (be brief).

_____

_____

_____

continued

FORENSIC EXPERT QUESTIONNAIRE *(Continued)*

What was your most devastating testimonial experience? State the facts and the circumstances of the disaster (be brief).

_____

_____

_____

How could the disaster have been averted, in your opinion?

_____

_____

How do you handle that effort? _____

_____

What percentage of the time do you consult regarding the discovery process without ever being asked to formulate opinions on the ultimate issues? _____%.

How do you track your effort through a forensic assignment; that is, how do you remind yourself of what must be done next?

_____

_____

_____

_____

How often do you have a chance to meet and discuss the case with other experts dealing with different aspects of the same inquiry?

Often _____ Seldom _____ Never _____

Do you attend experts' pretrial planning and testimony preparation conferences?

Often _____ Seldom _____ Never _____

What percentage of the time has the opposition been able to see your entire working file on the case? _____% If the answer is zero, did the opposition make effort to see your file?

Yes _____ No _____

Was that effort resisted by the attorney on the case?

Yes _____ No _____

What is the single most important admonition you ever received about the testimony or deposition process? _____

_____

What is your preference regarding use of demonstrative materials, charts, drawings, and models? _____

_____

How would you improve the effectiveness of such demonstrative items? _____

_____

_____

Do you prepare testimony differently depending on the forum?

Yes _____ No _____. If yes, what do you do differently between court and administrative testimony? _____

_____

_____

_____

Do you prefer to work against a hypothetical question?

Yes _____ No _____. If so, do you assist in drafting the questions? Yes _____ No _____.

How do you maintain your professional competence?

_____

Are societal memberships valuable for that purpose? Please explain. _____

_____

Have you ever turned down a case? Yes _____ No _____. On how many occasions? _____. For what reasons have you turned down assignments? _____

_____

_____

continued

FORENSIC EXPERT QUESTIONNAIRE *(Continued)*

Do you routinely check out the client and the attorney?

Yes ـــــــــــــ   No ـــــــــــــ. How do you go about that checking?

_____

_____

What factors do you consider in deciding whether a case is worth your effort? ___

_____

_____

Do you usually use an engagement letter or agreement?

Yes ـــــــــــــ   No ـــــــــــــ. If yes, please submit a copy of your usual fee agreement with your response.

If you have ever had a fee dispute in a forensic case, what was the cause? ____

_____

_____

How did it turn out? _____

_____

What usual sources do you use for the investigative work you do? List those sources most frequently used. _____

_____

_____

Do you regularly receive attorney assistance in evaluating whether the evidence you are getting is admissible? Yes ـــــــــــــ   No ـــــــــــــ. Do you believe basic evidence information would be valuable to you?

Yes ـــــــــــــ   No ـــــــــــــ.

Are you usually asked to prepare written reports?

Yes ـــــــــــــ   No ـــــــــــــ. If not, what are the benefits of not doing a written report? _____

_____

What are the safeguards you take when doing destructive testing?

_____

_____

What is your biggest problem in communicating with lawyers?

_____

_____

What can be done to correct those problems? _____

_____

_____

When on a forensic assignment, do you usually consult with other professionals?

Yes _____ No _____.

Do you usually reveal those consultations in your reports?

Yes _____ No _____.

Do you believe you understand the term "discovery"?

Yes _____ No _____. If yes, indicate your understanding of

what the discovery process is about. _____

_____

_____

Do you know the three main purposes of a deposition?

Yes _____ No _____. If yes, state what you think the pur-

poses are. (1) _____

(2) _____

(3) _____

When and how do you communicate with experts on the other side?

_____

_____

_____

Are you uncomfortable with the question-and-answer process?

Yes _____ No _____. If yes, what bothers you? _____

_____

_____

continued

FORENSIC EXPERT QUESTIONNAIRE *(Continued)*

How would you improve on the process? _____

_____

_____

What is the most traumatic, disappointing, or shocking experience you have ever had acting as a forensic expert? _____

_____

_____

_____

Describe any cases in which attorneys have attempted to shade, color, or actually manipulate your independent expert opinion. _____

_____

_____

_____

Indicate the problems of preparation which you have experienced in working, both with and without attorneys, as an expert witness. _____

_____

_____

_____

Indicate any items of judicial impropriety, rudeness, discourtesy, or ineptitude which you have experienced. _____

_____

_____

_____

Indicate problems you have had with getting paid for your services as a forensic expert. _____

_____

_____

_____

What unhappy experiences have you had with regard to the destruction of documents, evidence, samples, specimens, or other necessary materials? _____

_____

_____

_____

Indicate whether you ever had any experience with other experts who falsified data, modified reports, or altered their reports or basic foundation information. _____

_____

_____

_____

What are your ideas about licensing or certification of forensic experts? _____

_____

_____

_____

What professional societies or associations do you belong to and what offices do you hold in any such societies or associations?

_____

_____

_____

What kinds of things do you see as being necessary in the universe to upgrade the quality of forensic testimony in our courtrooms? _____

_____

_____

_____

What is credibility? _____

_____

How do you go about enhancing yours? _____

_____

_____

Do you keep copies of all your expert reports and depositions?

continued

Yes _____ No _____. If yes, how are they maintained and indexed?

_____

_____

Do you find the forensic area worthwhile?

Yes _____ No _____. If no, how could it be more rewarding

for you? _____

_____

_____

Are you interested in expanding your forensic activities?

Yes _____ No _____. How are you going about that expansion?

_____

_____

_____

How are others you know expanding their forensic practices?

_____

_____

_____

Do you have other thoughts on the subject? If so, feel free to jot them here. _____

_____

_____

_____

_____

_____

If you consent to the use of your responses, your name, address, phone number, and field of expertise in the book, please sign below.

_____
Signature

By answering these few questions, you will have helped considerably in the improvement of our judicial system.

Harold A. Feder

Appendix E
Federal Rules of Evidence 701 through 706

The Federal Rules of Evidence were chosen for inclusion because they tend to exemplify the current mainstream of legal thought on the subject. However, evidence rules in the various states vary considerably, and these rules have themselves been interpreted by many court decisions and opinions.

Rule 701: Opinion Testimony by Lay Witnesses
If the witness is not testifying as an expert, the witness' testimony in the form of opinions or inferences is limited to those opinions or inferences which are (a) rationally based on the perception of the witness and (b) helpful to a clear understanding of the witness' testimony or the determination of a fact in issue.

Rule 702: Testimony by Experts
If scientific, technical, or other specialized knowledge will assist the trier-of-fact to understand the evidence or to determine a fact in issue, a witness qualified as an expert by knowledge, skill, experience, training, or education, may testify thereto in the form of an opinion or otherwise.

Rule 703: Bases of Opinion Testimony by Experts
The facts or data in the particular case upon which an expert bases an opinion or inference may be those perceived by or made known to the expert at or before the hearing. If of a type reasonably relied upon by experts in the particular field in forming opinions or inferences upon the subject, the facts or data need not be admissible in evidence.

Rule 704: Opinion on Ultimate Issue
(a) Testimony in the form of an opinion or inference otherwise admissible is not objectionable because it embraces an ultimate issue to be decided by the trier-of-fact.

(b) No expert witness testifying with respect to the mental state or condition of a defendant in a criminal case may state an opinion or inference as to whether the defendant did or did not have the mental state or condition constituting an element of the crime charged or of a defense thereto. Such ultimate issues are matters for the trier-of-fact alone.

Rule 705: Disclosure of Facts or Data Underlying Expert Opinion
The expert may testify in terms of opinions or inference and give reasons therefore without prior disclosure of the underlying facts or data, unless the court requires otherwise. The expert may in any event be required to disclose the underlying facts or data on cross-examination.

Rule 706: Court Appointed Experts

(a) Appointment. The court may on its own motion or on the motion of any party enter an order to show cause why expert witnesses should not be appointed, and may request the parties to submit nominations. The court may appoint any expert witnesses agreed upon by the parties, and may appoint witnesses of its own selection. An expert witness shall not be appointed by the court unless the witness consents to act. A witness so appointed shall be informed of the witness' duties by the court in writing, a copy of which shall be filed with the clerk, or at a conference in which the parties shall have opportunity to participate. A witness so appointed shall advise the parties of the witness' findings, if any; the witness' deposition may be taken by any party; and the witness may be called to testify by the court or any party. The witness shall be subject to cross-examination by each party, including a party calling the witness.

(b) Compensation. Expert witnesses so appointed are entitled to reasonable compensation whatever sum the court may allow. The compensation thus fixed is payable from funds which may be provided by law in criminal cases and civil actions and proceedings involving just compensation under the Fifth Amendment. In other civil actions and proceedings the compensation shall be paid by the parties in such proportion and at such time as the court directs, and thereafter charged in like manner as other costs.

(c) Disclosure of Appointment. In the exercise of its discretion, the court may authorize disclosure to the jury of the fact that the court appointed the expert witness.

(d) Parties' Experts of Own Selection. Nothing in this rule limits the parties in calling expert witnesses of their own selection.

Note: At this printing one of the Rules is subject to probable redrafting. The proposed changes are included here in anticipation of Congressional enactment.

(Proposed) Rule 705: Disclosure of Facts or Data Underlying Expert Opinion The expert may testify in terms of opinion or inference and give reasons therefor without first testifying to the underlying facts or data, unless the court requires otherwise. The expert may in any event be required to disclose the underlying facts or data on cross-examination.

Appendix F
Sample Engagement Letter

I SCOPE OF WORK

II TIME REQUIRED

Work under this agreement will commence upon receipt of authorization to proceed. It is estimated that work under Part I can be completed in _____ to _____ weeks.

Delays caused by major changes in the project plans or by circumstances beyond the control of the engineer will extend the time of completion.

III PAYMENT

Payment for engineering services is based on the time required to accomplish the work and is computed by multiplying direct salary cost by a factor that accounts for overhead, including payroll, unemployment and other taxes, general and administrative expenses, and profit. Hourly rates currently in effect range from $60.00–$95.00 for principals and associates, $30.00–$65.00 for engineers and hydrologists, and $25.00–$35.00 for technicians, draftsmen, and technical typists. Personnel are assigned to the job in accordance with the type of work involved and the professional services required. Expenses incurred directly in connection with the project are billed at cost plus 10 percent to cover handling and administration.

The work described under Part I above represents our best estimate of what will be required based on the information provided. As the work proceeds and additional facts are developed, it may be necessary to undertake additional work, and some items described may not be needed. For these reasons we can provide only an estimate of the time and cost of doing the work. We believe the work described under Part I can be accomplished for between _____ and _____.

Every effort will be made to complete the work as economically as possible. Invoices will be submitted monthly for time and expenses incurred. Terms of payment are net 30 days. Overdue accounts are subject to an interest charge of 1.5 percent per month, and work will stop whenever payment is overdue more than 75 days.

IV SPECIAL SERVICES

Services in addition to those described under Part I will be performed or obtained for the client's account upon request at rates currently in effect. Special services may include, but are not limited to, expert testimony, appearances at public meetings, soil investigations, topographic and land surveys, including establishment of boundaries, well drilling, well and acquifer testing, electric logging, water quality sampling and analysis, preparation of construction drawings and specifications, and material testing.

Acceptance of this proposal and authorization to proceed with the work can be indicated by signing one copy and returning it to us for our files. The terms of this proposal will be honored for a period of 30 days from date of submittal only.

We appreciate your considering our firm and look forward to working with you.

Very truly yours,

LEONARD RICE CONSULTING WATER ENGINEERS, INC.

For: _____

Contracting Agency

/11b

By: _____

Authorized Signature/Title

Date: _____

Appendix G
Scope of Services

Furnished by Madsen, Okes and Associates, Inc.

1. PLANNING MEETING

    1.1 Meet with client.
    1.2 Establish scope of services.
    1.3 Set up project team.
    1.4 Assign tasks and establish lines of communication.
    1.5 Set schedule for work.
    1.6 Determine project cost budget.

2. DISCOVERY

    2.1 On-site: all parties.
    2.2 Off-site:
        2.2.1 Client's offices.
        2.2.2 Other offices.
    2.3 Other sources.

3. DOCUMENT DATABASE AND INDEXING

    3.1 Catalog and organize documents.
    3.2 Select documents for indexing.
    3.3 Code documents.
    3.4 Input documents into computer.
    3.5 Quality control and editing of index.
    3.6 Final output—selected sorts and document packets.

4. PROJECT ANALYSIS

    4.1 Review contract documents.
    4.2 Identify potential deficiencies.
    4.3 Analyze problems:
        4.3.1 Changes/extra work.
        4.3.2 Differing site conditions.
        4.3.3 Weather.
        4.3.4 Delay impacts.
        4.3.5 Acceleration.
        4.3.6 Other.

5. SCHEDULE ANALYSIS

    5.1 Review as-planned schedule.
    5.2 Establish as-built schedule.
    5.3 Include delays:
        5.3.1 Contractor delays.
        5.3.2 Owner-caused delays.
        5.3.3 Excusable delays (noncompensable).
    5.4 Collapsed schedule to establish responsibility for delay.

6. CLAIM ANALYSIS-ENTITLEMENT

    6.1 Review and analyze documents—by problem.
    6.2 Review identified entitlement—by problem.
    6.3 Analyze entitlements.
    6.4 Develop conclusions.

7. CLAIM ANALYSIS—QUANTUM

    7.1 Review original bid and estimate.
    7.2 Review contractor's cost records.
    7.3 Review alleged damages from contractor's claim.
    7.4 Analyze damage computations.
    7.5 Develop conclusions.

8. LITIGATION SUPPORT

    8.1 Litigation strategy.
    8.2 Interrogatories and responses.
    8.3 Depositions.
    8.4 Preparation of documents and visuals.
    8.5 Expert testimony.

9. MEETINGS AND REPORTS

    9.1 Monthly project meetings and reports.
    9.2 Internal roundtables.
    9.3 Final report.
    9.4 Litigation report.

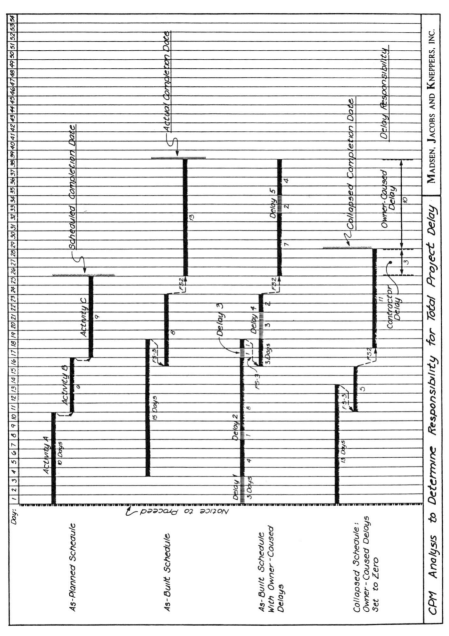

Figure G.1 Critical path for forensic assignment.

Appendix H
Information the Expert Needs
for Case Evaluation

Furnished by Kenneth R. Feder

I. Investigation activity (verify all facts in reports and secure copies of all investigation reports)
   1. Police investigation reports
   2. Insurance company report of accident (if applicable)
   3. Driver's report of accident
   4. Other reports (witnesses, occupants, etc.)

II. Facts of accident
   1. Date of accident
   2. Time: determine accurately daylight or darkness
   3. Road type
   4. Condition of road surface
   5. Grades of all roads or streets
   6. Obstructions to view
   7. Stop and Go signals (locations, positions of colors, timing)
   8. Signs (shape, color, mounting position)
   9. Pavement markings (lane lines, No Passing lines, pedestrian walks, stop lines)
   10. Verify accident diagrams: make sketch for comparison
   11. Location of all roads
   12. Direction of approach of all vehicles
   13. Area of impact (designate)
   14. Position of rest of all vehicles
   15. Position of any bodies or debris
   16. Position of all physical structures
   17. Operator's physical condition (BA, CO, etc.)

III. Vehicle condition
   1. Check involved vehicles (photographs)
   2. Description (year, make, model, color, passengers, type of transmission, type of engine)
   3. Condition before accident (brakes, tires, steering)

    4. Description of damage (all vehicles, all structures)
    5. Location of damage on vehicles
    6. Amount of damage
    7. Record of any previous repairs or problems

IV. Photographs
    1. Obtain photographs
    2. Road or street approach
    3. Accident location: photograph from several angles
    4. Positions of vehicles at rest
    5. Damage to vehicles before they are moved
    6. Damage of vehicles after accident
    7. Damage to any structures or utilities
    8. Physical evidence (skid marks, scuffs, gouges, scrapes)

FIRE INSPECTION REPORT

Severity Code
1 = Slight
5 = Totally

Interior Burns

Carpeting	No	Yes	Front ____	Middle ____	Rear ____
Carpet Pad	No	Yes	Front ____	Middle ____	Rear ____
Floor Board	No	Yes	Front ____	Middle ____	Rear ____

Seat cushions burned from top down?   No   Yes   1 2 3 4 5
Seat cushions burned from bottom up?   No   Yes   1 2 3 4 5

Instrument Panel   No   Yes   1 2 3 4 5

Accessories present:
    Radio/Stereo   No   Yes   1 2 3 4 5
    CB   No   Yes   1 2 3 4 5
    Radar Detector   No   Yes   1 2 3 4 5
    2-way Radio   No   Yes   1 2 3 4 5
    Mobile Phone   No   Yes   1 2 3 4 5

Ignition Switch   On   Off   Melted out   Undeterminable

Roof Cap   No   Yes   1 2 3 4 5
Windshield   No   Yes   1 2 3 4 5
Sunroof   No   Yes   1 2 3 4 5
Driver Vent Window   No   Yes   1 2 3 4 5
Driver Window   No   Yes   1 2 3 4 5

Left Rear Window	No	Yes	1	2	3	4	5
Rear Windshield	No	Yes	1	2	3	4	5
Right Rear Window	No	Yes	1	2	3	4	5
Right Front Window	No	Yes	1	2	3	4	5
Right Vent Window	No	Yes	1	2	3	4	5

Unassociated objects found in vehicle:

Front _____

Middle _____

Rear _____

Abnormal substances sample taken?   No   Yes

Location of longest burn time of interior _____

Comments: _____

_____

_____

Exterior Burns

Location of hot spot(s) _____

Location of any spill patterns _____

Burn patterns from top to bottom? _____

Burn patterns from bottom to top? _____

Areas of burn: _____

			Spot	Burn		Warped	Buckled
Hood	No	Yes					
Grill	No	Yes	1	2	3	4	5
Left Front Fender	No	Yes	1	2	3	4	5
Left Front Door	No	Yes	1	2	3	4	5
Left Rear Door	No	Yes	1	2	3	4	5
Trunk/Hatchback	No	Yes	1	2	3	4	5
Right Rear Door	No	Yes	1	2	3	4	5
Right Front Door	No	Yes	1	2	3	4	5
Roof Cap	No	Yes	1	2	3	4	5
Left Front Wheel Well	No	Yes	1	2	3	4	5
Left Front Tire	No	Yes	1	2	3	4	5
Left Rear Wheel Well	No	Yes	1	2	3	4	5
Left Rear Tire	No	Yes	1	2	3	4	5
Right Rear Wheel Well	No	Yes	1	2	3	4	5
Right Rear Tire	No	Yes	1	2	3	4	5

Right Front Wheel Well   No   Yes   1   2   3   4   5
Right Front Tire   No   Yes   1   2   3   4   5

Engine Compartment

Location of longest burn time _____

Supportive evidence (hot spots, fuel burn pattern, plastic melt, wire-loom melt)

_____

Location of any hot spots _____

Comments: _____

_____

_____

Checklist of parts:

____   Oil dip stick   ____   Coolant levels

____   Transmission dip stick   ____   Coolant hoses & clamps

____   Oil filler cap   ____   Fuel line clamps

____   Radiator cap   ____   Fuel filter clamps

____   Battery   ____   Injector hoses

____   Air cleaner   ____   Spark plug wires

____   Air cleaner cartridge   ____   Fuel pump lines & clamps

____   Crank case oil level   ____   Carburetor needle & seat

       Sample taken? Yes No   ____   Carburetor lead plugs

____   Transmission oil level   ____   Charcoal canister & lines

Engine block cracked or holes?   No   Yes   Location _____
Freedom of crankshaft rotation?   No   Yes   360°   180°   90°
Engine mains, rods, and pistons inspected?   No   Yes   N/A
Oil filter cartridge?   Tight   Loose   Missing
Crank case drain plug?   Tight   Loose   Missing
Transmission oil drain plug?   Tight   Loose   Missing
Oil leak patterns?   No   Yes   Undeterminable
Wiring loom fuse link?   Open   Closed
Wiring loom routing?   Correct   Incorrect
Wiring loom stiffness/balling?   Normal   Damage due to fire   Fused
Wiring loom ground outs?   No   Yes
Wiring loom pinched?   No   Yes

Wiring loom frayed?   No   Yes
Interior wiring loom routing?   Correct   Incorrect
Interior wiring loom stiffness/balling?   Normal   Damage due to fire   Fused
Interior wiring loom ground outs?   No   Yes
Interior wiring loom pinched?   No   Yes
Interior wiring loom frayed?   No   Yes

Comments: _____

Trunk Compartment

Location of longest burn area _____

Location of hot spots _____

Burn patterns from top to bottom _____

Burn patterns from bottom to top _____

Normal items found in trunk?

   Spare   Hand tools   Other _____

Abnormal items found? _____

Underside Vehicle Inspection

Fuel tank
Filler cap?   Tight   Loose   Missing
Amount of fuel in tank?   Full   3/4   1/2   1/4   Empty
Drain plug?   Tight   Loose   Missing   N/A
Type of tank?   Plastic   Metal

Number of tanks & location _____
Switching valve connection?   OK   Not OK
Switching valve clamps?   OK   Not OK
Inlet line and clamp to tank?   OK   Not OK
Return line and clamp to tank?   OK   Not OK
Fuel line routing and clamps?   OK   Not OK
Clam shelled?   No   Yes
Abnormal tank condition?   No   Yes
Filler neck clamps and connection?   OK   Not OK
Filler neck burn pattern?   OK   Not OK
Catalytic converter for hot spot?   OK   Not OK
Underbelly bubbling?   No   Yes

Comments: _____

_____

_____

Procedures
Exterior
Interior
Engine
Interior Electric
Fuel Tank
Underbelly

Additional inspection for Motor Homes

Highest degree of burn location? _____

Continuous burn pattern progression? Normal Abnormal _____

Unconnected hot spots? None Abnormal _____

Unconnected burn progression? None Abnormal _____
Accessories found:

_____	Stereo	Personal effects:
_____	CB	_____ Pots & Pans
_____	Radar Detector	_____ Silverware
_____	Television	_____ Canned goods
_____	Stove	_____ Tools
_____	Microwave	_____ Clothes
_____	Refrigerator	_____ Portable Radios
_____	Auxiliary Generator	_____ Guns
_____	Roof Air Conditioners	_____ Fishing Equipment
_____	Propane Tank	_____ _____
_____	Heater	_____ _____

Windshield _____

Left Side Windows _____

Rear Windows _____

Right Side Windows _____

Door(s) _____

Appendix I
Collection of Physical Evidence
(Chain of Custody)

A. Obtain it legally.

1. Warrant
2. Consent
3. Incidental to Arrest
4. Subpoena

B. Describe it in notes.

1. Location, circumstances, and how obtained
2. Date and chain-of-custody notation
3. How is the item identified?

C. Identify the item properly.

1. Use initials, date, and case number.
2. Preferably on the evidence itself. Liquids, soils, tiny fragments must be placed in suitable containers, sealed and marked on the outside.

D. Package the evidence properly. One case to a box.

1. Use suitable containers such as round pill boxes, plastic vials, glass or plastic containers, strong cardboard cartons.
2. Seal securely against leakage.
3. Package each item separately—avoid any appearance of leakage or contamination.
4. If wet or bearing blood, air dry before packaging (except arson cases where hydrocarbons are present).

E. Maintain chain of custody—keep it short.

1. Same person or persons that recovered the evidence should initial, seal and send evidence [or deliver it to an evidence locker].
2. Maintain the evidence in a locked vault, cabinet or room until shipped [or needed for tests, discovery or trial].
3. [When transporting the item always use registered mail.]
4. [Each person who takes physical custody of the item must sign for the item as custody is taken.]

Courtesy U.S. Department of Justice, Federal Bureau of Investigation, *Handbook of Forensic Science*, p. 100, revised March 1984. Bracketed material supplied by the author, not the FBI.

222

Appendix J
Outline for Preliminary Verbal Report

The following items should be included as part of a verbal preliminary report to attorney or client.

1. Restate assignment: this will enable you and the recipient of the report to make sure the focus of the inquiry is still on track.

2. Briefly summarize what has been accomplished:
- The parties involved
- The witnesses interviewed
- Physical things inspected
- Any precautionary steps to preserve evidence
- The sites inspected
- Tests conducted
- The dates of your work thus far
- Reports and literature reviewed

3. Monetary considerations: state how much you have expended in the way of investigative time and costs, particularly if there are budgetary constraints. You may also be called on to project how much additional money is needed for the remaining investigative effort.

4. Tentative conclusions: state what you believe to be the result of your investigative assignment thus far: what happened, who was involved, how it happened, when and where it happened, and what caused the event.

5. Investigative product thus far developed: itemize such things as laboratory tests, photographs, data compiled, specimens and samples collected, and all other tangible things that you have either located, identified, or have in possession.

6. Additional effort required: discuss areas of investigation yet to be accomplished. Obtain agreement from the client or attorney to your continuing investigation.

Appendix K

Sample Interrogatories and Request for
Production to Expert Witnesses

SAMPLE OF INTERROGATORIES AND REQUEST FOR PRODUCTION
TO A PARTY CONCERNING EXPERT WITNESS

_____, by counsel of record, _____, submits the following Interrogatories to _____, to be answered concerning that party's expert witness, pursuant to Rule 26(b) (4) and 34, of the Federal Rules of Civil Procedure, which are to be answered separately and fully in writing, under oath, within thirty (30) days after service. Answers must be updated as additional responses become available.

1. Identify each person assisting in answering this discovery and denote which questions are answered by which person.

2. State the names, addresses, and occupations of such person.

'3. State all areas of specialization of the expert's occupation or profession.

4. Describe all professional or social relationships the expert's have with _____ at the present and at any time in the past.

5. State when the expert's were hired and by whom. Attach copies of all correspondence or notes of telephone conversations between experts and the hiring party or counsel.

6. What relationships of a social or professional nature do the expert's have with _____'s counsel? Have the expert's ever been engaged as an expert or testified for _____'s counsel previously? If so, provide all details of each testimonial or forensic engagement.

7. What is the expert's formal education and employment experience in detail? Attach a current curriculum vitae or detailed resume.

8. What is the expert's agreement for compensation with the hiring party? Include all amounts paid or to be paid and attach copies of the engagement agreements, billing, and timekeeping sheets.

9. State the exact manner in which the expert became familiar with the facts of this case. Detail each and every one of the expert's efforts and include the time devoted to each step.

10. What was the expert's specific assignment? Describe each and every action taken in completing such assignment.

11. What is the subject matter of the expert's prospective testimony in the case? How was that assignment given? Produce all documentation of that assignment. Produce all of the expert's files with regard to assignments as they now exist, in original form, without addition or subtraction, and in the original file folders. If material is in computer storage, print it out and produce the printout.

12. Provide copies of all documents obtained or generated in the course of employment as an expert in this case including, but not limited to:
   a. All notes made of conversations with other witnesses, parties, other experts, or attorneys for the hiring party;
   b. All reports or writings examined in arriving at the expert's opinion;
   c. All correspondence with the hiring party and their counsel;
   d. Any other documentation generated in arriving at conclusions;
   e. All investigative reports obtained prepared by others, or generated by the expert;
   f. Any photographs, recordings, drawings of calculations prepared as part of the expert's study; and
   g. Any documents which the expert located, specifying the source of such documents.

13. How much time has the expert spent on this project? Allocate such time to each particular task performed.

14. Give the name, address, and telephone number of any attorney, witness, party or other expert with whom the expert has conferred about this assignment. Detail the response or information obtained from any such person.

15. State what experience the expert has had with similar or comparable projects. What prior expert testimony or reports has the expert ever prepared or given concerning a project similar to that of this case.

16. State whether any field investigation was performed. Give the name, address, and telephone number of any person with whom the expert met during such field investigation. Detail the time devoted to such effort.

17. Provide a bibliography of all documents, books, publications, treatises, or any other written material upon which the expert relied in forming opinions. Be page specific.

18. Provide a bibliography of all documents, books, publications, treatises, or any other written material considered by the expert to be authoritative on the subject matter of projected testimony.

19. State the facts, opinions, and conclusions to which the expert intends to testify at trial or hearing in this case.

20. What other additional specific opinions and conclusions did the expert reach concerning this project?

21. Give a summary of the technical, factual, professional, or scientific basis and ground for each opinion reached by the expert to support each conclusion or opinion.

22. State the expert's reasoning by which each conclusion or opinion (in paragraphs 19 and 20) is supported or reached, based on the information in paragraph 21 above, or otherwise.

23. What additional assignments has the expert been given which have not yet been completed?

24. What additional work do you believe will be necessary for the expert to complete prior to trial or hearing?

25. When is the expert expected to complete such assignments?

These are continuing interrogatories and requests for production. You must supplement your responses in a prompt and timely fashion.

Appendix L
Guidelines for Deposition
and Trial Testimony

Instruction for Witnesses Prior to Giving Testimony

FEDER, MORRIS, TAMBLYN & GOLDSTEIN, P.C.
150 Blake Street Building
1441 Eighteenth Street
Denver, Colorado 80202
Telephone: (303) 292-1441

A deposition is the means of recording testimony of a party or witness prior to trial. Your deposition may be taken and recorded before a court reporter, television camera, or recorder. You will be sworn to tell the truth as you would be when testifying in court or administrative hearing.

In deposition you may be asked questions by lawyers representing either side of the controversy. The court reporter records your answers in shorthand or on the stenographic machine. Later the entire proceeding is transcribed for your review and approval. Changes should be made only to correct transcription errors.

The care with which you give answers on deposition and in trial is extremely important. You are testifying under oath. Your testimony may be used to impeach you if inconsistencies develop. If you admit crucial facts during your deposition, you will be hard-pressed to deny them later. Testimony is a way of conveying information from you as a witness to the judge, jury, or dispute-resolution body which will decide the case.

The purposes for which deposition testimony may be taken are:
1. To gather new information or confirm existing facts
2. To lock you into a position for trial or hearing
3. To size you up as a witness
4. To develop what appears to be a lie or an inconsistency and then use that point for purposes of impeachment

---

Remember the following rules. They will help make your testimony less complex and more persuasive.

In order to enhance the effectiveness of your testimony at deposition, trial, or hearing we have prepared guidelines based upon our experience with many witnesses in different cases. These guidelines apply whether you are in court for testimony, testifying on deposition, or at some other dispute-resolution proceeding. Consider the following suggestions:

1. Tell the truth.
2. Prepare yourself by review of the facts.
3. Remember that most questions can be answered:
   "Yes"
   "No"
   "I don't know"
   "I don't remember"
   "I don't understand", or
   By stating a single fact.
4. If "yes" or "no" will do, that should be your answer.
5. Limit your answer to the narrow question asked. Then *stop talking.*
6. Never volunteer information or answers.
7. Do not assume you must have an answer for every question.
8. Be cautious of repeated questions about the same point.
9. Do not lose your temper.
10. Speak slowly, clearly, and naturally.
11. Your posture should be forward, upright, and alert.
12. Do not nod or gesture in lieu of an answer.
13. Don't be afraid to ask for clarification of unclear questions.
14. Do not be afraid of the examining attorneys.
15. Be accurate about all fact conditions, damages, and injuries.
16. Restrict your answers to facts personally known to you.
17. State basic facts, not opinions or estimates, unless they are asked for.
18. Be cautious of questions that include the word "absolutely" or "positively."
19. Remember, "absolute" means forever, without exception.
20. Be cautious about time, space, and distance estimates.
21. Do not guess if you do not know the answer.
22. Do not fence, argue, or second-guess the examining counsel.
23. Admit that you discussed your testimony previously if you did.
24. Do not memorize a story.
25. Avoid such phrases as "I think," "I guess," "I believe," or "I assume."
26. Maintain a relaxed but alert attitude at all times.
27. Do not answer too quickly—take a breath before answering each question.
28. Do not look to counsel for assistance.
29. Make sure you understand the question before answering.
30. Do not answer if you are told not to do so.
31. Never joke during a deposition or testimony.
32. Do not exaggerate, underestimate, or minimize.

33. Dress conservatively in clean clothes.
34. Be serious before, after, and during testimony.
35. If you make a mistake, correct it as soon as possible.
36. Remain silent if attorneys object during the examination.
37. Listen carefully to dialogue between attorneys.
38. Avoid mannerisms that signal nervousness.
39. Do not use technical language without translating it for your lay hearers.
40. Speak simply.
41. Do not discuss the case in the hallways or restrooms.
42. Do not converse with opposing parties, attorneys, or jurors.
43. Tell the truth.

Appendix M

Deposing an Adverse Witness

by Clifford L. Somers

This outline is intended as an aid to taking the deposition of an adverse expert. It should be used as guide, not as a script.

I. Background and Qualifications
   A. Obtain résumé, curriculum vitae, bibliographies, and lists of presentations.
   B. Education and Training
      1. What schools or training courses has the expert attended?
      2. What on-the-job training received?
      3. What degrees or certificates obtained and when?
      4. What licensing, specialty certification, or other professional accreditation received, from whom and when?
      5. Have expert's accreditations ever been questioned, investigated, suspended, or removed?
      6. Has the expert ever been sued as a result of professional activities?
   C. Litigation Experience
      1. Has the expert testified in a lawsuit before?
      2. Where, when, and how often?
      3. How much of the witness's income is derived from testifying and preparing to do so?
      4. Does the expert advertise his or her services, and if so, where and when?
      5. How did the witness get into this case?
      6. Has the witness served for this lawyer or his or her firm before, and how often?
   D. Publications
      1. Has the expert ever published any original work on the subject of this lawsuit?
      2. Review the expert's bibliography and presentations with him or her as to their bearing on the current action.
   E. Research
      1. Has the witness ever done research relevant to the subject at issue?
      2. If so, get details as to when, where, under

*Courtesy of *For the Defense*, Defense Research Institute, Vol. 31, No. 7, July 1989, pp. 24–29.

what circumstances, and for whom.

3. Were the results published, and if so, where can you get a copy?

F. Professional Organizations
   1. As to a physician, to what hospital staffs does he belong?
   2. As to all experts, get details as to which organizations they belong to and any positions held.
   3. Have they ever had their privileges or memberships thereon questioned, investigated, suspended or removed? Get details.

II. Materials Provided
   A. Records
      1. Get a complete list.
      2. From what source were they derived?
      3. Are they copies and if so, from what source were they copied?
      4. Is the witness expecting to examine more records and if so, what records, when, and from where?
      5. Were there any records the witness wanted but couldn't get?
   B. Literature, Tables, and Standards
      1. From what precise source were they obtained?
      2. Who obtained them?
      3. Were copies retained by the witness?
      4. Is this material authoritative, useful, persuasive, generally relied on in the industry, etc?
      5. Is the expert aware of any literature that is relevant but still in preparation or in the process of being published? Get details.
   C. The Specific Product in Suit
      1. Was the specific item that allegedly injured the plaintiff examined?
      2. How was it obtained? Trace the chain of custody.
      3. How was it identified?
      4. Were photographs taken, and if so, where are they?
      5. If it was a similar product, but not the same one, what differences were there?
      6. Where and how was the similar product obtained?
   D. Oral Information
      1. From whom was the information obtained and when?
      2. What information was obtained?
      3. What part did the information play in the witness's activities?
      4. What notes or records were made of the oral information and where are these?
   E. Other Materials
      1. What other materials or information was gathered and used?
      2. When and where and from whom obtained? Where are these materials now?
      3. Is anything else expected and if so, what, when, and from whom?

III. The Task of the Expert Witness

A. What was the Task
   1. Has the expert ever done this task before? Get details.
   2. Did they do what they were asked to do in this case?
   3. Did they do anything beyond what they were asked to do?

B. Defects
   1. What do you understand to be a "defect"?
   2. Do you differentiate design defects, manufacturing defects, defective warnings, and other defects? Get details.

C. Standards
   1. What is your definition of "standard of care"?
   2. How do you know what the standard is in this case?
   3. Describe any field experience you may have in practicing under these standards?
   4. If the standards are derived from a publication, which one specifically?
   5. If there are governmental or industry standards, did you help to prepare such standards? Give relevant details.

IV. Who Gathered Information for the Expert
A. Did you personally do all the work that led to your opinions?
B. Give full names, addresses, titles and qualifications of others involved in gathering and evaluating data.
C. What did each of these people do?
D. Were you actively involved

in their work or did you supervise?
E. Were you present at all times while the others performed their work?
F. Give full names, addresses, titles, and qualifications of any independent consultants whose input was received.
G. What did they produce?
H. How was it used?
I. Explore qualifications and hearsay problems.

V. Terminology
A. All non-lay terms of any complexity or strangeness must be defined.
B. Never forget that the jury may not know a term just because you are familiar with it.
C. Never fear appearing ignorant. Require the expert to explain in simple language all technical terminology.

VI. What Was Done
A. Records Reviewed
   1. Describe the time spent and the thoroughness of your review.
   2. What part did records play in the formation of opinions?
B. Technical Publications
   1. How were manuals and other technical publications obtained?
   2. Do you have copies?
   3. What part did the publications play in the formation of opinions?
C. Products
   1. Who examined or worked on the products at issue?
   2. What was done with or to the products?

3. What findings were made?

4. What is the significance of the findings?

5. Were photographs, microscope slides, videotapes, x-rays or other pictorial or graphic records made?

6. Who has these visual records?

7. What do they demonstrate?

D. Computers

1. Describe the type of computers used in gathering and analyzing information?

2. Who used the computers?

3. What sort of special software was used?

4. Describe what was done with the computers?

5. Do you have copies of any printouts of results?

6. What do the results mean to the expert's opinions?

E. Other Equipment

1. Describe all scientific or technical equipment and machinery used in gathering and analyzing information.

2. Was the equipment calibrated? When and how?

3. Who operated the equipment and what did he do?

4. What were the results?

5. Where are the results recorded?

6. What do the results mean to the expert's opinions?

F. Anything Else Done to Reach Opinions

1. What was done?

2. Who did it?

3. What were the results?

4. What do the results mean to the expert's opinions?

VII. Opinions

A. Lay Them Out

1. Have the witness list each professional opinion reached or category of opinion.

2. Read the list of opinions back to be sure you have it right.

3. Get the witness to agree you have them all, and that your list is accurate.

B. Facts

1. With respect to each opinion, get a recitation of the operative facts on which it is based.

2. If it is not stated or clear, get a citation to the source of each fact.

3. Get a list of any assumptions made about the facts.

4. What is the basis of the assumptions?

5. Make the witness agree you have all the relevant facts for each opinion.

C. Reasoning

1. With respect to each opinion, get an explanation of the reasoning process from facts to conclusions.

D. Causal Relationship

1. With respect to each opinion, get an explanation of its causal or other relationship to the case.

2. Get an explanation of the interrelation of multiple factors.

3. Be sure proper legal tests are met, such as "reasonable medical probability or scientific probability," etc.
4. Get an appointment of causes to effects if possible.

E. Standards
1. Are the opinions based on proper industry or professional standards?
2. Would the majority of the expert's peers agree with the stated opinions?
3. Are there any respected minority opinions in the field?
4. Does the witness concede the legitimacy of minority or differing views in the field?

VIII. Concluding
A. Other Work
1. What additional responsibilities or participation does the expert expect to undertake in this case?
2. When is it to be done?
3. If none is to be done, does the witness feel what has been done is sufficient basis for the opinions rendered?

B. Have all the witness's professional opinions or conclusions reached in this case been explored in the deposition?
1. If not, what else is there? Follow up as above.
2. Does the witness feel he or she has had a fair chance to state these other opinions or conclusions?
3. Is there anything the witness would like to add so as not to be misunderstood?

Appendix N
A Proposed Code of Conduct

AMERICAN ACADEMY OF FORENSIC SCIENCES
JURISPRUDENCE SECTION
CODE OF PROFESSIONALISM

Preamble

This Code of Professionalism was proposed by the Jurisprudence Section of the American Academy of Forensic Sciences to provide guidance to its members in the performance of their professional relationships with forensic experts.* The goal of the Code is to assist members in achieving the highest quality of professional conduct and to promote the cooperation between lawyers and forensic scientists which is essential to protect the legal interests of the public they serve.

In order to meet the public's need for legal services, lawyers and the quality of the service they provide must command the respect of the public as well as the other participants in the legal process. The fundamental principles set out in this Code are to provide an ethical framework for the Jurisprudence Section's members, although each lawyer must decide for himself the extent to which his conduct should rise above these minimum standards. The desire for the respect and confidence of the members of the society in which he serves and of the members of his profession should motivate him to maintain the highest possible degree of ethical conduct.

Lawyer professionalism includes accepting responsibility for one's own professional conduct as well as others in the profession and includes a desire to uphold professional standards and foster peer regulations to ensure each member is competent and public-spirited. Professionalism also includes reinforcing and communicating the ideals of professionalism among our membership and eliminating abrasive or abusive conduct with others, particularly our colleagues in the forensic sciences. Such behavior does not serve justice, but tends to delay and sometimes deny justice.

Compliance with the rules depends primarily upon voluntary compliance, secondary upon reinforcement by peer pressure and public opinion and finally, when necessary, by enforcement by the Court's inherent powers and ethics rules already in existence. The Academy, of course, may still sanction its members who are in violation of its Code of Ethics contained in the By-laws. Also, each state where the attorney is individually licensed may sanction the attorney for any violations of his state's Codes or Rules of Professional Conduct.

Terminology

1. "Belief" or "Believes" denotes that the person involved actually supposed the fact in question to be true. A person's belief may be inferred from circumstances.

---

*Special thanks to Professor Carol Henderson-Garcia, Nova University Law School, for this material, which is copyrighted by Professor Henderson-Garcia. (This code is undergoing revision as of September 1993.)

2. "Expert" denotes a person who possesses special skill, training and knowledge in a vocation or occupation.

3. "Knowingly," "Known," or "Knows" denotes actual knowledge of the fact in question. A person's knowledge may be inferred from circumstances.

4. "Reasonable" or "Reasonably" when used in relation to conduct by a lawyer denotes the conduct of a reasonably prudent and competent lawyer.

5. "Reasonable belief" or "Reasonably believes" when used in reference to a lawyer denotes that the lawyer believes the matter in question and that the circumstances are such that the belief is reasonable.

Rules

1. I shall treat all expert witnesses with professional courtesy and will acknowledge their obligations to their codes of ethics or conduct, and will not ask them to breach their legitimate confidential relationships with their clients or patients.

2. I shall verify the credentials of any expert witnesses I use.

3. I shall not knowingly proffer an expert witness with fraudulent credentials.

4. I shall report fraudulent experts to the appropriate authorities.

5. I shall not pay an excessive fee for the purpose of influencing an expert's testimony or fix the amount of fee contingent upon the content of his testimony or the outcome of the case. I will communicate to the expert that he is being paid for his time and his expertise, not the nature of his opinion.

6. I shall refrain from making any material misrepresentation of the education, training, experience or expertise of the of the expert witness. I shall not misrepresent nor mischaracterize an expert witness' credentials, qualifications, data, findings or opinion. I will not withhold nor suppress any relevant facts, evidence, documents or other material at my disposal that may be relevant to the expert's opinion.

7. I shall not request nor require an expert to express an opinion on matters outside his field of expertise or within his field of qualifications to which he has not given formal consideration.

8. I shall not attempt to prevent opposing counsel from communicating with my expert witness, nor will I instruct my expert witness to not communicate with opposing counsel about the subject of a lawsuit unless such contact is otherwise prohibited or regulated by law and the parties' attorneys have consented.

9. Any and all demonstrative evidence shall not be intentionally altered or distorted with a view to misleading the court or jury.

10. I shall keep all consulting and testifying experts reasonably informed of the status of the matter in which they are engaged and promptly comply with reasonable legally permissible requests for information.

11. I shall compensate the expert for the total amount of the undisputed portion of the fee agreed upon between the expert and the client or attorney representing the client.

Appendix O
Index to *The Demonstrative Evidence Sourcebook*

INDEX to *The Demonstrative Evidence Sourcebook*

TABLE OF CONTENTS

237

The Demonstrative Evidence Sourcebook, Douglas Filter, Staffort Hart Publications, Inc., 1985.

GLOSSARY

Accident reconstruction. The engineering and scientific process by which the dynamics of accidents are established.

Action plan. An organized approach to accomplishing complicated tasks.

Administrative board. Nonjudicial tribunal for determining controversies, essentially involving administrative agencies at any level of government.

Administrative hearing. Judicial or legislative proceedings conducted by an administrative agency at any level of government.

Administrative law. The so-called fourth branch of government, most closely allied with the executive branch, including boards, tribunals, and officers of various Federal, state, and local bureaus.

Answer. A paper (pleading) which recites a civil defendant's response to claims of plaintiff and which may include defenses and claims on behalf of defendant against plaintiff.

Arbitration. An organized process outside of a courtroom for resolving disputes between persons or entities.

Assumption. Fact or information not actually known, but believed to be so. Assumptions should almost never be used by an expert.

Attorney work product. The thought processes of an attorney preparing a case for trial, including books, papers, writings, notes, and other tangible things that evidence the attorney's effort. These items are generally privileged and cannot be obtained during discovery.

Bench. The location in a courtroom where the judge sits; hence, the judge. Also, a reference to the judiciary.

Case decision. Determinations by courts which provide guidance to attorneys and experts on the legal requirements of evidence, testimony, and substantive law.

Case plan. An organized analysis of a project, essentially a budget of time and effort.

Chain of custody. A mechanical method for keeping track of physical and tangible items of evidence during the dispute-resolution process.

Comparative fault. A legal doctrine which weighs the fault or liability of various parties to an event; a method by which the responsibility of the parties to an event is proportioned based upon their respective conduct.

Complaint.   A paper (pleading) which sets forth a civil plaintiff's claims.

Condemnation.   A process by which government or governmental entities can take private property for public purpose upon paying just compensation.

Conflict of interest.   Any situation which, because of prior relationships or known information, creates a division of loyalties making independent representation impossible.

Contributory negligence.   A doctrine of law providing that a party who participates in conduct which causes the injury, loss, or damage can make no recovery whatsoever in a court proceeding.

Credibility.   The believability of a witness.

Cross-examination.   The phase of the dispute-resolution process in which opposing counsel asks questions of witnesses in order to test the truth, accuracy, or thoroughness of direct testimony.

Curriculum vitae.   A resume.

Defendant.   A person or entity against whom a civil or criminal action has been brought.

Demonstrative evidence.   Charts, graphs, drawings, computer graphics, models, audio and video presentations, or any other device used to demonstrate, characterize, or explain verbal testimony.

Deposition.   Testimony given outside the presence of the trier of fact in the presence of a court reporter, counsel, and the parties, for the purpose of finding out what you know, determining what sort of witness you will be, and locking you into a position.

Destructive testing.   A process by which tangible items are actually disposed of during an examination.

Direct examination.   That procedure during a trial or hearing which first presents a witness's testimony to the trier of fact.

Discovery.   Those processes used before a trial in order to uncover the facts of the case.

Dispute-resolution process.   Trials, hearings, arbitration, mediation, or other ways in which disputes between individuals and entities are resolved.

Engagement letter.   A contract of employment used by expert witnesses when engaged for forensic investigation, consultation, and testimony purposes.

Exclusion of witnesses.   A rule whereby a hearing officer or trial judge may bar from the court parties who will testify except during the time of their actual testimony.

Expert opinion.   A major exception to the general rule of evidence which otherwise requires testimony be based upon personal knowledge. Because of their knowledge, training, and experience, experts are allowed to render opinions about what happened rather than merely recite what their senses recorded.

Expert testimony. Presentation of verbal or written evidence in the dispute-resolution process in a scientific, professional, technical, or specialized field, usually beyond the knowledge of laymen.

Expert witness. A person who by reason of education, training, or experience has special knowledge not held by the general public.

Expertise. Special skill or knowledge in a particular field.

Fact witness. A person who testifies in a dispute-resolution process about information gained from the senses (touch, sight, smell, sound), whose task it is to accurately report those observations.

Federal Rules of Civil Procedure. Those organized processes which govern trials and preliminary matters in the United States courts.

Federal Rules of Criminal Procedure. Those organized processes which govern trials and preliminary matters in the United States courts involving criminal proceedings.

Federal Rules of Evidence. A body of evidentiary rules used in Federal court, adopted in many state courts, and generally constituting a summary of the law of evidence in many jurisdictions.

Final status conference. A process by which expert witnesses can fine-tune preparation for trial or hearing testimony.

Forensic witness. A person who testifies at a dispute-resolution trial or hearing based upon scientific, professional, technical, or specialized knowledge, training, or experience. A person who is allowed by law to give opinions in law-related settings rather than merely recite facts gained from the senses. Forensic opinions are sought to explain past, present, and future events.

Foundation. The factual, technical, or scientific basis which supports testimony, specifically expert opinion and conclusion.

Frye rule. A law of court which provides that in order for an expert witness to testify concerning scientific, technical, professional, or specialized matters, the opinion testimony must be based upon a reasonable degree of acceptance within the scientific, technical, professional, or specialized field of the processes utilized by the witness to reach the conclusions tendered.

Hearing. An organized process by which the contesting parties present their evidence and testimony.

Hearsay. A statement of conduct made by a witness outside of the presence of the trier of fact with no opportunity for cross-examination by the opposition. There are certain exceptions to the hearsay exclusion which are based on indicators of reliability attending such declarations or conduct and which make them admissible.

Hypothesis. A rational configuration of assumed facts subject to establishment by specific proof.

Hypothetical question. A question posed to an expert based on assumed theories of factual events. For example, "If A, B, and C exist, what is your opinion as to D?"

Impeachment. An attack on a witness which questions credibility, believability, or opportunity for testing or observation.

In camera. An "in chambers" hearing which is conducted in a judge's chambers without the presence of the jury.

Indictment. A paper by which a grand jury brings criminal charges against an individual or entity.

Information. A paper by which a district attorney brings criminal charges against a person or entity, without the grand jury process.

Interrogatories. Written questions proposed to a party to which specific written responses under oath are required.

Judgment. A decision by a trial or appellate court.

Lawyer. An attorney, counselor, or advocate serving as representative of a party in the dispute-resolution process.

Learned treatise. A book, publication, journal, or any other professional, scientific, technical, or specialized writing which is considered authoritative in a particular field.

Motion in limine. A motion to limit testimony or evidence in a contested proceeding.

Negligence. Failure to exercise that degree of care which a reasonably prudent person would have exercised under usual circumstances and conditions; conduct marked by carelessness or neglect.

Opinion witness. A forensic or expert witness who is entitled to render opinions, as opposed to testifying about factual matters based upon the senses.

Ordinance. The method of enacting laws by municipalities.

Plaintiff. A person or entity that brings a civil action.

Pleading. A paper prepared by an attorney which is filed with a court, which contains a factual or legal position for a litigant, usually with copies provided to all other parties to a case.

Preliminary opinion. The first stage of an expert witness's opinion-forming process. Early judgments are made about a case, subject to later verification based upon additional investigation.

Presumption. A rule of law which states that if certain facts exist, then other conclusions, as a matter of law, are deemed to exist. For example, "If A and B are true, then C, as a matter of law, must also be true."

Privilege. Those communications, written or verbal, between certain classes of persons which cannot be reached by the opposition in the dispute-resolution process.

Professional negligence. Failure of a professional person to perform or conduct themselves in accordance with the standards of care and attention usually displayed by persons in that field in the same or similar circumstances.

Prosecutor. The attorney who represents the people (the prosecution) in a criminal case.

Protocol. A series of steps, processes, or procedures usually followed in a scientific, technical, professional, or specialized area.

Reasonable probability. That degree of certainty, necessary to support expert opinion, which suggests that an event is more likely than not to occur.

Request for admission. A discovery process by which one party requests the other party to admit that particular facts or circumstances are true or certain events actually occurred.

Request for production. A written request to a party to produce documents and other tangible things for copying or inspection.

Resume. A summary of a person's background, training, education, and experience.

Rules of evidence. Rules that determine what is and is not admissible in various dispute-resolution processes. They may be enacted by the legislative bodies, determined by appellate decision, or controlled by court order.

Rules of practice. Guidelines for conduct of parties who appear before courts and tribunals. These rules direct how certain steps are to be accomplished.

Sanction. The process by which a court punishes parties, witnesses, or attorneys for failure to comply with the rules of the forum.

Statute. An enactment by a legislative body which constitutes the law of particular state or country.

Summary of voluminous data. Charts, graphs, drawings, or other compilations that summarize numerous entries.

Testimony. The process of conveying information from a witness to a judge, jury, arbitration or other hearing panel.

Testing. A means of analysis, examination, or diagnosis.

Tort. A wrongful act involving injury or damage to persons or property for which a civil action may exist.

Toxic tort. An act or event by which a contaminant or pollutant is introduced into the environment, causing injury or damage to persons or property.

Transcript. A written version of verbal statements.

Trial. The method by which disputes are resolved in the court system, with either a jury or judge as the trier of fact.

Trier of fact. The judge, jury, administrative body, board, or arbitration panel which determines the fact issues of the controversy in the dispute-resolution process.

Verdict. A trial decision by a jury in a criminal or civil case.

Voir Dire. The examination by which attorneys or the court are allowed to question jurors as to their fitness to serve as impartial triers of fact. Also, the examination conducted by an attorney or the court in a trial or hearing by which a witness or a document is tested for reliability. Expert witnesses are sometimes subjected to *voir dire* examination before being allowed to render opinions.

BIBLIOGRAPHY

A Guide to Forensic Engineering Expert and Service as an Expert Witness, Association of Soil and Foundation Engineers, 1985.

American Journal of Family Law, "The Use of Financial Experts in Marital Litigation: The Attorney's Viewpoint and the Expert's Viewpoint", Howard W. Broecker and Robert E. Kleeman, Jr., vol. 1, No. 3, Fall, 1987, p. 277.

Civil Engineering, "The Engineer as Expert Witness," James E. Hough, December 1981, pp. 56-58.

Commercial Arbitration Rules, American Arbitration Association, as amended and in effect April 1, 1985.

Cross Examination of An Expert Witness, R. Mark Halligan, For The Defense, DRI, September, 1990.

Dealing With the Lawyer As Expert Witness, Louis M. Brown and Ruth C. Tachna, The Practical Lawyer, October, 1985, p. 11.

Effective Presentation of Experts, Mark L.D. Wawro, Litigation, Vol. 19, No. 3, Spring, 1993, p. 31.

Excluding, Limiting or Mitigating the Opinion of the "Professional Testifier" in a Products Case, Jack F. Dunbar and Francisco J. Colón-Pagán, For the Defense, D.R.I. April, 1993, p. 12.

Expert Witnesses – Criminologists In the Courtroom, edited by Patrick R. Anderson and L. Thomas Winfree, Jr., State University of New York Press, 1987, p. 208.

Expert Witnesses: Direct and Cross-Examination, William G. Mulligan, Wiley Law Publications, 1987.

Expert Witness Handbook: A Guide for Engineers, D. G. Sunar, Professional Publications, Inc., San Carlos, California, 1985.

Expert Witnesses in Civil Trials, Mark A. Dombroff, Bancroft Whitney Co., 1989.

Forensic Sciences, Matthew Bender, 1989, edited by Cyril H. Wecht, M.D.

Forensic Science Handbook, N. T. Kuzmack, Legal Aspects of Forensic Science, R. Saferstein, Ed., Prentice-Hall, Englewood Cliffs, NJ, 1982.

Galileo's Revenge – Junk Science in the Courtroom, Peter W. Huber, Basicbooks, 1991.

Going by the Book – Direct and Cross-Examination of Medical Experts, Russ Herman, Trial Magazine, ATLA, August, 1991.

Handbook for the Executive As A Witness, Alfred Tealy, United States Trademark Association, 1983.

Handbook of Forensic Science, U.S. Department of Justice, Federal Bureau of Investigation, revised March 1984.

How To Be An Effective Expert Witness, Terry Rankin, Jr., Office of Continuing Education and Extension, College of Engineering, University of Kentucky, April, 1985.

Is the Appraisal Witness Qualified?, Society of Real Estate Appraisers, Wallstein Smith, Jr., 1979.

Lawyers Desk Reference, Harry Philo, Bancroft Whitney and Co., 1987.

Natural Resources & Environment, "Science in the Courts," edited by Neil Orloff and Sheila Jasanoff, vol. 2, 1986, pp. 3-70.

On the Witness Stand, L. Wrightsman, C. Willis, and S. Kassin, Sage Publications, Beverly Hills, CA, 1987.

Qualifying and Attacking Expert Witnesses, Robert C. Clifford, Lloyd Publishing, 1989.

Rules for Admissibility of Scientific Evidence, West Publishing, St. Paul, MN, 1987.

Shepard's Expert and Scientific Evidence Quarterly, Shepard's/McGraw-Hill, Inc., P.O. Box 35300, Colorado Springs, CO 80935-3530.

Ten Commandments (More or Less) for the Expert Witness, 2nd Edition, Alfred R. Pagan, Better Roads, Rosemont, IL, 1987.

Testifying In Court: The Advanced Course, Medical Economics, Oradell, NJ, 1972.

Testifying With Impact, Arch Lustberg, Association Department, U.S. Chamber of Commerce, Washington, D.C., Revised Edition, 1983.

The Admissibility of Expert Testimony in Christophersen vs. Allied-Signal Corp.: The Neglected Issue of the Validity of Nonscientific Reasoning by Scientific Witnesses, Edward J. Imwinkelried, Denver University Law Review Vol. 70, No. 3, 1993 Centennial Volume, p. 473.

The Art of Advocacy: Expert Witnesses (A Video Series), N.I.T.A., Notre Dame Law School, Notre Dame, IN 46556, 1988.

The Pathology of Homicide, Chap. XVI, The Pathologist As Witness, Lester Adelson, Charles C. Thomas, publisher, 1974.

The Proper Care and Feeding of Your Forensic Engineer—A Practical Guide For Using Engineering Expert Services, Richard K. Herrmann and Daniel W. Luczak, Forensic Technologies International Corporation, 1986.

The Psychologist As Expert Witness, Theodore H. Blau, Wiley Law Publications, 1984.

The Scientist and Engineer in Court, American Geophysical Union, Washington, D.C., 1983.

Trial Advocacy, J. W. Jeans, West Publishing, St. Paul, MN, 1975.

Weinstein's Evidence: Commentary on the Rules of Evidence for the United States' Courts and State Courts, J. B. Weinstein and M. A. Berger, 3 vols., (Matthew Bender, New York, 1981).

Winning with Experts, Nancy Hollander and Lauren M. Baldwin, Trial Magazine, ATLA, March 1993, p. 16.

Witnesses In Arbitration, Edwin Levin and Donald Grody, Bureau of National Affairs, 1987.

INDEX

INDEX